Reinventing the River City

GEOGRAPHIES OF JUSTICE AND SOCIAL TRANSFORMATION

Reinventing the River City

RIPARIAN INFRASTRUCTURE, CINCINNATI ELITES, AND THE OHIO RIVER

RAYMOND PETTIT

THE UNIVERSITY OF GEORGIA PRESS
Athens

Athens, Georgia 30602
www.ugapress.org

Set in 10.5/13.5 Minion 3 by Mary McKeon

Printed digitally

EU Authorized Representative
Easy Access System Europe—Mustamäe tee 50, 10621 Tallinn, Estonia,
gpsr.requests@easproject.com

Library of Congress Control Number: 2025042216
ISBN: 9780820374901 (hardback)
ISBN: 9780820374918 (paperback)
ISBN: 9780820374925 (epub)
ISBN: 9780820374932 (PDF)

For NZ and Boots

CONTENTS

FIGURES

ACKNOWLEDGMENTS

I am obsessed with Cincinnati. Much to the annoyance (and occasional amusement!) of everyone around me, everything is an excuse to mention Cincinnati. Did you know that Cincinnati has some of the world's greatest Ordovician fossils? That it has the largest collection of Italianate architecture in the United States? That cornhole originated in Cincinnati? That it has really good ice cream? I am fascinated by every detail and idiosyncrasy.

Reinventing the River City is deeply rooted in this love for Cincinnati. For that reason, I want to first acknowledge the outsized role that the people of Cincinnati have played in shaping this book. I am grateful to the multitude of Cincinnatians who have influenced and motivated me over the course of my life. When I came home to do this research, they showed unnecessary kindness and patience in the face of obtuse pestering. I hope they find something here that resonates with their experiences.

I am particularly thankful for the specific Cincinnatians, living and dead, who are named in this book. While I may disagree with some of their actions, I hope I accurately captured their original desires and intentions because I believe they were almost all genuinely driven by a desire to improve the city.

Among the vast array of Cincinnatians, I should also make special mention of my family. My parents, my siblings, and my extended family have been overwhelmingly supportive of my academic interests. Showing admirable Midwestern bluntness, they have also asked me what this stuff was all about and challenged me to make it interesting to them.

I also cherish my friends in Cincinnati. Gathered at different moments, it has been an honor to get to know each of your different slices of the city. To everybody at the Cincinnati Interfaith Workers Center, on many levels, it has been extremely helpful to fight with you all to change our city while also working on this project.

Closing out the Cincinnati section of these acknowledgments, thank you to everyone at the libraries that made this work possible, including the incredible teams at the University of Cincinnati Archives & Rare Books, the Public Library of Cincinnati and Hamilton County Inland Rivers Library, and the Cincinnati History Library and Archives. You all went above and beyond as I came in to scan stuff during my lunch break, asked to review materials during renovations, or emailed for a third time about that missing Hudson Biery letter. Special mention also goes to the Symmes Township Branch Library and Ohio Book Store as places near and dear to me.

I would also like to thank several individuals residing outside of Cincinnati. I have not followed much of a traditional academic path, but I am lucky that I have found brilliant mentors and brilliant friends along the way. The City University of New York, first at Hunter College and later at the Graduate Center, made for a surprisingly supportive environment to a Cincinnati-obsessed kid. The CUNY system is a marvel, one I am forever lucky to have found.

Jeff Maskovsky, thank you for taking me on as an advisee early in my doctoral studies and then providing useful advice (sometimes ignored) as I fitfully groped for a project, got distracted, and moved through the process in my own way. You taught me what urban anthropology could accomplish, and I hope this work reflects the excitement I feel about the field. Jackie Brown, you were the professor for literally the very first college course I ever walked into. You helped me embrace anthropology as a way that I could critically explore my passion for Cincinnati. Dána-Ain Davis, Neil Smith, Don Robotham, Kate Crehan, Michael Blim, Tom McGovern, and all of the CUNY Department of Anthropology faculty sparked so many ideas found here.

My CUNY anthropology cohort somehow found the perfect balance of being demanding yet never competitive. Friends like Nazia Kazi, Megan Hicks, Ryan Mann-Hamilton, and Yesenia Ruiz come around infrequently. Arguing was fun, laughing was fun, dancing was fun, complaining was fun. Also, my deep appreciation to the Fall 2017 Writing Group. Due to a trick of fate, we spent a lot of time reading my chapters. It helped me enormously, teaching me to focus on writing what I assumed was the background story. Many thanks to Julie Skurski for organizing the group and for her guidance throughout.

Thank you also to the thoughtful non-CUNY folks who helped shape this work. First, sincere gratitude to Uwe Lübken and David Stradling, who both inspired me with their work on Cincinnati and provided valuable feedback. Thank you to the four (!) reviewers who helped take this from a raw, convoluted dissertation to a story that might engage a broader audience. Thank you also to the University of Georgia Press for believing in this work and having the patience to see it evolve. Many thanks as well to the Etla Residency Writing Fellowship for some space and time to finish the manuscript.

I owe a great debt to the large body of Cincinnati scholarship, but I would like to call particular attention to Rhoda Halperin's *Practicing Community* (1998). In her book, Halperin provides a rich ethnography of the mixed-race low-income communities that have long occupied the riverfront in Cincinnati, as well as efforts to disinvest in and displace these residents. In many ways, I conceived of *Reinventing the River City* as a complement to Halperin's study, examining city elites' rationales and goals in seeking to transform the Ohio River and the city's riverfront.

Finally, to the people I most closely share my life with: Geo, from scanning documents at the archive one hot summer to coordinating around countless mini-writing sessions, you have been there for me throughout. I have read so many "Without your help none of this could have happened" platitudes in acknowledgment sections, but it is very real. I am also so thankful for my children. You are thoughtful, funny, loving little monsters who inspire me every day. I hope you find as much joy and inspiration in your home as I have.

Reinventing the River City

INTRODUCTION

On Monday, September 4, 1911, a crowd of fifteen thousand descended on the village of Fernbank, thirteen miles downriver from the center of Cincinnati. They came to celebrate the opening of the Fernbank Dam, the latest in a system of lock and dam structures being built by the U.S. Army Corps of Engineers on the Ohio River. The Ohio River had long been a major freight artery for the United States, but seasonal variability of water levels severely limited its navigability. Designed to enable year-round shipping on the river, proponents claimed the new lock and dam system would "make the Ohio Valley the center of the country's commerce and wealth, as well as of its population and manufactures" (OVIA 1906, 52). Cincinnati merchants had been a driving force in moving forward the entire Ohio River lock and dam project, believing that its completion would create the opportunity for their city "to have and to become the greatest inland seaport city in all the land" (OVIA 1909, 18).

As the U.S. Army Corps of Engineers finished work on the Fernbank Dam, Cincinnati elites organized to celebrate this major milestone. The Cincinnati Fernbank Dam Association hosted a five-day citywide commemoration to mark the occasion, which featured aviation exhibitions, an automobile race, a parade focusing on the history of navigation, nightly acrobatic showcases, swimming and rowing contests, a steamboat flotilla, a band competition, and many, many speeches. The massive event brought out tens of thousands to take part in the various festivities.

The program encountered an unfortunate hitch at the Monday kickoff event in the village of Fernbank. Attendees felt flummoxed. They had come to see a dam, but all they could find was the Ohio River. "'But where's the dam?' the visitors cried in chorus. 'Please mister, kindly show it to us.'" Disappointment reigned when the dam tender replied, "'Taint here. . . . It's lying down on the river bed'" (*Cincinnati Post* 1911a, 1). Rainfall in previous days had raised the Ohio River's water level and made navigation feasible without the aid of damming. In response, the dam master had lowered the dam so that ships could pass directly through the area.

The next day, a ceremony took place to christen the dam with bottles of water drawn from the Pacific Ocean, Atlantic Ocean, Panama Canal, and Gulf of Mexico, "symbolizing the commercial union of all the waters of the world with that of the Ohio River" (*Cincinnati Enquirer* 1911, 18). Heavy rain and fog, plus the continued absence of the dam, forced the ceremonial party to pull their boat into an inlet and pour out the bottles there. Meanwhile, watchers from the far shore could see neither the dam nor the christening. "'It's an outrage,' thundered Mayor Stuart of Fernbank, who was on the boat, as he observed the voters of his village, assembled on the river bank, fade away in the distance. 'Five years we have been waiting for this and now—.' Words failed the Mayor" (*Cincinnati Post* 1911b, 7). The event organizers hoped their star attraction would soon make an appearance in the face of mounting frustration, but with strong rains, the dam remained hidden during the weeklong celebration.

The Fernbank Dam owed this special disappearing ability to its Chanoine design. Invented in France during the nineteenth century, Chanoine dams featured a series of giant slats, called wickets. In times of high water, the dam master could lower the wickets to the riverbed, enabling ships to pass directly downriver and avoid delays necessitated by passing through a lock. During low water, the slats went back up, creating the dam and maintaining a navigable channel depth. Despite its inauspicious beginnings, Cincinnati residents became fiercely proud of their new dam, taking boat excursions from the city center to marvel at this feat of engineering. On its completion, Cincinnati promoted the Fernbank Dam as the largest Chanoine dam in the world (*Scientific American* 1911).

The Fernbank Dam symbolized the beginning of a new chapter in Cincinnati's relationship with the Ohio River, or "Old Man River" as many called it. In the nineteenth century, Cincinnati had been subject to the river's fickleness. The city depended on the river even as it suffered from its unpredictable behavior. Low water or river ice halted shipping, sudden flooding besieged the riverfront, and growing pollution made the water undrinkable. Despite this, the city tolerated this volatility throughout the nineteenth century: "Nothing adverse to 'the River' was ever long remembered; only the ice floes and floods were blamed" (Ambler 1932, 21).

In contrast, across the twentieth century, Cincinnati elites worked to make the Ohio River a more reliable partner for the city—one they could depend on

FIGURE 0.1. An image of Fernbank Dam with wickets lowered in the center of the river. Produced by the Feicke-Desch Printing Co. and selected from the Cincinnati & Hamilton County Public Library's Clyde N. Bowden postcard collection.

for new initiatives around public health, economic development, and white supremacy. In the modern river city, Old Man River would benefit Cincinnati rather than terrorize it. Many contemporaneous water management efforts in the United States and Europe similarly attempted to make nearby waterways more productive (Blackbourn 2006; Cioc 2002; Pritchard 2011). The awesome power of rivers had to be made to serve humanity, to support the growth of populations, and to contribute to the improvement of daily life. Many believed that this required a forceful approach. Waterways needed to be "manacled, tamed, subjugated, conquered" (Blackbourn 2006, 5) to produce regional benefits and to minimize undesirable impacts like flooding or pollution. This drive to control waterways reflected a strong belief in the potency of science to gain mastery over natural features like rivers. Technical expertise from emerging fields like engineering and sanitation reinforced a conviction that rivers could serve any of a multitude of purposes. Riparian infrastructure helped make rivers more obedient and helpful via massive interventions encompassing entire watersheds.

Breaking from this approach, Cincinnati elites consistently sought to enlist the Ohio River as an active participant in their initiatives. Rather than focusing on controlling the Ohio River, Cincinnati elites moving into the twentieth century were primarily interested in collaborating with the river. They believed the Ohio River could be a productive partner to the city if encouraged properly through the creation of a durable relationship built on accomplishing a shared purpose. In fact, local elites agreed that seeking to dominate the river would actually have adverse or counterproductive outcomes. Many knew from direct experience that one could little anticipate the behavior of Old Man River, let alone control it. The use of riparian infrastructure would still play a critical role in establishing this new relationship. Cincinnati elites reconceptualized riparian infrastructure as a means for facilitating the involvement of the Ohio River in their projects. Conceived in this way, infrastructure could cultivate specific behaviors from the river instead of trying to compel them.

The Fernbank Dam offered a prime example of this attitude. Working with the Ohio River's fluctuations, the Fernbank Dam achieved the desired depths required for navigation while also appeasing the river captains eager to avoid unnecessary locking at times of high water. At the launch of the regional effort to build the Ohio River lock and dam system in 1895, Pittsburgh, Pennsylvania, coal merchant Captain John F. Dravo enthusiastically and explicitly endorsed the cooperative spirit of the Chanoine design. According to Captain Dravo, Ohio River commerce "must be a co-worker with nature to accomplish its purposes," and the Chanoine dam represented this cooperative wisdom by asking "those [Ohio River] waters just to wait a little while until we are ready to ship" (OVIA 1895, 20).

In recasting the Ohio River as a more trustworthy partner for the city, Cincinnati elites threw their energy behind addressing three particular problems: low water, flooding, and pollution. The first prioritized raising water levels on the Ohio River. Every year, low water disrupted shipping on the river, making it impossible to navigate for months at a time. The Fernbank Dam represented one piece of a massive decades-long effort to address this issue. Flooding represented another endemic problem along the river. Although riverfront neighborhoods had always bounced back quickly from flooding, leading to a general disinterest in trying to prevent the dangers of high water, the unprecedented Ohio River flood of 1937 finally moved many Cincinnati elites to reevaluate the dangers of flooding. Last, concern over stream pollution grew as more and more waste entered the river. Many local authorities had trusted the river to naturally filter out pollutants, but shifting policy debates sparked efforts to treat sewage before it was discharged into the Ohio River.

The organization and implementation of these riparian infrastructure projects overlapped with periods of dramatic change in Cincinnati itself. For much of the nineteenth century, Cincinnati had been a compact, walkable city, concentrated near the riverfront. As the twentieth century approached, the city grew rapidly, both in terms of population, as new, diverse waves of migrants boosted the number of inhabitants, and in terms of space, as Cincinnati absorbed surrounding suburban communities. Economic changes also restructured the city. Cincinnati began its history as a commercial powerhouse, but small-scale factories and then large-scale industrial production assumed a dominant economic role as the twentieth century drew close. Corporate consolidation and an emerging management class followed, before the city was transformed again by deindustrialization and shifts to a service economy in the twentieth century's waning decades. Throughout these transitions, numerous social movements, such as those led by labor, feminists, and environmentalists, also left lasting impacts on daily life in Cincinnati.

In the context of this shifting terrain, industrial elites, commercial elites, corporate elites, and numerous other local, regional, and national elite groups jostled with one another for their place in the city's hierarchy. The ongoing economic shifts that had characterized urban life in Cincinnati since its founding led to class instability. Different groups—elite or otherwise—consistently felt the need to reaffirm their relevance to the city and to secure additional advantages as a safeguard against being subordinated by other class formations. Building a rapport with the Ohio River increasingly surfaced as a useful advantage amid these intergroup struggles, an immensely powerful force that could be mobilized to support particular groups' objectives to the detriment of others. To take advantage of this untapped potential, the city's distinct elite groups eagerly claimed their own special privileged knowledge of what the Ohio River really wanted.

Consequently, groups of Cincinnati elites were not just taking a novel approach in collaborating with the Ohio River but also fought one another for the right to do so. The different groups of elites from Cincinnati and from farther afield promoted divergent views of how riparian infrastructure projects should proceed, presenting plans that they believed would also benefit their own class formations. The result is that, far from a straightforward story of Cincinnati elites collectively addressing low water, flooding, and pollution, each of these riparian infrastructure projects represented complex negotiations over governance and economic development in the city. As more riparian infrastructure came online, debates over how to best relate to the Ohio River shifted, often with overlapping interests embedded in the different infrastructural systems already built or planned for the future. The expansion of riparian infrastructure changed Cincinnati drastically, shifting the relationship between the Ohio River and the city in multiple ways. In the nineteenth century, Cincinnati held a place as one of the best-known river cities in the United States. The Ohio River acted as the central stage for almost all economic exchange and social interaction in the urban environment.

Local observers have argued that Cincinnati ceased to be a river city by the end of the nineteenth century, as residents turned away from the Ohio River (Stradling 2003). The unmediated engagement with Old Man River that had defined much of the prior era broke down as communities lost touch with the riverfront. What had once been core to almost every aspect of the city's life apparently became an afterthought, appreciated but far removed from its past importance. Just as the Ohio River apparently declined in relevance though, not so coincidentally, different elite groups had begun to announce their plans for how to best make the Ohio River and the Cincinnati riverfront productive. In many ways, these projects put in motion throughout the twentieth century arguably made the Ohio River even more important to governance, the local economy, and daily life in Cincinnati. Yet, this infrastructure also significantly remade what it meant to be a river city, shifting how people engaged with and depended on the Ohio River. Critically, the buzz of activity previously present on the riverfront faded, but it did not just inevitably disappear. Instead, elite infrastructure projects often forced social life away from the riverfront. In its place, elite forms of relating to the river arose, changing the feel of being on the Ohio River as well as who was permitted to occupy its spaces. These changes signaled the emergence of a new kind of river city, one that had its own riparian culture and economy, only less visible and accessible than prior arrangements.

Reinventing the River City follows the reordering of this relationship between Cincinnati and the Ohio River, tracking the changes that have unfolded from the late nineteenth century into the early twenty-first century. Some shifts have been gradual, others abrupt, but the trajectory has consistently positioned the Ohio River in a new role as a potent ally to those who want to reimagine the city. Whether as an asset, a resource, or a partner, the Ohio River is never far from discussions around Cincinnati's future development. The creation of dense networks of infrastructures along the riverfront have made this pivot possible, ushering in this modern river city. Evaluating these riparian transformations in Cincinnati provides insights into cities, rivers, and their relationship in modern history.

Before diving further into the relationship between the Ohio River and groups of Cincinnati elites, the remainder of this introduction provides basic orientation to the theory, methodology, and structure of the book. The material covered below provides an important backdrop for understanding Cincinnati's history with the Ohio River. For those readers who decide to skip ahead, the remainder of the book is still easily navigable. The terrain covered here is woven into the main narrative with explanation of key terms and concepts.

Diverse bodies of theory underpin *Reinventing the River City*. The following sections highlight those theoretical frameworks used most frequently: nonhuman actors, elite class formation, expertise and practical knowledge, and infrastructure. The focus is on showing how theory can be a tool to make sense of the socioeconomic processes described in this book as well as the significance of these events to a wider understanding of objects of study like rivers and cities.

Nonhuman Actors

The literature on nonhuman actors has exploded in recent decades, covering a complex and diverse effort to reorient the social sciences beyond a human-centric epistemology. Core to this view is an understanding that nonhuman actors have their own agency and can behave in ways that are hard to predict (Joyce 2003; Bennett 2005). Nonhuman actors, from viruses to continental plates to sewer systems, intervene in and modify the world around them, including other human and nonhuman actors. Even as humanity has emerged as the dominant force in shaping the world around us—a concept captured by the Anthropocene moniker—nonhuman actors continue to wield an incredible power to impact our environment and humanity itself (Latour 2005; Haraway 2016). Analyses of social processes that omit nonhuman actors are therefore often incomplete, failing to account for the multiple sources of agency that determine particular outcomes.

Within the field of nonhuman actor studies, rivers have attracted significant attention for being closely linked to the development of human society. Rivers supply drinking water, provide sustenance via fishing and irrigation, power mills and generators, serve as vital transportation links, and unleash destructive flooding on a massive scale, among many other roles that have proven critical to influencing patterns of settlement. From the urban perspective, until recently, almost all major cities depended on local rivers in one way or another, even as urban residents feared flooding or diseases born on river waters (Knoll, Lübken, and Schott 2017).

Historians have led the surging interest in understanding how rivers function as nonhuman actors, with early exhortations to consider waterways on their own terms (Worster 1985). Subsequently the field has produced a sizable number of "river biographies," works describing the transformation of rivers through human interventions, as well as how these rivers have in turn shaped daily life for humans.[1] These studies often concentrate on both the complexity and unpredictability of rivers, taking a holistic approach to examining rivers' capacities to impact human society via their energetic capacity, aquatic life, water levels, pollution load, sediment content, and multiple other characteristics. Through constant fluctuations and changes, rivers act in unexpected ways on human settlements.

The river biographies have also been crucial in understanding why efforts by human populations to control waterways have repeatedly failed, as well as how they have produced an endless chain of unintended consequences. A change in one aspect of a river's behavior can ripple across many other aspects of the riparian ecosystem in ways that are hard to anticipate and even harder to prevent. The damming of a river may disrupt downstream fishing industries, a modification to the river's channel may shift the local aquifer, or flood control measures may lower silt levels, decreasing the water's nutrient content. A key insight from this research has been that unruly rivers "constantly (or rather recurringly) remind urbanites that their attempts to control nature and keep it in check could only ever be fragmentary and never entirely successful in the long run" (Knoll, Lübken, and Schott 2017, 4).

Despite the importance of "river biographies" in understanding how rivers function as nonhuman actors, this book does not hew closely to this holistic approach. Instead, in analyzing collaborations between the Ohio River and Cincinnati-based elites, *Reinventing the River City* focuses on three specific aspects of the Ohio River's agency: navigability, flooding, and pollution. Those aspects of the Ohio River behavior connected to these three areas—such as changes in streamflow velocity, dissolved oxygen levels, and floodplain behavior—are therefore investigated. Other types of river usage that have not been as important to Cincinnati elites in the previous century—such as commercial fishing and hydropower potential—do not feature as prominently.

Reinventing the River City also explores the implications of humans building intentional relationships with nonhuman actors such as the Ohio River. There have been growing calls for humans to pursue more connections with the nonhuman actors around us, in the belief that this will produce a more sustainable path forward for human society. The thought is that close association with nonhuman actors will root human society in engagement and interdependency, rather than exploitation and ruin. As anthropologist Eduardo Kohn describes it, "There is something about our everyday engagements with other kinds of creatures that can open new kinds of possibilities for relating and understanding" (Kohn 2013, 7). Yet, there are potential shortcomings to any assumption that deepening relationships with nonhuman actors will inevitably shift humanity's trajectory toward mutual flourishing.

The core issue is that the preferences among different nonhuman actors can deviate significantly from expectations (Povinelli 2016; Tsing 2015). Many nonhuman actors actually thrive in the context of untenable practices like capitalist development because these conditions benefit or even heighten their agency. Whether bacteria that eat plastic, the vibrancy of life around radioactive sites, or rivers revitalized by infrastructure and debris, these "freak ecologies" defy easy categorization (Fletcher 2008). Efforts to establish better relations with nonhuman actors must therefore account for how those same nonhuman actors are currently thriving despite apparently unsustainable conditions.

In the case of the Ohio River, there is a long history of understanding the river as a nonhuman actor that behaves in ways both beneficial and detrimental to human society. Indigenous groups used the Ohio River extensively but built many of their communities along its safer, less flood-prone tributaries (Sleeper-Smith 2018). Settler colonial communities like Cincinnati knew the Ohio River as Old Man River—unpredictable and damaging but also generous and comforting (Grayson 1929). Many societies recognized rivers as volatile forces imbued with awesome and even sacred powers (Alley 2002; Lazzaro 2011; Torgersen 2018). Examining how groups of elites in Cincinnati have continued to invest the Ohio River with deep significance can act as a corrective to capitalist narratives of the separation of nature and human society.

Elite Class Formations

Elites are individuals who wield disproportionate power in society, able to compel human and nonhuman actors alike to follow their directives. The exercise of power is central here, especially in terms of determining the parameters that shape how others can pursue their everyday lives (Wolf 1990), for instance, by defining the field of economic actions or by maintaining control over the deployment of violence. Elites use dominance over a variety of social positions, such as control of public institutions or ownership of the means of production, to achieve these ends and benefit themselves over the long term (Khan 2012).

Elites are far from being just isolated actors who have accumulated power through their own ingenuity, charisma, or strength. Rather, elites are always embedded in a specific class setting. A class is generally recognized as individuals who have similar socioeconomic status, correlating with shared conditions of daily life and often comparable worldviews and goals (Warner and

Lunt 1941). Elites can broadly be understood as a class category, but there are many different elite class formations defined by a range of characteristics, such as their role in the economy or how they are embedded within racial dynamics. The result is an abundance of unique elite class formations, often with distinct perspectives that make it difficult to extrapolate from one group to another.

Furthermore, the relative power of elite class formations can fluctuate over time. They rarely represent a stable convergence of interests, as emerging sources of wealth or economic pressures can reconfigure elite groups' standing in specific places and periods. New economic opportunities, technologies, political conditions, and other factors propel new groups into dominant status and force existing elites to undergo dramatic changes or experience displacement (Blim 2016). Notwithstanding the threats posed by antagonistic forces, the interactions with other groups are critical to the process of elite class formation. Conflict, negotiation, subordination, and other forms of engagement delimit and sustain specific elite groups (Stone 1989). Beyond fights over resources and decision-making power, these interactions are often about who has the right to define what counts as elite status, as well as how this maps onto other linked categories like whiteness, masculinity, and urban identity (Bourdieu 1984).

Reinventing the River City examines these shifting dynamics of elite class formation in Cincinnati since the late nineteenth century. Different elite class formations have long sought dominance within the city, seeking control over sectors of the economy, trade routes, and political power. This has been not only about gaining a comparative advantage but also about asserting each group's centrality to Cincinnati's identity. Mastery over the Cincinnati riverfront and Ohio River have been particularly crucial, given their symbolic and economic importance. Moving into the twentieth century, claiming a privileged relationship with the Ohio River emerged as a potent strategy for different elite class formations wishing to buttress the interests of their distinct groups.

A core contribution of this book is examining what this relationship building with the Ohio River says about processes of elite class formation. Many studies have described elite attempts to control rivers and other nonhuman actors, but Cincinnati elites have shown a surprising willingness to move beyond efforts to simply control the Ohio River. This speaks to the fact that capitalist elites have long collaborated with nonhuman actors, fashioning durable, complex partnerships. As anthropologist Elizabeth Povinelli (2016) points out, far from underestimating the capacities of nonhuman actors, in their search for profits capitalists actually believe "nothing is inherently inert . . . and anything can become something more with the right innovative angle" (20). While capitalists might believe in a stark division of society and nature, they are also radically open to the behavior of any actor, human or nonhuman, that facilitates the process of accumulation. This engagement between Cincinnati elites and the Ohio River, with give and take on each side, provides important insights into understanding elite class formations and the potential of a more-than-human politics.

Expertise and Practical Knowledge

Reinventing the River City examines two epistemological approaches that have been central to elite class formation in Cincinnati: expertise and practical knowledge. Both are forms of producing information about how the world functions, observing our environmental surroundings to determine patterns and predict outcomes. Both also provide guidelines for how humans can affect the world around them, translating knowledge into action to achieve particular objectives. Controlling knowledge production is a critical source of power for elite class formations, enabling elites to influence how others see and understand actions unfolding around them (Wolf 1990).

Expertise asserts that scientific and professional training lead to improved objectivity and more rational decision-making. In this approach, experts are defined by their capacity to step outside of everyday life and analyze the world in abstract terms, drawing on academic disciplines to render the world intelligible (Mitchell 2002). The idea of using expertise to underpin governance was consolidated in the nineteenth century. Ruling elites in Europe expected experts—drawing on new scientific fields such as statistics, cartography, and hydrology—to improve human society in realms including transportation, agriculture, economics, and public health (Scott 1998; Joyce 2003). Governments used these approaches to guide interventions ranging from small-scale neighborhood projects to massive reconfigurations of national or international space, approaches that were deployed both at home and in the colonial context.

Historians of governance have described this deployment of expertise as a key to technocracy, the view that technical solutions are needed to resolve problems in the public sphere (Mitchell 2002; Joyce 2003; see Mukerji 2009 for earlier roots). Proponents of technocracy argue that experts are above political calculations. Expertise thus functions as an "anti-politics," disqualifying alternative proposals and debate as misguided or based on political interests, even—or especially—in cases traditionally understood as very political, such as with public financing (Brash 2011) and land reallocation (Ferguson 1990). The effectiveness of these expert solutions lies "precisely in the way they [are] realised as 'technical' and so *outside* the political" (Joyce 2003, 7, emphasis in original).

Unlike expertise, practical knowledge refers to ways of understanding the world through lived experience rather than formal training: individuals or collectives that have garnered knowledge through doing things directly rather than receiving theoretical or technical education (Fischer 2000). Often this information and its application is a source of local pride, used to differentiate one group from others. Practical knowledge is also closely related to epistemologies of local knowledge or traditional knowledge, all of which are seen to develop organically from specific contexts and to be sustained via informal networks (Antweiler 1998). With the rising importance of expertise, practical knowledge has frequently been looked down on, portrayed as inferior to expert knowledge or, at best, complementary.

As expertise has emerged as a tool of elite governance, many groups have seized on practical knowledge (or local knowledge) as a source of resistance (Scott 1985). In many places, the public has pushed back on experts as antithetical to popular decision-making, arguing that those closest to a problem are often best situated to develop a solution (Fischer 2000; Allen 2003). These critics often argue that technocratic experts make decisions based on elite interests rather than considering the common good. At the same time, practical knowledge is not just a tool of the oppressed but has also been shown to be effectively deployed in support of or in conjunction with technocratic regimes (Herzfeld 2005; Elyachar 2012).

Reinventing the River City follows this last thread, often exploring how practical knowledge and expertise worked toward common elite goals for Cincinnati, even amid disagreements. Local elites trying to position themselves as the preferred partner of the Ohio River have repeatedly claimed to know which infrastructural projects would be best for the city. As a result, frictions between different elite class formations often became epistemological debates about who had access to the best and most reliable information about the riparian environment and why this information should be used to design and implement effective river management strategies. While clearly concerned with the Ohio River, these conflicts have therefore also been deeply tied to how expertise and practical knowledge are deployed in pursuit of urban development within Cincinnati.

Expertise directed toward urban development has drawn deeply from the fields of urban planning, transportation management, and housing administration, among others (Fairfield 1994; Joyce 2003; Bocking 2006). Universities and groups such as the Urban Land Institute produce planning professionals who use zoning, population predictions, sustainability studies, and other tools to legitimize technical proposals in the service of urban development. Despite their diverse professional backgrounds and claims of neutrality, these experts in the United States have consistently favored urban growth as the most desirable path forward (Checker 2011).

Practical knowledge shows up in urban development efforts represented by a motley collection of opportunistic individuals without any particular professional formation, who use their connections, experiences, and intuition to reshape the urban environment. They may operate in the real estate sector, industry, cultural institutions, or multiple other heterogeneous settings, and often rely on intimate knowledge of the local context to benefit themselves. Neil Smith (1996) explores in depth for New York City's Lower East Side how some of the most successful developers in the 1990s were "mavericks," surviving and thriving by navigating the risk-filled frontiers of urban growth (14–16). Their practical experience enabled them to navigate the "locational seesaw" of opportunity in the urban environment (Smith 1996, 88). Although these individuals have varied backgrounds, their reliance on practical knowledge and instinct to drive speculative investments often puts them at odds with the more formulaic and conservative recommendations put forward by experts.

Despite these differences, expertise and practical knowledge have often served very complementary purposes in Cincinnati's debates around riparian infrastructure, serving as flexible rationales toward the same developmental ends (see Cowen and Shenton 1996). If one approach encountered difficulties, the other might present a viable path forward.

Infrastructure

Infrastructure has repeatedly been the terrain over which Cincinnati elites and the Ohio River have come together since the end of the nineteenth century. At different times, local lobbying organizations, technical associations, governmental advisory boards, and redevelopment corporations—bringing together representatives of elite interests from across the city—have each put forward their own infrastructural proposals about how to best approach the issues of navigation, flooding, and pollution. These infrastructures were meant to build on the growing rapprochement with the Ohio River while also structuring how the city (and region) would relate to this crucial waterway. In tandem, the Ohio River shaped these infrastructure projects and their outcomes via behaviors such as sedimentation, flooding, and the accumulation of sludge banks. *Reinventing the River City* examines both the role of infrastructure as providing the interface for this relationship and how infrastructure through its own agency has affected the Ohio River and daily life in Cincinnati.

This broad focus is not in any way to claim that infrastructure itself is a "coherent and stable historical object, that infrastructure is a neutral way of describing certain engineering works, regardless of historical period" (Rankin 2009, 61). Rather, as seen in the following chapters, these proposals reflected a range of goals and ideas for how the city should function. "Infrastructure" itself changed during the period covered here, from being called "internal improvements" in the nineteenth and early twentieth centuries and being promoted as "public works" around the mid-twentieth century, before gaining its current moniker. The histories of these different naming conventions in the United States reflect in part how actors conceptualized their projects and the kinds of objectives they laid out for their work, even as these same actors also pushed back on the limitations of these names and responded to other ideas, such as modernism and environmentalism, in justifying their visions.

While recognizing the historical instability of "infrastructure," this book assumes three baseline parameters: First, that infrastructures are networked objects that facilitate circulation, whether of people, information, freight, potable water, electricity, or countless other things (Larkin 2013). The desire for infrastructure is fundamentally rooted in improving the possibilities for specific human groups to access goods, ideas, land, and whatever else they may seek. Second, that infrastructures are (at least in part) made by humans, with the intention to enable improved circulation. Many networked objects created by nonhumans actually produce similar results to infrastructure without human intervention (for one very relevant example: rivers as transportation corridors), but the focus here is on networked objects planned or modified by humans with the intent to improve circulation. And third, the emphasis in this book is on the physical forms of infrastructure. While others have made compelling arguments for human relationships as a type of infrastructure (Simone 2004), the interactions between the Ohio River and Cincinnati elites at the center of this study have primarily taken place via tangible platforms. In summary, for this book, infrastructures are built interventions in the environment oriented toward increasing interconnectedness of people and places, as well as improving outcomes for human populations. Building on this definition, *Re-*

inventing the River City explores both the economic and social objectives of infrastructure.[2]

The economic role of infrastructure has long been a critical consideration. Many infrastructure projects have faltered or barreled ahead based on their perceived economic impact. Relative to cities like Cincinnati, urban growth proponents understand infrastructure as the base needed to enable redevelopment. Improvements in transportation, flood protection, and sewage treatment are seen to "prime the pump" to incentivize private development, which in turn leads to more taxable resources to direct toward even better infrastructure, which entices more investment, and so on, in a "virtuous cycle" (Laidley 2007). By mitigating obstacles like flooding and pollution, which could deter investment or exchange, these investments ensure that capital is able to circulate uninhibited, supposedly attracting more capital (Harvey 1982). In Cincinnati, the projects evaluated here all ultimately had the goal of either directly or indirectly remaking the riverfront as an attractive space for private investment. These interventions spurred cycles of disinvestment and redevelopment simultaneously aimed at making the city's waterfront neighborhoods and residents more economically productive.

Another crucial thread within infrastructure studies interrogates how these infrastructural systems organize daily life. Seen from this perspective, agencies overseeing local infrastructure organize both the Ohio River and the people of Cincinnati to perform in recognizable and acceptable ways (Linton 2010). According to historian Patrick Joyce, through its role in facilitating circulation, infrastructures "shape and delimit the way actions can be done" (Joyce 2003, 41), creating the parameters for both human and other nonhuman actors to perform. Infrastructure also plays a critical role in contributing to urban metabolism, the flows of energy, social interactions, and goods within a city (Kaika 2005). In particular, the speed and regularity at which infrastructure moves water through the city is a key factor shaping the rhythm of daily life. Human and nonhuman actors alike incorporate and embody these flows as they make their way through the city. The engineers managing the movement of water through Cincinnati by means of sewers, floodwalls, and water mains thus also help define elite urban governance and belonging—such as how they relate to concepts such as cleanliness, resilience, sustainability, and modernity (Gandy 2014).

Known as "technopolitics" (Joyce 2003; Mitchell 2002), these efforts to define the conditions of everyday life means infrastructure becomes a key site for how individuals and groups build an urban identity as well as struggle over who is included or excluded from these categories (clean vs. dirty, modern vs.

backward). Despite this, human and nonhuman actors regularly subvert, repurpose, or ignore the infrastructures around them, limiting their intended effects. Humans consistently meddle with infrastructure while nonhuman actors often escape from, corrode, or destroy the very infrastructure meant to facilitate their circulation.

Finally, infrastructures also have their own liveliness. As nonhuman actors themselves, infrastructure's behavior can conform to expectations or deviate in unexpected ways. The materiality of infrastructure—its form, its composition, its decay—impacts the world these systems help create (Joyce 2003). Infrastructure can inexplicably cease to work, generate unintended consequences, or continue to affect other actors once decommissioned. These are salient reminders about infrastructure's own potency when considering the budding relationship between Cincinnati elites and the Ohio River. Infrastructure is far from an inert bridge between the two and instead has played an active role in determining how this partnership has unfolded.

Methodology

To understand the dynamics between the Ohio River, Cincinnati elite groups, and riparian infrastructural systems, this book builds on the methodologies laid out in assemblage theory. As a methodology, assemblage theory has been used extensively to analyze how technologies are coproduced by a range of human and nonhuman actors, particularly relevant to examining the infrastructural debates at the center of *Reinventing the River City*. Assemblage theory grounds the analysis of social relationships in a lively materiality, diverging sharply from a view of human agency operating on an inert, nonsocial world.

In its application, assemblage theory builds on work developed by actor-network theory (ANT), which has had its primary application in the fields of science, technology, and society studies. Developed by philosopher Bruno Latour and others, ANT is a tool based on the "tracing of associations" (Latour 2005, 5). In the ANT framework, both human and nonhuman actors are understood as "mediators," who, through their relationships, "transform, translate, distort, and modify the meaning or the elements they are supposed to carry" (38). In describing these actor-networks, it is crucial to take seriously "the ability of each actor to make other actors do unexpected things" (129) and thus alter how technologies are conceived, implemented, and operate. In turn, technologies themselves, such as infrastructures, also act to shape the networks that form around them. ANT calls for the social to be understood as constantly in process, either involving the formation of new connections or requiring active work to sustain existing relationships (Law 1994).

The ANT approach is clearly useful in terms of conceptualizing and tracking relationships between the Ohio River, Cincinnati elites, and riparian infrastructures, drawing attention to the unstable networks that shape, maintain, and eventually abandon water management systems. However, there are specific drawbacks to the way ANT defines its field of inquiry. First, ANT has left scientific expertise in a privileged position at the center of the networks that surround technologies. Latour insists that science is uniquely responsible for the "social construction of facts," meaning that even though science is inextricable from the practices surrounding it and is subject to alteration by other actors, it is only the scientist that produces "the most ascertained, objective, and certified results ever obtained by collective human ingenuity" (Latour 2005, 89–90). Second, Latour has insisted on only studying relationships in the depths of praxis. In doing so, ANT adamantly rejects the analytical utility of social concepts like inequality and power if they are not readily apparent in specific interactions. Latour claims that the reliance on these structural concepts leads social scientists to hunt for data that conforms to their expectations rather than looking at what is really going on in a particular time and place. Critics of Latour point out that "any consideration of matters like masculine supremacy or racism or imperialism or class structures are inadmissible because they are the old 'social' ghosts that blocked real explanation of science in action" (Haraway 1992, 332). As a result, ANT provides little encouragement to consider why specific actors are included or excluded from scientific practices, or how social processes are shaped by systems of oppression or exploitation.

Assemblage theory provides a powerful remedy to these issues. Originally laid out by the philosopher Gilles Deleuze and psychoanalyst Félix Guattari (1987), assemblage theory provides a framework for understanding fluid and contingent relationships involving human and nonhuman actors without privileging human agency. An assemblage perspective also emphasizes the multiplicity of experiences, in that any given assemblage includes interpretations and activities that may not be consistent with one another. The constitution of an assemblage thus includes many different and cross-cutting registers. According to philosopher Jane Bennett, an assemblage is "a living, throbbing grouping whose coherence coexists with energies and countercultures that exceed and confound it" (Bennett 2005, 445).

These prompts to investigate multiplicity and uncertainty are particularly relevant to *Reinventing the River City*. In analyzing shifting infrastructural debates, the arguments made by different elite class formations, as well as between proponents of expertise and practical knowledge, appear deeply contradictory but also share aligned trajectories that contribute to their effectiveness in transforming Cincinnati's urban environment.

Moreover, within assemblage theory, there is no perspective that provides the most complete or objective information available. Instead, all viewpoints, whether that of a scientist, a civic booster, an infrastructural system, or the Ohio River, are partial, contingent, and limited. An assemblage is a "web with an uneven topography" (Bennett 2005, 445), meaning it is explicitly shaped by the distribution of power through processes such as imperialism and sexism. These social structures make some relationships more prominent and others more marginal, as well as enable some individuals to occupy more powerful positions and force others into subordinate roles or exclude them all together. This contoured description of assemblage contrasts sharply with Latour's view of ANT, which rather than highlighting the unevenness of relationships "has tried to render the social world as flat as possible in order to ensure that the establishment of any new link is clearly visible" (Latour 2005, 16). Whereas ANT prioritizes commensurability in studying actor relationships, assemblage theory urges researchers to examine structural disparities.

Assemblage is a methodological tool particularly relevant to understanding the materials analyzed in *Reinventing the River City*. This book draws predominantly from archives in Cincinnati, looking at the documents produced by the elite-driven associations that formed to address these issues of navigation, flooding, and pollution. Rather than one-sided technical reports or public documents, the bulk of the materials produced by these groups include convention proceedings, meeting minutes, correspondence, and debate summaries. These archival sources are complemented by seventeen interviews involving an intentionally diverse range of actors—including engineers, realtors, conservationists, public relations practitioners, educators, urban planners, and business owners—who have helped shape infrastructural projects affecting the Ohio River and riverfront in recent decades, as well as ethnographic fieldwork attending events and meetings concerning the Ohio River and Cincinnati riverfront. These varied source materials capture the active relationships and engagements involving a wide range of local development actors, providing crucial insight into the conversations taking place among different elite class formations, as well as how they engage with the Ohio River.

What is unique about the materials covered here is that most of them are explicitly dialogical, capturing multiple points of view in conversation with one another. Most technical forums intentionally avoid this narrative mode, instead adopting an authoritative impersonal voice stressing coherence (Mitchell 2002). The materials at the center of this study are unusual in relying on debate and discussion for their legitimacy, presenting disparate voices and creating meaning out of this engagement. As a methodology, assemblage shows how the interaction of these (carefully selected) voices—and their dissemination—proactively frames elite relationships with the Ohio River as well as the crafting of urban governance strategies.

The contributions of nonelites and nonhuman actors remain difficult to trace, but oral histories and newspaper articles play an important part in helping to surface the perspectives that many elites tried to sidestep. Assemblage theory provides a means to grasp how all of these actors create and operationalize social groupings and networks, often in ways that are highly uneven, contradictory, or exclusionary.

Book Structure

The histories told in *Reinventing the River City* move back and forth between the Ohio River and the Cincinnati riverfront, following the riparian infrastructure projects that often contained discordant understandings of the best and highest use for these spaces. Across the Ohio River Valley, focus is primarily on the main stem of the Ohio River as the dominant concern for elite groups in Cincinnati. This is complemented with occasional explorations of the Ohio River's numerous tributaries, many of which have unique histories of their own. In Cincinnati, the emphasis is on the city's central riverfront, which has retained a symbolic importance as the city's birthplace and as a critical node linking the city to the Ohio River. The book also engages with developments along the length of Cincinnati's larger metropolitan riverfront, including communities in Northern Kentucky that often developed their own approaches to riparian infrastructure. The emerging narrative shows a depth of relationship between the Ohio River and Cincinnati that is fiercely local while also pointedly regional and national in its implications.

In the following section of this book, the prologue, I explore the histories of the Ohio River and the Cincinnati riverfront prior to the twentieth century. I focus specifically on the deep connections between the idea of the Ohio River and the idea of Cincinnati, how things like nomenclature, identity, and local economic dynamics have formed in the relationship between the two. The Ohio River's behavior has regularly affected the Cincinnati riverfront, and inversely, developments in Cincinnati have had significant implications for the Ohio River. Because of this focus, the prologue is not a comprehensive geological or historical overview of the Cincinnati and Ohio Valley region prior to the twentieth century, but rather a relational one highlighting their intersections over time.

The first three chapters each explore the histories of a specific river management problem—low water, flooding, and navigation—and how Cincinnati elites promoted riparian infrastructure for these issues as well as how the Ohio River supported or impeded these efforts. This thematic chapter organization enables a diachronic investigation of how and why specific groups of elite actors consolidated around distinct infrastructure projects for the Ohio River. Elite groups often had minimal concerns about the unintended consequences resulting from their projects. For example, the chapter on the Ohio River lock and dam system does not extensively describe how this new infrastructural system affected river hydraulics and ecology because the commercial elites that promoted the lock and dam system were not concerned by what were, for them, tangential changes in the Ohio River's behavior. Instead, the responses to these changes, largely organized around concerns over pollution, were driven by a different group of elites interested in maintaining a reliable supply of clean water. At the same time, because each of these distinct projects lasted decades, there are important overlaps in actors and time periods that are highlighted throughout.

The first chapter examines the history of navigation infrastructure in Cincinnati. As mentioned, seasonal fluctuations in river depth presented a persistent obstacle to providing regular boat service on the Ohio River, hindering Cincinnati's river economy as rail corporations extended their transportation dominance. In response, a group of ship captains, merchants, and civic leaders in Cincinnati formed the Ohio Valley Improvement Association (OVIA) in 1895 to lobby the federal government to improve navigation by deepening the river. This group called for the U.S. Army Corps of Engineers (USACE) to build a series of dams on the Ohio River, such as the Fernbank Dam discussed at the beginning of this introduction, which would slow down the water as it headed downstream, creating a chain of pools connected by locks at each dam. Cincinnati merchants and the USACE used a combination of practical knowledge and scientific expertise to advance their project, even though it was strongly opposed by conservationists who advocated for the scientific management of Ohio Valley water resources. By promoting a view of the Ohio River as a cantankerous actor—that only those with years of maritime experience in the region could truly understand and work with—the OVIA was able to overcome powerful conservationist protests.

The second chapter explores how the 1937 Ohio River flood sparked a reevaluation of flood control in Cincinnati. Severe flooding in the early twentieth century, as well as decades of lobbying, had finally unlocked federal funding for levees and other flood control measures across the country. In Cincinnati after the 1937 flood, initial belief that only a massive floodwall could protect the city quickly gave way to a heated debate involving city government officials and local business interests, pitting engineering experts and riverfront businesses who argued for comprehensive flood protection infrastructure against a faction of urban planners and redevelopment advocates who argued for a much-reduced floodwall. Local professional interests eventually aligned with the city's urban planning experts to curtail the floodwall plans, arguing that it would restrict the city's future development and that the river's unrestricted flow needed to be respected. In doing so, these urban planners also deployed the Ohio River as an ally over the next decades to slowly eat away at the buildings left on the central riverfront, enabling the central riverfront to eventually be targeted for destruction by urban renewal initiatives.

The third chapter investigates Cincinnati's long relationship with pollution. Across the nineteenth century, even as sewers proliferated, Cincinnati residents and businesses still dumped most of their waste directly into the Ohio River with little treatment. With surging national debates around pollution control policy, a group called the Cincinnati Stream Pollution Committee, formed by the Cincinnati Chamber of Commerce, began to push for a comprehensive pollution treatment approach embracing the entire Ohio Valley. The Cincinnati Stream Pollution Committee, including sanitation engineers, government officials, marketing experts, and industrial representatives, lobbied eight states to join an interstate compact called the Ohio River Valley Water Sanitation Commission (ORSANCO). Through this process, industry, which had long been resistant to pollution oversight, was able to maintain an active role in determining what counted as pollution and how it should be treated, while also preempting national regulations for pollution treatment. This engagement with sanitation expertise also changed industrial perceptions of the Ohio River, with industrialists arguing for the first time that a clean river was fundamental to economic growth in the region.

These threads—navigation, flooding, and pollution—come together in the fourth chapter, in which I discuss two parallel riverfront redevelopment efforts. Ethnographic fieldwork carries the book's narrative into the present and examines how these infrastructural legacies continue to shape elite relationships with the Ohio River and Cincinnati riverfront, examining two very different visions of the "working river" and the "luxury river." My investigation of the "luxury river" focuses on The Banks, a mixed-use development on the central riverfront. Built between the Ohio River and the nearby Fort Washington Way bypass, The Banks has been lauded as a sustainable, resilient project that many city officials claim has, at long last, realized the economic potential of the riverfront. While The Banks has received significant acclaim, the chapter also focuses on efforts to redevelop Cincinnati's ports and promote the "working river." The River Advisory Council and, later, the Central Ohio River Business Association pushed to expand the federally defined boundaries of the Ports of Cincinnati & Northern Kentucky, finally succeeding in 2015. As a result, Cincinnati is now considered one of the country's largest inland river ports, a marketing boon for the city's maritime industries. While the leaders behind The Banks and the Ports of Cincinnati & Northern Kentucky have competing visions of how the riverfront should be seen, they have also drawn on the same infrastructural histories embedded in the landscape to legitimize their efforts, including arguments about environmental impact, flood resiliency, and the importance of navigation. In this context, riparian infrastructure has been increasingly promoted by local elites as a crucial public good, even as they used infrastructure to reinforce exclusionary access to the riverfront and the Ohio River.

I conclude the book with a brief consideration of the future of the Ohio River and Cincinnati riverfront. Since the late nineteenth century, Cincinnati elites have reshaped what it means to be a river city, assembling an urban landscape where the river is critical to daily life and the local economy but also far removed and often inaccessible for residents. I ask, What would it look like for community-driven decision-making to consider the interlocked questions posed by pollution, flood control, and navigation, and how might we get there.

PROLOGUE

Cincinnati, Nineteenth-Century River City

It is common to hear in Cincinnati that the city would be nothing without the Ohio River. An economic lifeline, the city owes its location and early growth to the Ohio River's funneling of migrants and commerce to the area. Many local residents also recognize that, inversely, Cincinnati has had a profound impact on the Ohio River. The metropolitan population has shaped the river in countless ways since the city's founding. The Ohio River and Cincinnati are therefore closely connected. Recognizing these linkages, this prologue follows geographer Erik Swyngedouw (1999) in avoiding an arbitrary division of nature from society by presenting hydrological data, maps, and ecological descriptions that naturalize the Ohio River basin and then describing how Cincinnati has been built on top of this preexisting context. Nor is this prologue an all-encompassing history of human occupation in the area, covering thoroughly the Indigenous and colonial history of the region. Rather, the emphasis here is on providing an intertwined history of the river and the city, charting how the relationships between the Ohio River and Cincinnati shaped the emergence of the latter as a river city in the nineteenth century.

Geologically speaking, the Ohio River is a relatively new river, about 400,000 years old, younger even than many of its tributaries (White, Johnston, and Miller 2011).[1] The name itself is much more recent, derived from an Iroquois name, which the French translated as "beautiful river" and began to call "La Belle Riviere." The Ohio River moniker came into common usage among the English settler colonial population only in the mid-eighteenth century, in an effort to avoid using the French name for the river (Dunn 1912).

The function of the Ohio River as well as its extent and appearance have changed significantly over the course of its existence. Along much of its length, the Ohio River replaced the ancient Teays River, which flowed northwest—from modern-day western North Carolina to northern Illinois—instead of the Ohio River's present southwesterly direction. Glaciers descending from the north disrupted the Teays River's course starting approximately two million years ago, forming massive lakes where ice dams interrupted the river. When these lakes overflowed, the floods scoured new channels that make up much of the present Ohio River's passage (White, Johnston, and Miller 2011). The Teays River's former channels can still be found across the landscape. This includes a defunct tributary called the Cincinnati River, a massive waterway in its own right that extended northward from the Teays River. The wide valley that used to hold the Cincinnati River has offered some of the flattest terrain in the hilly Cincinnati region, hosting the city's industrial heart as well as the southerly flowing Mill Creek.

The 981-mile-long Ohio River begins at an arbitrary starting point adjacent to downtown Pittsburgh, Pennsylvania, at the junction of the Allegheny and Monongahela Rivers. The river then extends to Cairo, Illinois, where it joins the Mississippi River. Due to abundant precipitation across the watershed, the Ohio Valley makes up only 16 percent of the total Mississippi basin's surface area, but accounts for more than 40 percent of its final discharge. Despite the large amount of water moved by the river, as a more recent feature of the landscape the Ohio River itself has a relatively narrow valley, with limited floodplains until closer to its terminus.

The symbolic importance of the Ohio River has shifted along with its route. Many Indigenous groups considered the river the primary waterway in the region and used it as a central feature of the landscape. Over the centuries, Indigenous settlement patterns along the Ohio River experienced significant population shifts due to factors like climate change, warfare, and increasing pressure from European colonialism (Drooker 2002). French colonial interests, which claimed the entire Mississippi River basin in 1682, saw the Ohio River as an important route for trade and the supply of French military fortifications. After the Treaty of Paris in 1763 shifted the claim to the British, they used the river as a dividing line between southern areas slowly opening to white settlement, and an "Indian Reserve" to the north. After U.S. independence, the Ohio River became a vital route for waves of white settlers moving westward, a powerful early symbol of the country's Manifest Destiny and drive toward expansion (Gruenwald 2002), while Indigenous peoples saw it as the main route of the young nation's genocidal push through the region (Ostler 2015). Even as the westward migration of white settlers continued, the Ohio River became an important border as part of the Mason-Dixon Line, separating slave-owning states in the South from wage-labor states in the North. This Ohio River area therefore served as an important borderland to connect the different formations of white supremacy in the North and the South (Salafia

2013). Meanwhile, Black communities referred to the Ohio River as "River Jordan" in recognition of its emblematic role on the Underground Railroad and the route to freedom (Trotter 1998).

As the first major city to emerge along the Ohio River, and located close to its midpoint, Cincinnati's history is deeply rooted in both the geography and the symbolic importance of the river. Though the pattern of U.S. settler colonialism is often portrayed as isolated families of white homesteaders slowly expanding outward into a wild frontier, in fact, urban settlers often arrived first, attempting to predetermine the routes to be taken by later arrivals, as well as operating as military outposts to subdue Indigenous populations (Wade 1959; Mahoney 1990). Covering the Cincinnati area, John Cleves Symmes purchased more than 300,000 acres in present-day southwest Ohio from the U.S. Congress (WPA 1943). In 1788 three groups founded villages in this territory, with Symmes's chosen settlement, North Bend, joined by two other early communities, Columbia and Losantiville. All three were located on the banks of the Ohio River.

The first residents of Cincinnati founded the town in 1788 with the name Losantiville, which meant "town across from the mouth of the Licking River" in a mixture of Latin (*os*), Greek (*anti*), and French (*ville*), with the "L" standing for the Licking River, a tributary that flowed into the Ohio River from Kentucky. Two years later, in 1790, the recently appointed governor of the Northwest Territories, General Arthur St. Clair, pushed to change Losantiville's name to Cincinnati, in honor of the Society of the Cincinnati, a group of veterans from the U.S. War of Independence, to which he belonged. The group's name came from Lucius Quinctius Cincinnatus, a Roman citizen-soldier who had served as dictator while defending the ancient Roman Republic from an Aequi invasion but quickly relinquished his role once the Romans had defeated the threat. Early U.S. leaders celebrated Cincinnatus as a patriotic model due to his dedication to democracy.

In 1789 a U.S. military detachment chose to base a new garrison, Fort Washington, in the burgeoning town. The site sat above the most frequent flooding and also provided a vantage overlooking the mouth of the Licking River, a vital corridor into the Kentucky interior, which at that point contained the largest white settler population in the region. From this position, military commanders reasoned that the garrison could forestall hostile incursions by Indigenous groups targeting Kentucky's settler communities (Stradling 2003). With the presence of Fort Washington, Cincinnati became an important center for military campaigns against Indigenous peoples throughout the Northwest Territories (Taylor 2004). The U.S. military used Cincinnati as a logistics base to launch campaigns against the Shawnee, Miami, Lenape, and other Indigenous peoples in the region, which concluded with the forced westward displacement of most of these peoples in the first decades of the nineteenth century.

Even after the garrison at Fort Washington relocated directly across the river to Newport, Kentucky, in 1804, Cincinnati residents played a key role in remaking the Ohio Valley as a domain of white settler colonialism. Merchants and wholesalers built up Cincinnati as a trading post, maintaining commercial connections along the valley's waterways. Migrants descending the Ohio River in skiffs, keelboats, or flatboats stopped in Cincinnati to purchase the supplies they needed to settle further downriver or to disembark and continue on foot to the newly conquered interior areas of Ohio and Indiana (Wilhelm 1991).

The Ohio River riverbed was primarily characterized by a sand and gravel base, with frequent islands, though less so in the middle third of the river. The river dropped gradually, from 217 meters above sea level at Pittsburgh to only 88 meters when connecting with the Mississippi River (White, Johnston, and Miller 2011). The result, especially after the upper section, was a slow-moving river, with only one significant section of rapids, near Louisville, Kentucky. The main channel of the river shifted frequently, winding through unpredictable sandbanks and sandbars, submerged trees, and hidden rocks. A journey along the river could easily turn treacherous, with pilots forced to guess the location of the best route. In the early nineteenth century, many travelers relied on the most recent edition of Zadok Cramer's *The Navigator* to avoid these potential hazards (Mahoney 1990). The introduction of steamboats in 1811, making upstream travel widely accessible for the first time, further reinforced Cincinnati's role as the center of the Ohio Valley, with the busy Public Landing receiving goods and traders from across the region. Soon the Cincinnati riverfront became known as the region's "storefront" and the Ohio River as the city's "Main Street" (Gruenwald 2002; Bigham 1991).

Cincinnati's hinterlands encompassed a diverse and promising combination of natural resources and landscapes. The series of glaciers that formed the course of the Ohio River had significantly shaped the geomorphology of the region. To the north of the Ohio River, the glaciers left a large band of relatively uniform, newer, and more fertile soil well suited to agricultural exploitation. To the south of the Ohio River, the quality of older soil deposits varied greatly depending on local conditions and the more irregular topography (Mahoney 1990, 13). Near Cincinnati itself, the hilly, wooded terrain near what had been the southern extent of glacial expansion presented less attractive prospects, but the emergence of the Cincinnati market saw interest in this area as well. Before their forced removal, centuries of agriculture and land stewardship led by Indigenous women had left the landscape as "a kind of paradise" according to historian Susan Sleeper-Smith, with the cultivation of rich croplands, flood-absorbing wetlands, and environmental niches for diverse foodstuffs such as apples and nuts (Sleeper-Smith 2018, 5). Under settler colonial occupation, the region supported the lucrative production of tobacco and hemp in Kentucky, as well as hogs, cattle, and corn in Ohio and Indiana. These goods fed into Cincinnati's commercial engine, routing products to the bigger southern and eastern markets. Moreover, the deposits of salt, iron ore, and coal concentrated upriver of Cincinnati, as well as abundant timber, much of it close to the river, helped drive urban growth and early production of goods like pork (giving the city the nickname of Porkopolis), whiskey, and basic agricultural implements (Wilhelm 1991, 78).

The early city gained fame for its rapid growth and bustling economic energy, though several visitors recorded mixed impressions. One particularly notable observer of early Cincinnati, Frances Milton Trollope, wrote *Domestic Manners of the Americans*, a well-known travel book about the United States. Immensely popular in Britain, the book takes a largely negative view of the United States, with particular focus on the author and her family's two years living in Cincinnati. According to Trollope:

> We had heard so much of Cincinnati, its beauty, wealth, and unequalled prosperity, that when we left Memphis to go thither, we almost felt the delight of Rousseau's novice, "un voyage à faire, et Paris au bout!" —As soon, therefore, as our little domestic arrangements were completed, we set forth to view this "wonder of the west" this "prophet's gourd of magic growth,"—this "infant Hercules;" and surely no travellers ever paraded a city under circumstances more favourable to their finding it fair to the sight.... But, alas! the flatness of reality after the imagination has been busy! I hardly know what I expected to find in this city, fresh risen from the bosom of the wilderness, but certainly it was not a little town, about the size of Salisbury, without even an attempt at beauty in any of its edifices, and with only just enough of the air of a city to make it noisy and bustling. (1832, 51)

Trollope goes on to deplore the poor sanitation, lack of artistic expression, and rough mannerisms that characterized the early city. Her business venture in Cincinnati, an upscale bazaar near the riverfront, failed quickly, and the family left after slightly more than two years in the city.

Pushing back on these and similar criticisms, residents of Cincinnati sought to develop the city as an early scientific and literary center as well as a beacon of refinement and culture. Numerous local elites gathered firsthand information about the characteristics of the Ohio Valley, working to define a region still mysterious to both its settler colonial communities and exterior audiences (Hendrickson 1973). Local doctor Daniel Drake produced some of the earliest geological, meteorological, and epidemiological studies of the region, as well as founding the Western Museum Society and Western Academy of Natural Sciences to begin to catalog and display the resources found across the Ohio Valley. Charles Cist, a local publisher and statistics enthusiast, produced some of the earliest statistical analyses of urban life in the region, documenting Cincinnati's growth and early history, as well as compiling popular stories about the white pioneers and their encounters around the city (Cist 1845). Cincinnati elites also founded a number of regional periodicals in Cincinnati, seeking to shape a distinctive new cultural identity for the rough-and-tumble West (Katz 2002).

An idea of expertise guided these early efforts to explore and describe the Ohio Valley. Binaries of white expertise and Indigenous ignorance underpinned settler colonialism in the area and helped justify the displacement and domination of Indigenous groups. Individuals like Daniel Drake argued that Western knowledge was universal due to its adherence to rational thought and Indigenous knowledge unreliable and too directly tied to nature. In his *Discourse on the History, Character, and Prospects of the West* (1834), Drake claimed that "the civilizing of the Indians is beset with difficulties not easily surmounted; but who can say that our efforts have been always well directed? or cease to regret, that they [Indigenous peoples] have perished by our presence, as the young corn dwindles and dies beneath the shade of the beautiful sugar-tree, while both belong to one kingdom of nature?" (21).

Drake's imagery, where Europeans ("the beautiful sugar-tree") naturally overshadow and choke out Indigenous peoples ("the young corn"), was typical of the time. White colonists thought they would replace native populations because they were more civilized and better capable of cultivating the land, while Indigenous peoples were incapable of progress, most pressingly due to their lack of interest in owning property. This belief, reiterated in countless early publications and stories, created an indelible link between expertise and whiteness in the Ohio Valley.

At the same time, these explorers and cataloguers documenting (and benefiting from) discoveries across the Ohio Valley were almost all men, who believed their gender as well as their race made them capable of the self-control and rational thinking necessary to undertake unbiased observation. Cincinnati's emerging patriarchal society imposed a different role on white women. Local white elite men portrayed elite white women as inclined to ignorance due to being confined to the domestic sphere as well as due to a perceived tendency for emotional responses. As a result, women were seen as lacking capacity to be objective and impassive, disqualifying them from scientific or commercial pursuits (McNeil 1998). Instead, expectations fell on middle- and upper-class white women in Cincinnati to educate the public about morality, as with local writer Harriet Beecher Stowe's *Uncle Tom's Cabin*. These women were also expected to promote the cultivation of refinement, such as the instructive domestic scenes found in the works of local female artists such as Lilly Martin Spencer (Katz 2002).

These efforts to build Cincinnati's reputation as a center of sophistication contrasted sharply with the city's primary source of prosperity, the steamboats plying the Ohio River. Life on the river had long had a reputation for being outside the norms of regular society, defined by transitory populations less interested in the politics of respectability. After decades of development, steamboats had become massive, each a "world in miniature" with sleeping quarters, large dining and entertainment halls, and freight storage. Many steamboats visiting smaller towns also served as de facto grocers, general stores, bars, blacksmiths, or whatever else was needed at their ports of call. The hundreds of steamboats docking at Cincinnati Public Landing each year brought a steady stream of freight and passengers from far afield. Alongside the steamboats, a motley collection of irregular crafts, from small-scale fishing boats to peddlers to shantyboats, brought variety and diversity to river society.

Steamboats represented an alluring site of danger. Built to be light and fast, they are described by historian Walter Johnson as enormous "bubbles" floating on top of the river (Johnson 2013, 92). Unsurprisingly, these fragile ships were notoriously prone to accidents. Snags (sunken trees stuck in the riverbed that easily could punch holes in boat hulls), sandbars, boiler explosions, and ice floes sank steamboats at alarming rates, causing the loss of life and freight (Gruenwald 2002; Johnson 2013; Allen 1991). Moreover, steamboat racing was a popular pastime on the Ohio River. Captains pushed their vessels to the limit to delight their passengers and attract fame. The inherent risks of racing caused more accidents. Frequent losses and high profits defined steamboat shipping, making it an unpredictable economic pursuit for the ship captains who were frequently owner-operators of their crafts.

In response to cutthroat competition, many ship captains went to great lengths to adorn their boats with intricate woodwork and fanciful decorations, seeking to convince potential clients of their trustworthiness through an attractive appearance (Johnson 2013, 101). These "floating palaces" brought into proximity a diverse collection of people from different economic and racial backgrounds, as well as enabling the mingling of sexes. In this mobile society, individuals could more easily step outside of their normal social roles, further spurring a sense of the unknown. The experience of traveling with this mix of strangers in a confined space was unusual in the antebellum period, as was the ubiquity of drinking, gambling, and carousing usually found onboard, abetted by travelers often carrying significant savings with them as they migrated along the frontier between the slaveholding South and wage-labor North. Black passengers on the Ohio River were constantly under suspicion of being escaped slaves, using the riverboats to flee bondage. Slave hunters frequently prowled steamboat decks, searching for bounties. This potent mix further added to a sense of danger and excitement around the river (Johnson 2013).

Despite being a vital component of Cincinnati's steamboat economy, the Ohio River was not always a cooperative partner. Countless stories describe these willful expressions of the Ohio River as "Old Man River" (Grayson 1929). Old Man River was neither malevolent nor kind, prone to destroy just as much as to provide. Still, as a commercial lifeline, the river was unreliable. Depending on one's location in the Ohio Valley, the river system was only navigable from two to ten months per year. Ship captains had to wait for spring and autumn freshets to open the river after winter ice and summer low water had made the channel impassable (Mahoney 1990). These spring and autumn freshets, when the river rose after snowmelt or periods of extended rain, were crucial to river navigation but also carried the risk of flooding, particularly in spring. Any flooding meant disruptions to business and social life as people waited for the waters to abate.

The federal government reluctantly authorized minor improvements to the river in the antebellum era, primarily focused on making shipping easier, including dredging, snag removal, and building structures like wing dams that helped concentrate the channel (Shallat 1994). In 1830 private investors opened the Louisville and Portland Canal to circumvent the Falls of the Ohio, the only significant rapids along the river. Despite these investments, travel on the Ohio River remained precarious and irregular. These vagaries carried over to high freight costs, which rose considerably as reports of flooding or low water filtered through a dispersed communication network (Mahoney 1990). Farmers, miners, small-scale manufactories, and others reliant on river transport had to accommodate shipping price uncertainty, limited seasonal availability of cargo space, and constant risk of loss.

The Cincinnati riverfront acted as an interface between more staid urban life and the adventure of the river. "At midcentury, Cincinnati business still centered about the public landing. Steamers came and went, whistles blew, the wharf was piled high with merchandise and crowded with people. When a packet was in dock it seemed as if the whole world were there. The men of the boats were of a fabled race—pilots in their 'Texas' high above the river, suave gamblers, and the roustabouts, singing chanteys while bearing the river's trade up and down the gangplanks" (WPA 1940, 199).

Early in its development, Cincinnati's residents and businesses concentrated near the two-block-long Public Landing, a city-held commons along the river where anyone could dock or draw water for their needs. Over time, the city slowly spread into a wide U-shaped basin behind the riverfront, as well as expanding east and west along the riverbanks and across the river into Kentucky, primarily in the towns of Newport and Covington. The city's population boomed as local merchants and workshops required significant labor to meet the demands of the rapidly expanding settler population across the Ohio Valley (Ross 1985). Beyond its commercial activities, Cincinnati began to produce a wide range of goods, including carriages, soap, steamboat engines, and barrels, alongside longer-established concerns like local meatpacking businesses and distilleries.

An intense regional labor shortage due to this early economic expansion helped drive high wages for Cincinnati workers. This attracted interest among white immigrants from the East Coast in the first half of the nineteenth century, and then increasingly from overseas, particularly from Germany and Ireland (Stradling 2003). Black immigrants, mostly from the South, also began to arrive very early in Cincinnati's history (Taylor 2004). These Black residents, alongside the remaining Indigenous population, occupied the bottom of the racial hierarchy in Cincinnati, while whites of English or Scottish descent dominated local positions of power (Ross 1985).

Even with the expanding city, the central riverfront remained the focus of early Cincinnati's public life—the place where people went to shop, find work, draw water, and hear the news. The presence of shops, housing, markets, popular places of entertainment, and employers such as small-scale factories and warehouses ensured that Cincinnatians visited the riverfront regularly. A visitor to the waterfront might find Methodists baptizing converts in the river or roustabouts reveling at notorious saloons and hotels in the area, such as the Silver Moon Lodging House (Grayson 1929, 62, 77).

With many urban residents living close to their place of employment, Black and Irish residents increasingly occupied the housing in the downtown riverfront area. Men from both communities competed for unskilled jobs on the Cincinnati docks or among the area's manufactories, or were employed on steamboats as cooks, barbers, or stewards. Meanwhile, women used the river for their work as washers, as well as engaging in sex work in the brothels and bars in the area and occasionally taking jobs in the paper mills and other small-scale workshops near the riverfront (Ross 1985). White Cincinnati residents began to call sections of the riverfront area Little Africa or Bucktown because of the predominance of Black residents, while adjacent Gas Alley (near the city gasworks) was known for its Irish population (Taylor 2004; Dannenbaum 1984). Significant intermixing defined the riverfront overall. Merchants and early industrialists forcing Black and Irish workers to compete for jobs created tension between these groups, contributing to race riots on the downtown riverfront in 1829, 1836, and 1841. Cincinnati's white residents believed the local government failed to enforce the Ohio Black Laws, which had been designed to discourage Black migrants from settling in the state or finding local employment that white residents believed belonged to them (Trotter 1998). This further exacerbated animosity toward Cincinnati's Black residents.

While the central riverfront remained a vibrant if disreputable area, other riverfront areas began to differentiate themselves during the antebellum period. Some adjacent riverfront neighborhoods, like the Fulton district to the east of the city center (named after the steamboat innovator), began to focus more exclusively on production. The Fulton area included many of Cincinnati's largest boatyards, offering higher-paying employment in specific trades as the city became one of the largest ship producers in the country (Lewis 2016). Across the river, Covington, Kentucky, developed as a thriving German residential community. The city was closely connected to Cincinnati but also began to serve as an economic outlet for the interior Bluegrass region of Kentucky, with rail links and agricultural processing facilities, such as cigar factories for Kentucky's tobacco.

Cincinnati's growth in the first half of the nineteenth century—as well as the interlinked growth of mining, agriculture, and logging across the Ohio Valley—had already begun to affect the Ohio River. Forests along the riverbanks provided fuel for steamboats, but by the mid-nineteenth century most timber stands near the river had been cleared. This deforestation increased water runoff from storms, contributing to flooding as well as eroding riparian hillsides and moving more soil into the Ohio River. Deforestation also led to increased reliance on coal as a steamboat fuel source, and therefore mining. Drainage from mines would increasingly alter the river's chemistry, making it more acidic and harming aquatic life, though this impact was minimal at the time. Finally, as a source of drinking water, the Ohio River posed dangers. Cincinnati residents and businesses dumped their waste into open sewers running along the city streets, which drained directly to the river. In theory, this sewage would be diluted and flushed downstream with minimal local impact. In practice, this enabled the spread of disease, particularly cholera. A devastating infection, cholera spread rapidly both in Cincinnati and across the Ohio Valley, abetted by the constant flow of steamboat arrivals and departures. Epidemics hit the city hard in 1832, 1849, and 1866. Although closely studied by Daniel Drake and others, the link between cholera bacteria, drinking water, and human waste was little understood until the late nineteenth century (Carter 1992; M. Smith 2016).

The Civil War brought both economic booms and radical shifts for the Cincinnati economy. The conflict cut off Cincinnati's critical southern market, but at the same time, military production underpinned a major industrial expansion in the city. Steamboats shipped goods both upriver and downriver to support the massive Union armies. Despite this, traditional local steamboat trade declined as Cincinnati's regional market connections fell apart. Moreover, the Civil War saw a massive expansion of railroad usage to provision troops in far-flung locales. Hostilities dampened the normal bustle of river life, shifting the environment from one of excitement to a deep sense of tension and uncertainty. Even given the economic boosts provided by federal government spending, Cincinnati elites emerged from the Civil War unsure of what the coming decades would bring.

Moving into the 1870s, the Ohio River remained an indisputable force in the city, as Cincinnatians continued to be subject to Old Man River's shifting whims. Lack of year-round navigation, consistent flooding, and exponential growth in waste disposal continued to shape daily life in the city. Cincinnati's elites explored a number of ways to respond to these issues, combining scientific innovations and political maneuvering to adjust the city's relationship with the river. Many of these efforts focused on proposals to control the risks posed by the Ohio River, such as through filtration systems for the city waterworks, levees for flood control, and increased dredging of the channel bed to improve navigation. Prominent Cincinnatians hosted one-time conventions beseeching federal intervention on these issues, organized new municipal government departments, and invested in new technologies, but they were largely unable to change the Ohio River's behavior.

In the postbellum period, railroads further pulled economic opportunity away from the riverfront. One boatman, returning to the Cincinnati riverfront in the 1880s after a long absence, cried after seeing the changes in the area, devastated that the railroads had brought "down the curtain on the good old days of steamboating" (Grayson 1929, 73). With the steamboat economy faltering, journalists and city leaders relentlessly depicted of the city's central riverfront as an unsavory, dangerous area due to its connections to racial intermixing and labor unrest (Trotter 1998). As railroads gained prominence, steamboat journeys lost their luster, and the river became known as the "poor man's highway" (Ambler 1932).[2]

This decline of river transportation was accompanied by a more definitive shift in Cincinnati's central riverfront neighborhoods toward entertainment and illicit activities, bucking the moral conventions of both white and Black communities living in other sections of the city (Taylor 2004). Local journalist Lafcadio Hearn provided a rare window into life on the riverfront during this period. With an eye for lurid detail, his newspaper articles from the 1870s reinforced perceptions of river life as debaucherous, driven by deep links to Blackness:

> Shortly before daybreak on Saturday morning a drunken negro was pulled out of the river at the foot of Broadway by two watchful patrolmen, who subsequently experienced considerable difficulty in bringing the man to the station-house, as he was actually insane from poisonous whisky, and struggled with maniacal fury. By the time he had been brought, dripping wet and muddy, to the office of the Hammond Street Police Station, the force of his mania had fairly expended itself, and he stood before the desk with an air of frightened bewilderment, like a sleepwalker suddenly aroused from his dangerous dreams.
>
> "What's your name, Mr. Tired-of-Life," humorously asked the humorous Sergeant.
>
> "My name," answered Tired-of-Life, in a voice husky with whisky and river water, "is Albert Jones."
>
> "Albert Jones!" exclaimed the Sergeant, in a tone of serious surprise; "that man can imitate the whistle of any boat on the Ohio or Mississippi River. Give us the Wildwood or the Andy Baum, old fellow!"
>
> The prisoner's face suddenly brightened; he drew himself up with something of a rough pride and exclaimed in the tone of one long accustomed to interest a crowd, "Gentlemen, I will show you the difference between the whistle of the Wildwood and the Andy Baum. Listen to the Wildwood—coming in."
>
> He suddenly threw up both hands, concave-fashion, to his mouth, expanded his deep chest, and poured out a long, profound, sonorous cry that vibrated through the room like the music of a steam whistle. He started off

> with a deep nasal tone, but gradually modulated its depth and volume to an imitation of the steam-whistle, so astonishingly perfect that at its close every listener uttered an involuntary exclamation of surprise. (Hearn 1953, 9–10)

Hearn's story intentionally blurs the boundaries between the Ohio River and its denizens. Albert Jones is the human embodiment of a steamboat even when he is so intoxicated that he had just nearly drowned himself. His deep experience with river life is evident, and he knows the intrigue it provides for the more land-bound residents of Cincinnati, who are both attracted to and repelled by his lifestyle. Hearn provided numerous similar accounts, from scenes of Black female sex workers swimming in the moonlit Ohio River to more macabre tales of flood victims returning from the grave to host a ghostly party in an abandoned riverfront dance house. Taken together, they describe a riverfront that existed outside of strict government control and social norms—aided by the transitory nature of the Ohio River itself. The riverfront defied the rest of the city with irregular racial and gender mixing even as it continued to attract visitors (Taylor 2004).

Already preoccupied with revitalizing the river economy, urban elites also felt increasing anxiety about this changing riverfront and the need to discipline its unruly inhabitants. In this sense, elite efforts to tame the Ohio River were often deeply intertwined with desires to tame riverfront populations. If Old Man River could be made to behave, so might his riverfront dwellers. Toward the end of the nineteenth century, many merchants, tradespeople, and small-scale industrialists on the riverfront were increasingly concerned about the future of their investments and were looking for new options to transform local possibilities. Hopes to resolve both issues increasingly coalesced around an ambitious plan to dam the Ohio River, enabling year-round navigation and reorganizing social life along the riverfront.

CHAPTER 1

Ohio Valley Navigation and the City, 1895–1929

After decades of strenuous lobbying, Ohio River navigation advocates wanted to throw a party. On October 17, 1929, a flotilla of twenty-four steamboats gathered in Pittsburgh for a "Celebration of the Opening of the Ohio River Nine-Foot Stage." Over the next nine days, the parade traveled downriver, stopping at cities along the way to commemorate the opening of the very last of the Ohio River locks and dams, located outside Cairo, Illinois. The U.S. Army Corps of Engineers constructed this system of fifty-one locks and dams over the course of fifty years, making year-round navigation possible on the Ohio River.[1] The Ohio Valley Improvement Association (OVIA), which had been lobbying for the river improvements since 1895, organized the festivities. The U.S. secretaries of commerce, war, and labor, alongside the minister plenipotentiary of Egypt and five railroad directors, took part in the opening ceremonies in Pittsburgh. President Herbert Hoover, an engineer by training, accompanied the cruise between Cincinnati and Louisville. In total, an estimated 500,000 people attended these OVIA riverfront events (OVIA 1929b).

One observer compared the OVIA's celebration to the yearly opening of the Great Lakes' shipping season. After winter ice receded, "it was necessary to get out brass bands and use much advertising space in the newspapers to get the public into the annual habit of utilizing the boats" (OVIA 1929b, 41). In the case of its celebratory flotilla, the OVIA wanted to reawaken the public to the potential of the river after decades of decline. To many Ohio Valley residents in the early twentieth century, river transportation appeared outdated and unnecessary. The speed and reliability of railroads—and later, cars—made river transport unnecessary. In response, the OVIA's flotilla of steamboats, with its dignitaries, pageantry, and speeches, announced a new navigational age, one relying on modern infrastructure to provide regular, cheap, and efficient freight transport by river. At the same time, the multiday celebration harkened back to the history of the river, with speeches on George Washington's cartographic forays into the Ohio Valley and the history of Blennerhassett Island, where Aaron Burr allegedly plotted to create a breakaway republic in Texas.

The seeds of this massive celebration can be traced to Cincinnati at the end of the nineteenth century. As that century came to a close, the city's river merchants were despondent. They watched as 1894 and 1895 produced some of the poorest navigation seasons in memory, with low water restricting shipping to only a few months. Meanwhile, the railroads seemed to go from strength to strength. Desperate to change their fortunes, Cincinnati's river merchants cast around for new ways of relating to the Ohio River, settling on an approach that relied on a novel combination of technical and practical knowledge to revitalize river navigation. This chapter explores how, despite a combative conservationist movement that wanted to see experts managing the Ohio River as a natural resource, Cincinnati's river merchants and the larger OVIA movement were successful in positioning the river foremost as a commercial space, one that required massive locks and dams to enable year-round navigation. In justifying their project, the OVIA and its partners at the U.S. Army Corps of Engineers employed a very different concept of expertise compared to the conservationists. They argued that depending on abstract scientific theories about river basins and annual rainfall was insufficient. Rather, one could only truly understand how to work with the Ohio River by bringing technical engineering skills together with deep personal experience developed over decades on the river.

Cincinnati river merchants were critical to creating and promoting this perspective, providing the leadership and resources to drive forward the lock and dam plan over almost four decades. Through their efforts, they also sought to rework how the city interacted with the Ohio River, drastically changing the meaning of riverfront life across the Ohio Valley.

Declining Trade on the Ohio River

Prior to the Civil War, Cincinnati's growth seemed unstoppable, amazing observers at home and abroad. Horace Greeley, the highly influential newspaper publisher and reformer, claimed in 1850 that the city was "destined to become the focus and mart for the grandest circle of manufacturing thrift on this continent" (Cist 1851, 257). Yet, in the postbellum period, newer cities like Chicago, Illinois, and St. Louis, Missouri, assumed expansive roles in the regional economy, facilitated by their closer relationships with booming frontier economies (Cronon 1992; Mahoney 1990). As Cincinnati's dominance over western and southern markets waned, so did its commercial bustle. Merchants had been key powerbrokers in Cincinnati for decades, but the city's diminishing role in provisioning the frontier—exacerbated by the economic crises of the 1870s and increasing labor strife in the city—cut into their business profits and undermined their political and economic power (Ross 1985). In response, many local elites increasingly invested in large-scale industrial production as a new source of capital accumulation, moving into the manufacture of carriages, furniture, liquors, and numerous other products.

Not all could make this transition easily though, and many of the city's merchants found it difficult to adapt to these new economic realities. By 1880, of the wealthiest manufacturers in the city, only 9.3 percent had started as merchants and moved into industrial production (Ross 1985, 223). River merchants were particularly hard hit, including steamboat captains and the commercial firms that heavily depended on the river for transportation, such as coal operators and wholesale grocers. As one local journalist observed, "Cincinnati for years has been known as one of the noted river towns of the country. Like all other places where the traffic by water was a source of commercial power, there has been a falling away at this port" (*Cincinnati Enquirer* 1887). River interests viewed the railroads as the primary source of their problems. From early on, local elites had been suspicious of the railroads, which would be "used for the transportation of *foreign* merchandise from the sea ports into the interior of the country, and thus bring it in competition with home products" (*Cincinnati Daily Enquirer* 1842; emphasis in original). These competitive fears were confirmed when railroads began to replace river shipping as early as the 1850s, providing faster and more regular transportation options. The Civil War accelerated these transitions. It was not long before rapidly growing railroad corporations were undercutting their steamboat competitors across the Ohio Valley, running rail lines parallel to the river and offering cheap shipping rates to hamstring transport by boat. In Cincinnati and elsewhere, railroads also bought harbor frontage to reduce available space for ships to land and purchased the operating rights for cities' docks or wharf boats in order to drive up landing charges.

Disputes broke out on the Cincinnati central riverfront as railroads expanded their activity in the area and river merchants resisted. One such conflict during the spring of 1882 concerned the right of freight trains to actively use the riverfront area during daylight hours for unloading freight (they were previously restricted to extensive usage of the area only at night). E. W. Kittredge, a local lawyer representing waterfront business owners before the

Cincinnati Board of Public Works, complained about "the effect the [rail] cars would have upon the river trade in blockading the streets leading to the river. There were at present about three hundred and fifty steamboats and barges plying into Cincinnati, with a tonnage of nearly one hundred million tons. It would require miles of freight trains to carry these loads. . . . The transfer of freight should be made at the other junction of the Railroad Companies at a point outside of the city, where they would have plenty of room to make their side-tracking" (*Cincinnati Enquirer* 1882). The Board of Public Works held five heated committee hearings on the subject. Strong interest among local merchants and industrialists forced the sessions to move to larger occupancy chambers. Finally, on April 4, 1882, the board rejected the daylight motion, urging the railroads to expand their own facilities rather than use the riverfront as an ad hoc terminal.

Despite this temporary victory, railroads continued to consolidate their grip over the transportation sector in Cincinnati and throughout the Ohio Valley. Leading river merchants were unsure of how to respond, with many clinging to the sparse freight shipments or passengers they could find. According to one steamboat captain, "We have been standing with folded arms and allowed this great river to be crippled by railroads" (OVIA 1895, 20); as another well-known ship operator described it: "When railroads came, we of the river ran away from the river. The railroads were going to absorb all the trade" (OVIA 1895, 41). Unsurprisingly, river trade declined steadily as railroads grew. Sixteen million tons of freight moved on the Ohio River in 1889, as well as 6.5 million passengers (OVIA 1899, 8). Those numbers dropped precipitously over the following years until traffic bottomed out at only 4.6 million tons in 1917, with negligible passenger totals (Robinson 1983).

The declining role of river merchants marked an important moment of social and economic transformation along the Ohio River. For many, the age of the river had come to an end. One ode to the river in 1889 noted, "The old-time steamboatmen are not all dead. . . . Many of them still linger on the stage of life, though in these days of rapid transit and railroad rush they are probably looked upon as superfluous. . . . Many of these men have sought other callings, and become prosperous and prominent, but whenever two or three of them gather together, the spirit of the old days will surely be present, and their thoughts and conversation will almost invariably be of the glories of the river in olden times" (*Cincinnati Enquirer* 1889).

The historian Reuben Gold Thwaites, a close colleague of Frederick Jackson Turner, decided to document the passing of the historic Ohio River, much as Turner had done for the western frontier. In 1894 Thwaites departed Pittsburgh with his family loaded onto the *Pilgrim*—a simple skiff without an engine—and floated down the Ohio River for six weeks, recording his observations. Intent like Turner on reconstructing pioneer life, in *Afloat on the Ohio* (1897) he describes the disappearing "river people"—fiercely independent, living off the river's bounty, and resisting the increasingly omnipresent effects of industrial life. The simple river lifestyle was being overtaken by the "noisy, grimy, matter-of-fact manufacturing towns" (6) springing up along the Ohio River. These new towns huddled around waterfront factories, which depended on the river for their water supply, to dump their waste, and occasionally to receive coal or to ship their goods (depending on local rail freight connections and prices). Thwaites everywhere noted "the appalling havoc which these . . . industries are making with the once beautiful banks of the river" (40).

The popularity of the railroads—"in sight of which we shall almost continually float, all the way down to Cairo, nearly eleven hundred miles away" (Thwaites 1897, 7)—reduced the number of people traveling on the Ohio River. By the time the Thwaites family began traveling downriver, passenger steamboats had almost disappeared. Only the Greene Line, between Louisville and Cincinnati, remained as the last regular packet service, a cooperative arrangement among independent ship captains to keep predetermined schedules along a specific route. Other captain-merchants on the river found fewer and fewer small towns that relied on them. These changes affected the number of people working on the river as well, since ancillary businesses like ship peddlers and fishing communities depended on the clientele provided by frequent river traffic. Similarly, boat-building industries suffered. Steel-bottom boats began replacing wood-hulled frames, leading to fewer boats being sunk by snags or other river debris. This meant the production of fewer boats and a consolidation of the traditional dry docks into a handful of businesses using industrial methods. Cincinnati had once been a leading boat builder, but all except one dry dock closed by 1901, and this last company only lasted until 1919 (White 1999).

Riverfront Tensions in a New Cincinnati

While Cincinnati's river economy experienced these significant setbacks, the city more broadly was undergoing major changes as well. With the city relying on the Ohio River as an economic artery for so long, it was unsurprising that declining river trade occurred in tandem with major social shifts in Cincinnati. Up through the Civil War, the city had been concentrated in a relatively small, walkable area, circumscribed by a ring of hills and focused on the riverfront. While specific neighborhoods were known for particular land use concentrations, class status, or racial communities, these differences were limited. Instead, most of this small urban center was defined by its heterogeneity. This shifted rapidly in the postbellum period, as the city's population became simultaneously more racially diverse and spatially segregated (Taylor 1993; Ross 1985).

Poor upland Southerners, Black and white, as well as immigrants from Central and Eastern Europe, poured into the city. Many of Cincinnati's wealthy English and German families moved to the city's new suburbs on the urban fringe, while middle-class residents pushed out after them. This left lower-income communities isolated in Cincinnati's older urban core for the first time. The newer arrivals settled in their own separate ethnic and racial neighborhoods in this area, facilitated by migrant networks and emerging practices of housing segregation. In parallel, industrial production grew rapidly on the western side of the city core, following the lowlands of the Mill Creek Valley. These changes further differentiated land use patterns across the city.

As residents and industry moved outside of the city limits, Cincinnati's municipal government pursued them, annexing surrounding towns. As a result, City Hall suddenly became responsible for a much larger area than it had governed previously. The enlargement of the city limits, combined with new levels of urban diversification, severely stretched Cincinnati's infrastructure, social services, and legal system in the closing decades of the nineteenth century. The local government scrambled to build infrastructure for its new communities, as arrangements for annexation often included provisions for providing water and sanitation, as well as an assumed responsibility for other growing demands like gas lines, street paving, and streetcar service. In addition, the government had originally built facilities for public education, medical care, and fire protection almost exclusively in the urban core. The city had to rapidly scale up these offerings in the face of distant demand, which in turn led to further strain on the city budget and bureaucracy.

Local officials also faced a rising tide of social discontent. Highly exploitative labor conditions brought on by rapid industrialization and the increased concentration of poverty in the urban core combined to increase unrest in the city. Cincinnatians saw police and the judicial system as ineffective and corrupt, and surging numbers of arrests did little to placate residents. These frustrations culminated in the most violent episode the city had ever known.

On December 24, 1883, William Berner, a white man, and Joseph Palmer, a Black man, allegedly robbed and murdered their employer. After a high-profile case, the court sentenced Berner to a reduced charge of manslaughter in March 1884 and gave him a twenty-year sentence; Palmer, the Black man, was tried separately and hanged after being found guilty of the full murder charge. With Berner's trial taking place a month after the worst flooding Cincinnati had ever seen, the city was already on edge. After the announcement of Berner's lenient conviction, outrage spread. Several days of protest culminated in a mob breaking into the city courthouse to hang Berner, though it dispersed after finding that he had already been sent outside of the city. The mob re-formed the next day and returned to burn down the courthouse, as well as loot and largely destroy the adjacent district. More than fifty people died in the violence.

The sustained fury of the riot—the largest in Cincinnati's history—brought to the fore long-simmering urban tensions. Many of the core issues remained unresolved. In 1886 a massive May Day general strike halted the city again and seemed at the point of returning Cincinnati to chaos. In this case, many local employers agreed to an eight-hour workday, which averted similar outbreaks of violence. Yet, these events and many other smaller incidents contributed to a local perception of Cincinnati as descending into disorder.

For local elites, the city's changing riverfront represented one of the most problematic areas, particularly the central riverfront in front of downtown. The area had been the antebellum city's center and most fashionable district, but by the final decades of the nineteenth century it had become a district of warehouses, shipping and rail facilities, factories, saloons, and low-rent apartments. Many new arrivals to the city first gained a foothold in this neighborhood. With the influx of both Black and European migrants after the Civil War, the area became known for its racial intermixing, increasingly frowned on as governments and businesses implemented strict segregation policies. The area also gained a reputation as Cincinnati's refuge for illicit entertainment and criminal activities. Sections of the central riverfront called Rat Row (for its Black residents) and Sausage Row (for its sex work) drew widespread public condemnation while also attracting residents from other areas of the city.

Moreover, the central riverfront hosted numerous shantyboats—floating houses that allowed their residents to maintain a flexible subsistence strategy. Due to shantyboat tenants' nomadic semiaquatic lifestyles, Cincinnatians largely viewed them as unreliable, filthy, and dangerous (Anderson 1957). During his journey downriver on the *Pilgrim*, Thwaites observed that "both in town and country, the riffraff of the house boat element are in disfavor" (54). Cincinnati's best-known colony of shantyboats, called Shantytown, was found under the Cincinnati Southern Railroad bridge tower, just west of downtown. The "most irritating type of thieves found refuge in [this] roystering hamlet in the shadow of the big bridge" (Grayson 1929, 241), and frequent news reports described the Shantytown squatters' criminality and lack of conformity to social norms, such as one woman reportedly involved in a domestic dispute while living in a separate shantyboat from her husband (*Cincinnati Post* 1889). Even though many of the "boats" were hardly waterworthy, many local officials were eager to force the Shantytown residents to permanently disembark or move on.

For the Cincinnati river merchants, overwhelmingly white men of English and German descent, their anxiety about the decline of the Ohio River as a productive economic space was compounded by what they perceived as the lackadaisical attitudes of these low-income riverfront residents. A reporter for the *Cincinnati Enquirer* captured this local elite viewpoint well in a February 1897 vignette about the Rat Row section of Front Street, describing the atmosphere as news spread of a fast-approaching river rise that would temporarily shutter most riverfront businesses. Walking through Rat Row's blocks of warehouses and tenements, the reporter observed:

> It was in "Rat Row," the famous residence of numberless colored denizens of the river front, that the most dramatic scenes were enacted. The water was just lapping the curbstones when The Enquirer skiff pulled up in front of the "Row." From every window a head protruded and feminine voices call to the men on the sidewalks below for news of the prospective flood.
>
> The probability that they would be driven from their homes did not seem to affect them greatly. A very bad piano in the row was having "Don't Love Nobody" hammered out of it, and the saloon near the corner of the row was doing more business than usual. In front of it a group of roustabouts congregated all afternoon and watched the river "come to git" them. . . .
>
> "That ole Mistah Rivah's mad foh suah," said one colored woman, with a piece of gaudy calico over her in lieu of a shawl. "I'm goin' to make my man get ouah things ready foh rent day."
>
> And it went on on Rat Row this way all day. In the ground floor of the row are a number of warehouses and stables, and the owners of these have taken most of their goods out and are prepared to move the rest hurriedly.
>
> Along the row stood [white] business men watching with knitted brows the rise of the river. To them it meant the loss of many dollars; the colored folks to whom it meant the loss of home and possibly life, watched it with as much laughter as they would a cake walk. (*Cincinnati Enquirer* 1897a, 10)

This dissatisfaction with the neighborhood and the apparent indifference to its poor inhabitants extended to any number of facets of daily life. An 1893 *Cincinnati Post* article investigating cholera preparedness decried the "filth" of Sausage Row, with the aggravated reporter describing the lack of concern he witnessed: "Colored folks employed along the river were gossiping idly about. They little knew, or, probably, cared, about the [cholera] danger which, with the coming of summer, will menace them" (*Cincinnati Post* 1893, 4). Moreover, the transient Black and white boat-hand population particularly troubled local elite class formations, both for their perceived loose morals and for their reputation to show up at election time as illegal voters (Tucker 1967, 14).

These perceptions underlined elite groups' central concern about the riverfront. River merchants not only had to tolerate the vagaries of the Ohio River but also had to rely on undesirable Black and Irish riverfront residents as a source of cheap labor. With declining commerce on the Ohio River and the riverfront seemingly becoming more disreputable by the day, Cincinnati's river merchants desperately sought any possibility that could change their fortunes.

River Merchants Reorganizing

With Cincinnati river merchants' considerable influence in the city's early years, they had played a prominent role in local government. Many held political office in the city, such as Richard Bishop, a very successful riverfront grocery wholesaler who was mayor from 1859 to 1861 before becoming governor of Ohio. Yet, the city's economic restructuring in the postbellum period led to a significant shift in local politics.

Beginning in the 1880s, Cincinnati's Republican Party built a political machine that dominated municipal government over the coming decades. Brushing aside earlier, weaker political machines, George B. Cox, or "Boss Cox" as he was known, led this powerful new urban political formation, navigating urban crises and challenges from opponents to maintain a strong grip on Cincinnati (Tucker 1967). The success of Boss Cox's machine came through a system of patronage via political appointments and contract awards, highly effective ward-level voter turnout operations and ballot stuffing, influence with local newspapers, and tight control over party nominations. One national journalist claimed that Boss Cox's machine was unparalleled in its efficiency, "the most perfect thing of the kind in this country" (Steffens 1905, quoted in Miller 1968, 823).

Many urban political machines relied on lower-class and populist politics, but Boss Cox initially established a close partnership with Cincinnati's business leaders drawn from the city's growing industrial sector (Miller 1980). As a result, rather than the machine nominating populist leaders representing the impoverished urban core, the Republican Party put forward a series of elitist, progressive-minded candidates, most drawn from the new affluent suburban communities. These politicians, including Mayor Julius Fleischmann, promised to run the city on firm business grounds, reforming and improving many of the failing city services. This partnership relied on strong support from the newer upper-class and middle-class suburban communities, while also using traditional precinct-level strong-arm tactics in lower-income neighborhoods to prevent the urban core from voting too strongly in favor Democratic candidates. Overall, this political alliance stabilized the city government and improved municipal services, even as complaints about the corruption of Boss Cox's machine continued and Democratic candidates occasionally succeeded in securing citywide office.

Where did Cincinnati's river merchants fit within this picture? Not prominently. They no longer held a dominant role in the city's economy and were therefore often an afterthought or even excluded from machine politics. Boss Cox had served as a steamboat cabin boy in his youth (Grayson 1929, 108), but reviving Ohio River trade or improving the riverfront failed to register as a priority for the largely suburban-based governing coalition. Simultaneously, Cincinnati's industrial elites embraced cultural refinement to distinguish themselves from the rest of the city (Haydu 2002). River merchants, particularly those who worked directly on the river, were a notoriously unpolished group that fit awkwardly within this trajectory. Many had worked their way up on steamboats and embraced the coarser mannerisms and practical experiences of river life. As a result, river merchants rarely occupied key roles in Boss Cox's machine, and some were even vocal opponents. For example, Albert Bettinger, one of the most well-known river advocates in the city, mounted a vice mayoral bid as part of an outsider Republican effort to take down Boss Cox's machine in 1907. The mainstream Republican ticket soundly defeated Bettinger.

Lacking a route to organize through municipal politics, the city's river interests sought another forum. They found one in an unlikely place. In February 1890 the Cincinnati Chamber of Commerce organized a Freight Bureau (Cincinnati Chamber of Commerce 1891). Railroad concerns in Cincinnati believed that the city was receiving discriminatory rail freight pricing and schedules, especially for transportation to the South. They agitated for the creation of the Freight Bureau to represent their interests in transportation disputes and promote the city's rail advantages. At its start, the Freight Bureau paid little attention to the Ohio River and shipping by steamboat.

Unsurprisingly, the third annual Freight Bureau banquet, held just before Christmas in 1894, was therefore a "gathering of the two classes most interested in the work of the bureau—the railroad men and their patrons" (*Cincinnati Enquirer* 1894). Yet, unexpectedly, the Ohio River prominently featured on the program as well (due in part to cancellations by other speakers). Lieutenant-Colonel Amos Stickney from the U.S. Army Corps of Engineers and Captain J. F. Ellison of the Pittsburg and Cincinnati Packet Company both spoke about the commercial potential of navigational improvements on the Ohio River, to a boisterous reception.

The 1894 banquet lit a spark among Cincinnati's river merchants. Suddenly they saw the Freight Bureau as a potential platform for their interests. Over the coming year, river merchants successfully pushed the Freight Bureau to also encompass river improvements. The Chamber of Commerce reported that the Freight Bureau had "extended its scope of service the past year [1895] by taking up the question of improvement of the Ohio River in the interest of the commerce and industrial prosperity of this locality" (Cincinnati Chamber of Commerce 1896, 94). The Cincinnati Chamber of Commerce became preoccupied with tapping the Ohio River as a neglected asset. The chamber's 1895 *Annual Report* bemoaned the sad state of the river and disruptions to trade: "As unsatisfactory as was the preceding year in the affairs of River Transportation in which this city is especially concerned, the year 1895 was even more unfavorable, from the same causes which prevailed in 1894, the low stages of water. The navigable period was exceptionally short, representing altogether about five months, for the entire year" (Cincinnati Chamber of Commerce 1896, 96).

One commodity in particular spurred the chamber's interest in improving the Ohio River: coal. With rapid industrialization in Cincinnati, coal became more critical to local factories with each passing year. Most of Cincinnati's coal supply came from Western Pennsylvania mines, shipped downriver by barge. Yet, annual incidents of low water on the river forced local industrialists to rely on rail freight, which was both more expensive and less efficient than shipping coal on the river. For example, even with rail freight substituting river transport in 1895, the total coal tonnage received in Cincinnati was the lowest since 1890, leading to local fuel shortages and hitting the city's lucrative coal transshipping trade. Moreover, the number of coal barges disembarking from Pennsylvania and West Virginia had begun to drop as these states' own industries consumed more and more of the supply. As a result, to the alarm of many, as 1895 concluded, Cincinnati had "very small [coal] supplies on hand, the reserves being close to exhaustion" (Cincinnati Chamber of Commerce 1896, 79). As much as anything, the coal supply situation pushed the Cincinnati Chamber of Commerce to support local river merchants desperate to find a way to improve the outlooks of their businesses.

To push forward this work, the Freight Bureau organized a Committee on Improvement of the Ohio River in 1895, charging it with the task of investigating the issues facing river transportation and providing recommendations about how to improve the situation. This committee became a platform for Cincinnati river merchants to not only reassert their importance in the city but also emerge as powerful players on the national stage.

Launching the Ohio Valley Improvement Association

In mid-August 1895 the Committee on Improvement of the Ohio River proposed hosting a regional convention to improve collaboration across the Ohio Valley. The idea's enthusiastic reception spurred immediate action. The group decided to capitalize on this momentum and organize the convention in short order. They selected two days, October 8 and 9, 1895, to host the meeting and began sending invitations to "delegates from every town along the Ohio from Pittsburg to Cairo, and also all Members of Congress, Senators, and Representatives from Pennsylvania, West Virginia, Ohio, Kentucky, Indiana, and Illinois" (*Cincinnati Enquirer* 1895).

In total, 162 delegates arrived, not including local attendees. The group of self-described rivermen met at the Grand Hotel in Cincinnati with the intention of founding "a grand co-operative movement, having in view the creation of a healthy public sentiment which will promote legitimate effort to secure, at the hands of the next Congress, such appropriation as may be necessary to carry forward, vigorously and practically, the work of improving the Ohio River" (OVIA 1895, 3).

On the second day of the meeting, the delegates decided to form a permanent body to carry this work forward, which they named the Ohio Valley Improvement Association (OVIA). Alongside the selection of OVIA officers from across the region, the convention chose an executive committee based in the Cincinnati area to oversee the day-to-day operations of the new organization. This group included Captain Paris Brown, a long-time riverman and mayor of Newport, Kentucky, directly across from Cincinnati, as well as J. F. Ellison, from the Pittsburg and Cincinnati Packet Company.

In their convention speeches, the newly minted OVIA members bemoaned the decline of the Ohio River as a navigable waterway. Their complaints focused on the lack of dredging and removal of snags (trees sticking out of the riverbed) that made the river treacherous for steamboats, the continued seasonal fluctuation of water levels that restricted navigations to only part of the year, and increasing settlement along the riverbanks, which they saw as using up water that should end up in the river and contributing to riverbank erosion. A U.S. Army Corps of Engineers officer, speaking at the 1895 convention, echoed these frustrations with the erratic behavior of the Ohio River, describing how, in terms of "direction the river is quite tortuous, passing from one curve into another," while the "water supply is extremely variable, which may be illustrated by the statement that the oscillation of water surface at Cincinnati from extreme low water to the greatest flood height is about 70 feet" (1895, 10–11). The Ohio River had long been known as unreliable and dangerous (as well as generous), but these complaints reflected a growing realization that inland waterway commerce might cease to exist unless the river environment underwent major changes to make it more conducive to shipping.

The convention participants pinned their river improvement hopes on the federal government. They wanted the U.S. Congress to authorize an increased investment in river upkeep to maintain a deeper and more-easily navigable river, aiding steamboats to compete with railroads. According to Cincinnati mayor John Caldwell, welcoming attendees in 1895, the group had "assembled to consider the needs of the great Ohio River, and to . . . take such action as will enable you to convince Congress of the justice and necessity of liberal appropriations for the improvement of the Ohio" (OVIA 1895, 5).

The *Gibbons v. Ogden* case in 1824 had vested the authority to regulate navigable interstate waterways with the U.S. Congress. Beginning that same year, Congress began passing yearly Rivers and Harbors Acts that established annual appropriations for waterways improvements. Despite this history of federal navigation investments, decades of political debates and negotiations around the scope and scale of waterways improvements had left the Ohio River surprisingly neglected. After *Gibbons v. Ogden* expanded congressional powers over water navigation, general distrust among government officials about expenditures on "internal improvements"—as infrastructure was referred to at the time—constrained federal spending in the antebellum period. Opponents viewed internal improvements as, at best, benefiting only specific localities (whereas federal funds should contribute to the prosperity of the entire nation) and, at worst, corrupt attempts to enrich individual builders and property owners (Larson 2001). Under U.S. presidents Franklin Pierce

(1853–57) and James Buchanan (1857–61), even minimal river interventions like dredging and snag removal essentially ceased (Shallat 1994). States, municipalities, and private enterprise were thus left to pay for improvements, limiting the size of the projects that could be undertaken.

A more assertive postbellum federal government, enlarged and emboldened after the massive Civil War effort, invested more into internal improvements (Larson 2001). The Rivers and Harbors Act of 1869 appropriated $2 million for improvements that year, $3.9 million in 1870, and $5.8 million in 1872, compared to a total of only $3.1 million for river improvements during the entire antebellum period (Lippincott 1914, 648). But, most of these funds went to the ascendant industrial North, deepening harbors in New York, Philadelphia, and Cleveland, Ohio, or for works to link the Great Lakes (O'Neill 2006, 54). Rather than large regional projects, most of these internal improvements focused on specific congressional districts. Representatives and senators frequently traded floor votes in order to garner support for water-related projects in their home territories. This small-scale "pork barrel" or "logrolling" approach came to dominate the politics of internal improvements. As a result, from 1824 to 1895, the Ohio River received only $5.5 million for improvements, mostly for snag removal and dredging, contrasted against the $7.6 million received by the Ohio River's tributaries over the same period (OVIA 1899, 12).

The first priority for the OVIA was therefore to increase the appropriations for the Ohio River. The association had numerous antecedents in the form of one-time conventions (also called memorials) bringing together interested parties from across the region to demand action on navigational improvements for the Ohio River. The OVIA's founders intended to supplant these one-time conventions, creating an ongoing organization with a more sustained impact. According to a steamboat captain from Pittsburgh speaking at the first OVIA convention, "In former years we have had meetings and passed resolutions, then gone home and acted as if everybody else was to do the work" (OVIA 1895, 40).

In its tactics, the OVIA represented an emerging means of political organization: the permanent interest group, also known as a lobbying group. Numerous trade organizations and social movements were adopting the permanent interest group model, which relied on membership fees to support year-round advocacy. Business interests like Cincinnati's river merchants embraced the lobby as a way to push for policy change that was not tied directly to local party politics and thus more responsive to their needs (Clemens 1997). River merchants and connected industries from across the Ohio Valley—and especially Cincinnati, which made up the bulk of the OVIA's membership and financial backing—planned to use the association as their own platform to address government officials, engineers, and the general public.

In order to improve navigation on the Ohio River, the OVIA focused its demands on the creation of a lock and dam system along the length of the entire Ohio River, from Pittsburgh to its connection with the Mississippi River at Cairo, Illinois. Approximately fifty dams would form slack-water pools, each pool extending miles backward until reaching the next dam farther upriver. This chain of connected slack-water pools would remove the seasonal threat of low water and guarantee a navigational depth of six feet (later adjusted to nine feet) throughout the year. The deeper water had the added benefit of making it less likely that ice would form in winter. The dams themselves were to be movable, known as the wicket or Chanoine design, so that segments of the dam wall could be lowered, allowing boats to float over them during natural periods of high water. This mitigated concerns among ship captains about boats being forced to pass through locks when river levels were naturally high enough for navigation.

Colonel William E. Merrill brought the Chanoine approach to the United States after studying engineering advances made on the Seine River outside Paris (Johnson 1991; OVIA 1925, 88), and the U.S. Army Corps of Engineers (USACE) had even built a Chanoine dam on the Ohio River near Pittsburgh to create a year-round harbor for the city.[2] Pittsburgh merchants and ship captains celebrated the Davis Lock and Dam, completed in 1885, especially after engineers enlarged its lock sizes to address concerns that a narrow lock would force ships to break apart their tows (a typical Ohio River tow at that time could include ten or more barges bound together) and reassemble them on the other side, another potential cause of delays. The Davis Lock was the largest lock in the world at the time of its construction.

Despite the popularity of the Davis Lock and Dam, by the time of the first OVIA convention in 1895, the federal government had no further plans to build additional locks and movable dams on the Ohio River. The OVIA called for an immediate plan covering the full length of the river. While previous Ohio River improvements had focused on dredging, snag removal, wing dam construction, and other interventions with only localized or temporary effects, the lock and dam system would remake the entire river, positioning it as a reliable, cheap, and modern shipping alternative for the region and country. This proposal for navigational improvements, embracing the 981-mile length of the Ohio River, represented an enormous project, well beyond any other internal improvements previously attempted. The technological challenges alone were daunting, as no system of Chanoine dams at this massive scale had ever been constructed. Securing congressional appropriations for such a project would likely be just as difficult.

Early OVIA Efforts

Through the OVIA, Cincinnati's river merchants discovered a renewed purpose. Here was a platform to realize their ambitions. Rather than sit idly and continue watching their fortunes suffer due to the unpredictability of the Ohio River, they could dream of a transformed Ohio River with booming waterborne commerce and thriving shipping businesses. The OVIA enabled Cincinnati's river merchants to begin building networks across the Ohio Valley and farther afield to realize these dreams.

Drawing attendees from across the Ohio Valley, early convention audiences consisted of "steamboat masters, pilots and clerks" as well as the merchants who owned the barges, packets, wharf boats, warehouses, and boatyards fundamental to river commerce (OVIA 1899, 32). Men made up the vast majority of the OVIA's membership, with only a few women joining them, such as Captain Mary Becker Greene, the only female captain in Ohio at the time and owner-operator of the Greene Line. Although the wealth and power of these rivermen paled in comparison to railroad corporations and other industries lining the riverbanks, the OVIA coalition began to expand shortly after its founding.

By 1902 the association's first president, John Vance—a former U.S. representative from the riverfront town of Gallipolis, Ohio—saw businessmen increasingly joining the steamboat captains and boat builders in the audience (OVIA 1902, 14), and by 1905, Cincinnatian Edwin Gibbs observed, "Today we have in our ranks the merchant, the manufacturer, the banker, the lawyer, all to such an extent that . . . the river is now in the woeful minority" (OVIA 1905, 39–40). This interest reflected growing discontent with the railroads, as both traffic congestion and "rail car famines" had begun to wreak havoc on freight schedules. Frustrations only heightened after the 1906–07 rail transportation crisis, when a cascading series of failures paralyzed the rail system across the country (Sloss and Martland 1984; OVIA 1924, 84). Given the many growing industries in the Ohio Valley that relied on a regular supply of coal to power their factories, the rail freight disruptions and a perception of price gouging in the first decade of the twentieth century contributed greatly to a broader interest in using the Ohio River as a transportation alternative.

In addition to growing industrial membership, the OVIA began to cultivate a close relationship with the U.S. Army Corps of Engineers. Started under President Thomas Jefferson, the USACE quickly gained a reputation as a highly selective, science-oriented branch of the military. Influenced by the scholarly and aristocratic French engineering tradition, USACE leadership used arguments about state-building and national defense to justify expanding their role as the leading engineering experts within the U.S. government. The Rivers and Harbors Act of 1824, an annual bill that established appropriations for waterways, named the USACE as the agency responsible for navigation improvements across the country, including harbor construction, dredging, snag removal, and building dams. By the second half of the nineteenth century, the USACE had "emerged as the nation's largest and most powerful water development agency" (Shallat 1994, 2). Still, the USACE faced deep skepticism, with critics portraying the technocratic corps as elitist, power hungry, and antidemocratic.

The rise of "pork barrel" politics in the second half of the nineteenth century limited the possibility of making internal improvements on the massive scale preferred by USACE officers. In response, the corps had learned to adapt by working closely with congressional committees and other federal agencies. This politicking kept the USACE relevant, but also led to attacks painting it as a servant to "pork barrel" politics, without its own vision or principles. As a result, by the time of the OVIA's founding, USACE leadership was in the strange position of being portrayed both as antidemocratic technocrats determined to reshape the country as they saw fit and inefficient servants of "pork barrel" politics that put regional interests above the nation (Shallat 1994).

Initially, the USACE appeared restrained in its support of the OVIA. At the OVIA's first convention, Colonel Stickley, in charge of Ohio River improvements at the time, made clear the organization's role as a neutral observer, stating, "It is the policy of the War Department to prohibit its officers from taking any active part in the matter of influencing legislation or urging appropriations for the improvement of the rivers and harbors in their charge" (OVIA 1895, 9–10). However, USACE officials stationed in the Ohio Valley quickly became crucial OVIA allies, working together with Ohio Valley river businesses to advocate for river improvements, producing economic studies to justify the project, and attending the OVIA's annual conventions to provide updates on the progress of works and renew their friendships with OVIA members. With time, it became difficult to distinguish between speeches by OVIA members and USACE officers, such as when Major E. L. Daley, a USACE division engineer, felt moved to claim, "I believe that you have all today seen enough to appreciate how worth while it is that we assure for navigators a continuous and dependable operation of this wonderful system, the Ohio Valley River navigation. (Applause)" (OVIA 1925, 11–12).

With the support of Ohio Valley industries and the USACE, the OVIA made slow but steady progress. The association continued to hold annual conventions, and its leadership lobbied the U.S. Congress persistently, coordinating with local politicians to pressure for annual or biannual Rivers and Harbors Act appropriations benefiting the Ohio River. Because the U.S. Congress refused to authorize the entire Ohio River project in one go, each lock and dam required individual appropriations, sometimes covering just a part of the work, such as for land acquisitions or surveys. This piecemeal funding made the process grueling and required a near-constant campaign to keep work moving forward. Despite these challenges, the OVIA members were in a festive mood by the time of their tenth annual convention, in 1904. Work had begun on twelve locks and dams along the length of the Ohio River, and members expected Congress could be convinced to fast-track the work in the coming years. As Albert Bettinger, a leading waterways advocate and aspiring politician from Cincinnati, optimistically declared at the tenth anniversary convention, "We [have] never had any very great difficulty in either satisfying ourselves or those who would listen to us, of the great merit of this improvement, and of the enormous advantage to an enormously large portion of our population that its consummation would afford" (OVIA 1904, 113).

Rise of the Conservationists

The Ohio Valley Improvement Association's advocacy for Ohio River improvements coincided with surging interest in waterways policy across the country. Groups were formed throughout the 1890s to address various water concerns. Western farmsteaders and engineers met in Salt Lake City, Utah, in 1891 to form the National Irrigation Congress (Pisani 1992). Planters from Mississippi and Louisiana formed the Mississippi River Improvement Levee Association in 1890 to request federal support for flood control works (O'Neill 2006). Following in the footsteps of the OVIA, numerous other navigation associations sprung up as well in the first decade of the twentieth century, such as the Lakes-to-the-Gulf Deep Waterway Association, the Tennessee River Improvement Association, and the Upper Mississippi Valley Improvement Association. In addition, at the very beginning of the twentieth century, the National Rivers and Harbors Congress (NRHC) launched as a nationwide effort to increase the size and frequency of Rivers and Harbors Act appropriations.

Unabashedly a lobbying group, the NRHC had no preferred waterways improvement strategy, but supported both large and small projects for navigation, irrigation, and hydropower development across the country. First launched in Baltimore, Maryland, in 1901, the organization fizzled until reinvigorated by Congressman Joseph Ransdell in 1905. The OVIA, as one of the strongest waterways groups in the country at the time, helped Ransdell organize a meeting to relaunch the group, and also shared some of its leadership and approaches with the organization. Responding to this lobbying, President Theodore Roosevelt urged increased waterways spending for a variety of projects across the country, as well as internationally, such as with the Panama Canal.

The conservation movement quickly began to exert a powerful influence on waterways planning. The U.S. conservation movement took shape over the second half of the nineteenth century as a call for the careful management of nature to benefit human society. Numerous thinkers laid the groundwork for the conservation movement, such as Henry David Thoreau and John Muir, but George Perkins Marsh made a critical contribution in *Man and Nature* (1864) by arguing that humans could degrade the landscape and exhaust natural resources, potentially leading to societal collapse. Conservationists successfully pushed for the federal government, with the support of public actors such as corporations and volunteer groups, to take an active role in the management of natural resources, including forests and mineral deposits. Implicitly or explicitly, conservationists largely assumed that white men would be the ones administering these natural resources and determining how they could be best used for the common good.

The conservation movement's influence over waterways groups grew rapidly once water itself was recast as a natural resource. Geologist and anthropologist William John McGee became particularly important in this effort (Linton 2010; Schmidt 2014). McGee, the founding president of the American Anthropological Association, was introduced to the conservation movement by his mentor John Wesley Powell, a geographer who had advocated for the importance of watershed management in governing the American West. McGee's writings on the relationship between the environment and human cultural development quickly made him one of "brains" of the conservation movement (Pinchot 1947; Hays 1959).

McGee had moved to St. Louis to organize "Anthropology Days" for the 1904 Summer Olympics and World's Fair, remaining in the city afterward to direct the St. Louis Museum. While in St. Louis, he was recruited by the Lakes-to-the-Gulf Deep Waterway Association to aid in the creation of a navigable deep-water channel from Chicago to New Orleans, Louisiana. This introduction to waterways policy shaped McGee's political and theoretical work for the remainder of his life (Schmidt 2014). Among his many projects, McGee wanted to introduce comprehensive surveys of water resources and standard units of measure for the different industries using water (1909). And as with his mentor Powell, McGee believed water resources should be managed according to river basins, drawing on geographic expertise and the emerging field of hydrology. These measures would improve control over water resources and avoid waste. In the tradition of Marsh's *Man and Nature*, McGee viewed the proper management of water resources as essential to ensuring population growth and national strength (McGee 1909). According to McGee, "No more significant advance has been made in our history than that of the last year or two in which our waters have come to be considered as a resource—one definitely limited in quantity, yet susceptible of conservation and of increased beneficence through wise utilization" (1909, 38).

Conservationists—after consolidating positions inside government agencies including the U.S. Geological Survey and the U.S. Forest Service—viewed water management as an important area to expand their influence. In 1907 President Theodore Roosevelt appointed the Inland Waterways Commission to survey U.S. water resources and create an integrated multipurpose water management plan. The conservation movement celebrated it as a turning point (Schmidt 2014). The initial rationale for forming the commission had been to consider how to improve inland navigation because of the 1906–07 railroad transportation crisis. The commission's objectives quickly expanded beyond navigation to embrace broad multipurpose water planning (Pisani 2006). Chaired by Representative Theodore Burton, a Progressive reformer from northern Ohio who also headed the House Committee on Rivers and Harbors, Roosevelt's appointees to the commission also included noted conservation advocates Gifford Pinchot from the U.S. Forest Service, McGee from the U.S. Geological Survey, Frederick H. Newell from the Reclamation Service, and Senator Francis Newlands from Nevada, among others.

The Inland Waterways Commission immediately began to work on a plan to integrate almost all of the major aspects of water management studied at the time—including hydropower, flood control, navigation, irrigation, and reforestation—in order to maximize the resources available in different river basins. The commission's foremost objective was to promote coordinated management among water's many different uses. This represented a stark departure from the water use policy of the time, which continued to be dominated by "pork barrel" legislative practices. The Inland Waterways Commission and allies in the conservation movement wanted to push back on the piecemeal "pork barrel" approach to waterways improvements. In particular, they wanted to target the USACE.

Inland Waterways Commission chair Burton had already been advocating reforms of the USACE to standardize and provide oversight of the corps' role in individual waterways projects. In 1902 Burton had led the creation of the Board of Engineers for Rivers and Harbors to provide a technical feasibility review and a cost-benefit analysis for all USACE divisional projects (Waugh and Hourigan 1980). Burton wanted the board to winnow out the smaller projects favored by congressional "pork barrel" and instead emphasize larger improvements that would have a significant impact. This work naturally fed into the Inland Waterways Commission (Hays 1959).

OVIA and the Conservationists

The OVIA occupied an uneasy position in this emerging discourse of efficient multipurpose water management. On the one hand, Burton considered the Ohio River lock and dam project, in its scale and objectives, as the perfect remedy to the readily apparent flaws of the "pork barrel" approach: "The Ohio is a great artery of commerce. Improvements have been made costing tens of millions of dollars for branch streams like the Big Sandy, the Kentucky, the Green, the Wabash, and even the Cumberland and the Tennessee. As a result there is a more uniform and at times a greater depth of water in the Kentucky and Kanawha Rivers than in the Ohio where they empty into it. . . . There are six feet in the pools in those rivers, and in the Ohio where they flow into it at times not more than three or four feet" (Crissey 1956, 100–101). The Board of Engineers for Rivers and Harbors that Burton had helped set up issued a special report on these Ohio River improvements in 1907 arguing that it was, "in the opinion of the Board, the one river of all others most likely to justify such work" (NRHC 1912, 224). Yet, significant concerns persisted.

First, many conservationists closely associated the Ohio River project with the USACE's leadership, which they saw as suspiciously pliant to local interests. OVIA members still felt it necessary to dispute claims of "pork barrel" even when the project was almost completed, with a speaker at the OVIA convention in 1924 describing how "hundreds, perhaps thousands of editors across the country . . . contemptuously cast aside the opinions of the Army Engineers and yell 'pork barrel! pork barrel! pork barrel!' every time a Rivers and Harbors Bill is under consideration" (OVIA 1924, 87). Moreover, the OVIA membership was drawn largely from regional businesses, such as barge lines and wholesalers, that represented smaller-scale economic interests. This difference helped conservationist critics paint the OVIA as limited and provincial in its vision.

The conservationists disliked the fact that the Ohio River lock and dam system focused exclusively on navigation. This fell well short of the multipurpose water management goals that conservationists aimed for, leading many critics to point out what the project could have accomplished if it had only been more ambitious. Burton felt that "we ought to treat water as an entirety: navigation, water power, purification of water, prevention of floods[,] and there is nothing better than this House can do than to frame some system under which they shall be treated, not merely in reference to navigation, as a separate unit, but to bring all together as an asset of this people as important as the land" (Crissey 1956, 99).

For their part, OVIA members were equally leery of a multipurpose water policy approach. Suggestions to incorporate other water supply considerations were regularly rejected in favor of a focus on navigation. At the OVIA's first convention, Cincinnati health officer Dr. Prendergast suggested "that while the commercial improvement was pushed, the sanitary part should not be overlooked" (OVIA 1895, 22). Captain George Anderson of Pittsburgh replied brusquely that "while he was not a sanitary expert, he had learned that the river purifies itself every ten or fifteen miles" and, moreover, the design of the movable dams proposed by the OVIA helped aerate water (23). OVIA convention audiences politely heard out similar suggestions to consider forest conservation or flood control over the years, but firmly rebuffed them (Hart 1957; Hays 1959).

OVIA resistance to overtures from the Inland Waterways Commission and the conservation movement came to a head in 1908. That year, William John McGee attended the OVIA's fourteenth annual convention in Louisville, Kentucky. After his initial enthusiasm for the work of the Lakes-to-the-Gulf Deep Waterway Association, McGee had fallen out with that group when it refused to adopt a multipurpose water management approach and instead maintained its emphasis on navigation. As a result, when he arrived at the convention representing the Inland Waterways Commission, the OVIA members and USACE officials were already deeply suspicious of McGee. They took offense to his claims that navigation groups like the OVIA and Lakes-to-the-Gulf

Deep Waterway Association considered water as "merely a body of liquid as is a lake or a sea" (Hays 1959, 104) and that these groups ignored the numerous other important uses for water.

Before he could even address the OVIA group at the 1908 convention, a number of speakers pointedly attacked McGee's conservationist platform. Congressman Swagar Sherley, a long-time member of the OVIA (and also an appointed member of the Inland Waterways Commission), put it bluntly: "I have the honor to be a member of the Commission appointed by the President for the conservation of the natural resources of America. . . . I am interested in the other projects that are being talked of; but I do not want to see those projects tied to the proposition of improving the Ohio River (Applause)" (OVIA 1908, 122).

At the same meeting, Major William Sibert of the USACE—who had formerly overseen the government's plan for improvements on the Ohio River but by 1908 had been transferred to working on the Panama Canal—spoke more pointedly: "It is thought that the people who are advocating a combination of all the above subjects ('flood control, forest preservation, prevention of the erosion of the soils, development of water power, etc.') as a plan of river improvement are unacquainted with the practical needs of navigation or the practical ways of providing such needs" (OVIA 1908, 60). Speaker after speaker drove home the point that the OVIA and USACE were solely interested in navigation for the Ohio River.

McGee got the message, responding that "the plan of improvement of the Ohio by means of the movable dam system, [is] an admirable plan, and perhaps not the one that would be adopted today were the question to come up: but, mark you, the question is not up. A plan has been adopted and is under way, and it is in accordance with that plan that future development must be carried forward. (Applause)" (OVIA 1908, 129).

After 1908 OVIA convention speakers occasionally presented information on other water-related topics, such as hydropower and sanitation, but its members did not seriously debate again about conservation and the consideration of water as a natural resource until the 1930s. Navigation remained the settled objective of the association, and it would be developed independently of other water management strategies. Indeed, members of the OVIA were so focused on their objective that they only very rarely even appealed to other benefits that would accrue naturally from the lock and dam system, such as increased water supply for cities along the Ohio River in periods of drought (OVIA 1929b, 51).

The OVIA successfully brushed back pressure from the conservationists and kept the focus narrowly on its lock and dam proposal for the Ohio River. Not only a sign of how powerful the OVIA had become, it also pointed to the faltering momentum of conservationists in the federal government. The multipurpose water movement lost influence with the end of President Roosevelt's term in office. Roosevelt's successor, President William Taft, felt less passion for coordinated federal resource management, and allowed the Inland Waterways Commission's mandate to lapse. Taft—from a prominent Cincinnati political family that supported the OVIA's efforts—favored limited executive powers and preferred to act only with congressional authorization (Hays 1959). In terms of waterways policies, he viewed navigation as the clearest area where the federal government had authority to advance work, and he moved to curtail other related projects, such as hydropower (Hays 1959).

At the OVIA's convention held in Cincinnati in 1910, Taft spoke strongly in support of the Ohio River lock and dam project, claiming that after any "calm and impartial consideration of all the project improvements for river transportation, there is none that offers so great a probability of success and benefit to the entire country as the improvement of the Ohio River" (OVIA 1910, 15). Taft's new policies and approach helped drive noted conservations like Gifford Pinchot out of the federal government. Moreover, McGee died in 1912, dealing another blow to the movement. As a result of these shifts, improvements driven by the USACE, regional water users, and sectional alliances in Congress eclipsed multipurpose water planning in the early twentieth century (Hays 1959; O'Neill 2006).

Lobbying for Navigation

In less than two decades, Cincinnati's river merchant had gone from being afterthoughts within their own city to becoming the hub of a powerful national lobby, capable of ignoring the conservation movement. How could this shift take place so quickly? On the one hand, the demand for coal continued to drive interests among businesses and government officials in Cincinnati and elsewhere. These parties wanted to see the Ohio River become a reliable coal freight transportation option. On the other hand, by the early 1910s shipping traffic on the Ohio River was lower than it had ever been, less than half of the levels seen in the closing decades of the nineteenth century. During World War I shipping dropped even lower, to almost a quarter of prior levels. Clearly, the OVIA could not just rely on growing demand for coal to legitimize its plans. Leadership had to have an effective strategy to drive support for the Ohio River lock and dam system, selling their dream for the river and keeping momentum going for the slow but steady completion of this internal improvement.

Understanding the success of the OVIA and Cincinnati river merchants requires a significant reevaluation of waterways policy debates in the United States at the beginning of the twentieth century. Many histories of the period lay the blame for the conservation movement's setbacks at the beginning of the twentieth century—and particularly the downfall of the Inland Waterways Commission—at the feet of associations like the OVIA that supported river navigation and, to a lesser extent, groups calling for federal management of flood control efforts (Hays 1959; O'Neill 2006). For those who supported the conservation movement's aims, this created distrust for lobbies including the OVIA, Lakes-to-the-Gulf Deep Waterway Association, and Mississippi River Improvement Levee Association.

In his influential text, *Conservation and the Gospel of Efficiency* (1959), prominent conservationist historian Samuel Hays characterizes these lobbies as operating mainly from personal or institutional interest rather than any visionary ambitions. Meanwhile the USACE is depicted as an entity that had strayed far from its scientific roots, more interested in preserving its power than examining the most rational and efficient approach that could be used to manage water resources in the United States. The USACE resisted the "coordination of navigation with any other water use" solely in order to "protect its own role in water development" (Hays 1959, 8). Congressional "pork barrel" corrupted the USACE even further, leading to it supporting the development of "many projects at once to satisfy a great number of localities rather than to construct the most important ones first" (274). On the opposite side, Hays portrays conservationists as a group of well-intentioned technicians, excited to use their emerging expertise to strengthen the country. The persistent narrative that has emerged from the histories written by Hays and his peers is that reactionary institutional and sectional interests such as the OVIA and USACE controlled decision-making around waterway improvements, to the detriment of the conservation movement's scientists and the U.S. public at large.[3]

Far from seeing themselves as simply maintaining the status quo, in the early twentieth century the OVIA and USACE viewed their work as groundbreaking. From their vantage, they had only recently reached a position where they could develop comprehensive solutions to the problems of navigation, which were markedly different from the problems of water resource management posed by the conservation movement. In the early years, OVIA members often portrayed themselves as fighting to overcome long odds to achieve their project. A U.S. representative from Indiana spoke at the 1907 convention of his desire to "commemorate and perpetuate the names of the pioneers of this movement, who for thirteen long years have struggled through disaster to achieve this present success" (OVIA 1907, 83).

This sense of struggle came from the annual need to secure renewed congressional appropriations for the Ohio River lock and dam system in order to continue advancing the project, as distinct congressional sessions considered each lock and dam along the length of the river separately, treating them as individual projects. OVIA leadership felt they had reached a major breakthrough when, in 1910, the U.S. Congress approved a Rivers and Harbors Act that committed the government to completing the lock and dam project within twelve years. They were dismayed to subsequently find out that this resolution in no way established any requirements for the next session of the U.S. Congress (OVIA 1923, 13). Even the USACE, often depicted by historians as the entrenched gatekeepers of U.S. water policy, had only been authorized by Congress as having continuing jurisdiction to administer the navigable waterways as part of the Rivers and Harbors Act of 1899 (whereas previously Congress had required official authorization for each new project). Beyond the political challenges of securing congressional approval , both the OVIA and USACE believed their Ohio River proposal represented an unprecedented change in how the country related to its waterways. To them, the Ohio River lock and dams project was in no way an obvious outcome, but rather a radical new idea that had to be advanced on multiple fronts.

The OVIA saw one of its primary contributions as educating the public around the benefits of improving navigation on inland waterways. USACE representatives and elected officials frequently portrayed the OVIA's contribution as one of "vision," the ephemeral work of building excitement for the potential of the new river. The organization's mission in 1900 described: "The CHARACTER OF WORK engaged in by the Association is educational, in keeping before the people . . . facts bearing upon the commerce of the Ohio Valley" (OVIA 1900, 6). At first the OVIA employed traveling agents to undertake these educational efforts; they crisscrossed the Ohio Valley, giving short public talks in order to increase membership and local subscriptions. Then, when J. F. Ellison assumed a dual secretary-treasurer role in 1904, he organized an OVIA Bureau of Publicity, expanding the group's activities to include direct mail solicitations and an emphasis on outreach to newspapers (OVIA 1904, 134–35). The OVIA worked closely with journalists to place promotional stories, from convention recaps to in-depth explorations of river trade. Later, radio increasingly became a forum for OVIA members to disseminate information. The OVIA organized its flotillas as public parades to attract attention to the river, an approach first suggested by an officer from the USACE. The association hoped these flotillas would "reawaken" the population to the river's potential, inciting wonder and nostalgia.

Through its materials and conventions, the OVIA pursued a strategy of activating a multitude of voices in promoting its work. For the OVIA to be successful, everyone involved had to spread the word. Convention attendees were encouraged to become agents for the movement however they could, making boosting the river and the recruitment of new members a part of their daily habits. For the OVIA, it was not necessarily about presenting a coordinated message that won support for its work, but rather the volume of messengers.

This stands in stark contrast to the approach taken by conservationists, who relied on a select few charismatic representatives to push out their message, including most prominently President Theodore Roosevelt and U.S. Forest Service chief Gifford Pinchot. This simplified control over who spoke for the movement, and was coordinated with an extensive publicity strategy activating the press, conferences, and interviews to disseminate conservationist views. In support of these publicity events, government agencies and conservationist groups sent massive reports and reams of data proving the claims of the movement's representatives. In one instance, William John McGee sent so much information out prior to a White House Governors Conference focused on conservation in May 1908 that newspapers published articles just about the overwhelming quantity of advance materials provided to their journalists (Ponder 1990, 552). The careful coordination between scripted publicity and scientific reports reinforced the expertise claimed by the conservation movement, presenting a united, technocratic voice to the public.

In contrast, the OVIA appeared as a cacophonous mishmash of waterway advocates, philosophically disjointed and often at odds with one another. Yet, the fact that member voices did not always agree was actually embraced. One of the OVIA's core promotional strategies was sharing the proceedings from its conventions, transcribing the speeches of dozens of water advocates from across the country each year. In sharing these proceedings, the OVIA put on display the differences between its members. On one level, disagreements between convention speakers set the parameters of discourse, containing dissent and providing the opportunity to rebut and diminish those who deviated from the OVIA's navigational objectives. This is exactly what happened to McGee when he tried to advocate for multipurpose water planning at the 1908 OVIA convening. More importantly though, convention proceedings allowed the engagement of two distinct groups core to the OVIA's strategies: the rough-hewn rivermen and the sophisticated USACE engineers.

Practical and Expert Knowledge on the River

Representing an uneasy alliance of two discordant approaches to understanding the Ohio River, the OVIA and the USACE quickly came to believe that the lock and dam project would only be successful if they brought together their unique skill sets into a new assemblage of waterways management. The emerging consensus around the need for navigational improvements on the Ohio River relied on two distinct understandings of how to relate to the Ohio River that most river inhabitants had previously seen as incompatible: calculated scientific expertise—embodied by engineering expertise—alongside practical and intuitive river knowledge—contributed by the OVIA's rivermen. This assemblage held potent crosscurrents as well as the tantalizing possibility of incorporating the Ohio River as part of its energies.

Whereas conservationists projected a firm belief in scientific expertise alone as the source of their convictions, the OVIA early on pushed the USACE's experts to accept outsider perspectives. At the first OVIA convention, Captain John Dravo, the prominent coal merchant from Pittsburgh, asked corps engineers to be "big enough and broad enough to accept suggestions from the practical man on the river, to add to the education of West Point the education of the Ohio River, as obtained by these men" (OVIA 1895, 22). In this argument, the vagaries and sudden dangers of navigating the Ohio River made practical knowledge crucial to transforming the Ohio River into a productive transportation system—knowledge that had to be gained through years of working on the river. Throughout the nineteenth century, rivermen had valued pragmatic solutions over technological advances, relying on intuition and expediency to succeed on the capricious river. Good steamboat pilots were known for their preternatural ability to anticipate shifts in the Ohio River riverbed.

The USACE leadership rapidly realized that this epistemological partnership could serve their interests, especially as they struggled to fight off the conservationists assailing their institution. At the 1908 OVIA convention, Major William Sibert of the USACE, as part of his pointed rebuke to McGee, made clear the implications of this approach, stating, "This is an age of specialists. It is the business of an ethnologist, for instance, to acquaint himself with the habits and customs of the various types of the human race, both antediluvian and modern, but he would hardly be expected to be an authority of equal weight upon the habits and customs of a stern-wheel steamboat with 20,000 tons of coal in tow in a five-mile current in a narrow channel of the Ohio River" (OVIA 1908, 60–61). Sibert argued that the success of the lock and dam project depended on intimately understanding the river and the particularities of transport on the inland waterways, scoffing at McGee's belief that a project could seamlessly combine navigation, hydropower, flood control, and other concerns and still be effective. In Sibert's view, McGee's background as an anthropologist and an academic suggested an abstract cross-cultural knowledge inferior to the practical skills that OVIA members had developed from their decades of intimate experience with Old Man River. Through their arguments, Sibert and the OVIA successfully portrayed the conservationists as out of touch, hopelessly disconnected from local realities.

This partnership was not only rhetorical but also implemented in the day-to-day work of building the lock and dam system, extending from the convention floor to the construction site. Corps engineers relied on steamboat pilots, old deckhands, and other river inhabitants to help them with their efforts. A deputy inspector with the USACE, who reviewed dam and lock works on the Ohio River, recounted his own run-in with one of these individuals:

> This *Armstrong* when I took over had just been reconditioned[,] and they had not completed all the insulation on the steampipes and that sort of thing in the engine room and the boiler room. So one day this shantyboat appeared on the scene and they pulled in and tied up there at Henderson Island and the old man in the rowboat came out to the boat and was greeted like a long lost friend and it turned out that he was an expert insulator. Probably the dirtiest human being I ever saw . . . but he did a beautiful job, so I inquired about that, and the story was at that time many of the shantyboat people were marvelous artisans and had definite trades and could really do a beautiful job of work when they felt like working. (Anderson 1957, 5–6)

In their work, corps engineers regularly depended on those who had developed their own particularized skills and knowledge of river life, even if it differed from their formal training. They needed these individuals to repair their boats, consult on construction techniques, and evaluate each project location so the engineers could tailor lock and dam designs to the specific site conditions.

This last point was important because the Ohio River posed unique challenges at every turn. The river's silt load wreaked havoc with lock and dam plans, confounding corps engineers trying to install the massive movable lock and dam systems. The silt gummed up the lock mechanisms, buried lowered wickets, and caused constant headaches for the USACE, especially since each dam was made up of dozens of separate wickets that the lockmaster would have to lower or raise depending on water height. Evan Bone, a corps engineer who worked on the Ohio River project over multiple decades, described how the "problem with silt was a problem all the way through, especially as they would get farther and farther down towards the source of the river" (Bone 1957, 3). The engineers tried various solutions, but "then they found out, the Old Man [River], the trouble with silt, came along again" (3).[4] The USACE also faced numerous other obstacles posed by "Old Man River," including sudden flooding that surged over cofferdams, runaway barges, and unstable sand foundations, all issues that delayed construction repeatedly over the course of the Ohio River lock and dam project. Given these issues, the USACE had to develop and test new construction methods and technical innovations at almost every site, but the engineers also had to be open to implementing informal—or less "by-the-book"—solutions to these problems.

Working with rivermen from Cincinnati and elsewhere, the USACE embraced the need to adapt to the demands of Old Man River rather than to simply impose engineering plans. The rivermen, who viewed the river as a thing literally alive and had learned to account for its shifts as best they could, provided advice on how to mitigate the silt issues and anticipate the river's moods (Johnson 2013, 88). Together, the OVIA and USACE repositioned the river as a potent force that had to be coaxed into sharing "the magnificent possibilities which are dormant in our rivers" (OVIA 1904, 100).[5] Through their partnership with OVIA rivermen, corps engineers learned to take significant direction from the river itself. The lock and dam system was not about dominating the Ohio River, but about compromise and cooperation. This understanding was well captured when, with the completion of the lock and dam system in 1929, the OVIA held a tongue-in-cheek ceremony celebrating the marriage of "Old Man River" and "Miss Movable Dam." The eight-piece Kentucky & Indiana Railway Terminal Company orchestra played a newly composed "Ohio River Song," and then a mix of men and women on the flotilla cruise assumed the roles of the wedding party, from the Bride to the Bride's Papa and the Flower Girl, much to the amusement of the assembled OVIA members. The ceremony was followed by music, dancing, and even a ventriloquist (OVIA 1929b, 171–72).

The Ohio River had made the creation of the lock and dam system difficult through the threat of flooding at construction sites, the constant unexpected accumulation of silt, and damp and strenuous working conditions that made workers sick. Yet, in the long term, the Ohio River actually proved amenable to this new idea of collaboration, largely conforming to expectations and facilitating elite control over this riverine space. As the project advanced, the river became more and more obliging after the opening of each new dam. OVIA members and corps engineers described the lake-like qualities of the river as the dams further slowed down and deepened the Ohio River. Sibert, by this point a USACE major general, speaking at the dedication of the last lock and dam in the system, Number 53, during the OVIA's celebratory cruise of 1929, asked, "Can you imagine a greater satisfaction to a man than to see, through his efforts, emerge from the sandy bed of the Ohio, locks and dams creating these placid pools with draft and width sufficient for the continuous use of men?" (OVIA 1929b, 204). The new river was so amenable that even before the completion of the full system in 1929, the USACE could create artificial rises at times of shallow water by letting water accumulate upriver, and then having each lock master lower their dams in a sequenced order as the high water moved downriver. The effect was to create surges of high water that flotillas of coal barges could ride to their destination, even in times of heavy drought (OVIA 1923, 57).

A New Water Management Approach

The USACE and OVIA's efforts to redefine the commercial relationship with the Ohio River were situated in a national setting experiencing radical transformations. Vast industrialization since the second half of the nineteenth century had brought rapid technological, demographic, and cultural shifts to communities across the United States, generating a sense of unease and disorder as well as a pressing question of how emerging forms of social life should be organized. Conservationists represented one expression of a push to rationalize and standardize the administration of entities such as city governments and corporations, collectively known as the Progressive movement. Relying on top-down, bureaucratic forms of social control, many of the most powerful elite class formations favored Progressive strategies to bring order to the chaos of mass industrialization. These were not the only proposals though, as antagonistic (and occasionally complementary) movements like the Populist Party sought to foster independent, localized forms of governance and enterprise (Wiebe 1967; Postel 2007). Rather than values of progress and efficiency, these groups tended to emphasize community solidarity and the importance of maintaining social norms (Doukas 2003).

Small-scale businesses, such as the rivermen behind the OVIA, favored those initiatives that resisted centralized control and coordination. Yet, rather than being a reactionary effort, in embarking on a partnership with the USACE, they brought forward a new assemblage of scientific engineering and practical knowledge underpinning complex and sophisticated governance and economic proposals—one that defied easy categorization. The rivermen represented a diminished elite group, but they also possessed a valuable potential economic function relative to coal shipments. Through the proposed Ohio River lock and dam project, they were able to offer the besieged USACE a means of consolidating its own power in a moment of considerable bureaucratic reorganization. This partnership (or "marriage" as they called it) of experiential and abstract knowledge contrasted not just with the conservationists' approach, but also with the vital currents of water management practices in the United States and abroad since the late nineteenth century.

First, many waterways advocates increasingly rejected local experience as untrustworthy and unproductive, instead elevating quantifiable hydrological observations and careful engineering plans as the only truly reliable way to derive the most benefit from water resources. In the United States, the water management approach put forward by William John McGee built on this perspective with deeper nuance. McGee lifted up the role of both human and nonhuman actors alike in shaping the world (what he and others called "Earth-making") and pointed to water as a uniquely powerful agent for influencing both geological and social change. Yet, even despite McGee's acceptance of the messy contingencies that came from recognizing how a host of powerful nonhuman actors (like rivers) would shape waterways policies, McGee failed to move beyond leaving humans, and especially scientists, in a privileged position where it was incumbent on them to tame nature (Schmidt 2017, 59). According to McGee, the scientist had a duty to improve human society and its relationship with the world through water management (Schmidt 2017, 73–74). In their formulation, the OVIA and USACE departed sharply from these views, foregrounding not only the contributions of nonscientists but the river itself.

Second, the ways the OVIA and USACE brought a gender perspective to the relationship between technology and nature diverges in subtle ways from their contemporaries. The domination of nature had been linked to the domination of women in Western society since at least the sixteenth century, creating an equivalency between the two that legitimized their subordination to the rationality and masculinity of science (Merchant 1980). Carrying forward this legacy, the conservation movement maintained a strict exclusion of women from scientific and expert leadership roles because women lacked the capacity to objectively manage nature, even while depending on extensive support from white women in popularizing its objectives (Merchant 1984). On the Ohio River, in celebrating the practical knowledge of rivermen, technical expertise took on a less masculine connotation, even to the extent of being portrayed as feminine at times, such as with the bride "Miss Movable Dam" in the OVIA's faux wedding as part of the 1929 celebratory cruise. This is not to say that women were in any consistent way welcomed into the Ohio River project. Women were almost always absent from OVIA conventions, though white women sporadically appeared as organizers of nighttime social events for attendees or in composing songs or poems about the river read during proceedings.

Still, technology played an important role in translating the work of the OVIA to female audiences, furthering its association with the feminine. At the 1908 convention in Louisville, President Vance of the OVIA concluded a session by inviting Louisville residents to a special presentation: "This evening at 8 o'clock we hope the citizens generally will avail themselves of the opportunity to bring their ladies, for there is a treat for them in the shape of the stereopticon lecture by Captain J. Frank Tilley, Secretary of the Pittsburg Coal Exchange. His lecture will be illustrated by lantern slides, and will show the process of the construction of locks and movable dams. He will begin with the unimproved river and build a dam before your eyes" (OVIA 1908, 50). The engineering logic presented on the lantern slides helped make the "unimproved river" (a rough and dangerous place) accessible to the white women attendees. These details point to a slightly different gender context for the OVIA and USACE's work, as the combination of both practical and technical knowledge troubled the easy affiliation of waterways expertise and masculinity.

Third, with its "gospel of efficiency," the conservationist movement largely approved of the massive corporations proliferating at the start of the twentieth century (Hays 1959). In their eyes, these enormous industries were the most capable of production at the scale and level of organization necessary to productively administer natural resources. Conservationists like Pinchot argued that centralized planning of industrial production "must replace competition so that manufacturers could produce with less waste" (Hays 1959, 126). Even Theodore Roosevelt, noted trustbuster, argued that corporations were actually more beneficial with the proper regulation (Muncy 1997), though for his part, McGee expressed deep distrust of corporations (Schmidt 2017, 85). To these conservationists, because of its ties to "pork barrel" appropriations, the USACE ended up serving unproductive small-scale regional business interests, an inefficient approach compared to the national reach and impact of the emerging corporate conglomerates. For its part, the OVIA presented the Ohio River, rebuilt through federal infrastructural investments, as the basis for a free competition between business owners, rather than as an object of centralized planning serving the interests of corporations. Members drew on the river's symbolic and historical importance as a commons to contrast it with the singular control exerted by massive corporate monopolies. As one speaker put it, seizing on anticorporate sentiment, there was no way a reconfigured Ohio River, freely accessible to whoever wanted to use it, could be "Morganized" (OVIA 1905, 5), referencing to financier J. P. Morgan's role in building multiple monopolies. The OVIA embraced the role of small-scale businesses like those owned by its rivermen members, lionizing the practical knowledge and unrefined business educations many of them had as important counterweights to the dangerous influence of corporations.

What emerges from this history is a widely different role for expertise in managing the Ohio River compared to what the conservationists were proposing at the time. Rather than a centralized technocratic approach, like with multipurpose water management, the USACE and OVIA promoted a hybrid of old and new knowledge, a diverse assemblage of disparate perspectives. This epistemological mixture preserved a strong connection to past ways of knowing and valuing the river, embodied by the traditions of the OVIA's overwhelmingly white rivermen, a group who represented themselves as self-made entrepreneurs tracing their origins back to the pioneer freeholder days of the Ohio River. The resulting assemblage left the highly educated and disciplined engineers of the USACE in the surprising position of trying to learn from the river rather than master it. In taking this approach, the OVIA and USACE were able to achieve considerable success in preserving the importance of navigation within the United States and its place within federal water policy, despite the fact that much of the public had viewed the Ohio River as the "poor man's highway" and a relic of the past at the end of the nineteenth century (Ambler 1932).

Cincinnati Riverfront

By the early 1920s, after slowdowns caused by World War I, the completion of the lock and dam system finally seemed like it would become a reality. Confronted with the realization of their long-term goal, OVIA members started to grapple with what came next. They recognized that a significant amount of pressure would fall on them for the Ohio River system to be successful. Ac-

FIGURE 1.1. Detail from the cover of the OVIA's *Official Program and Complete History: Ohio River Pageant and Dedication* for the inauguration of the lock and dam system in 1929, juxtaposing the river of pioneer times with the modern river.

cording to Senator Frederic Sackett, from Kentucky: "Naturally there comes the query if the rivers are improved will the public use them. The future of the completed Ohio will be looked to for the answer. No other body is so well placed as is the Ohio Valley Improvement Association to carry forward the work of selling a completed river to the people—to industry as a transportation system, and to popularize its use" (OVIA 1927, 75).

The OVIA ramped up its efforts to promote the modern river, with a series of pamphlets, speaking engagements, and events such as the 1929 celebratory cruise from Pittsburgh to Cairo announcing the opening of the new river. At the same time, one of its primary areas of preparation focused on the development of terminal facilities along the Ohio River. OVIA members saw new terminals as key to delivering on the potential of the lock and dam system, because any increase in shipping would be adversely affected if there was no cheap way to get freight on and off the boats for local consumption or transshipping. Senator Sackett, responding to his own challenge, claimed, "Loading and unloading facilities, therefore, become of prime importance in popularizing the use of the stream" (OVIA 1927, 75). Another presenter even suggested that, after the completion of the lock and dam system, OVIA's new slogan should be "Modern terminals for every landing" (OVIA 1929b, 175).

Members of the OVIA were active in waterfront redevelopment schemes across the Ohio Valley, but particularly in Cincinnati. Building on their role in founding the OVIA, Cincinnati merchants, river businesses, industrialists, and public officials had all continued to push for the success of the Ohio River lock and dam project. Over the OVIA's first three decades of existence, Cincinnati residents had provided close to 50 percent of all financial support for the organization (OVIA 1924, 11). During the 1929 flotilla to inaugurate the completed lock and dam system, OVIA members erected an obelisk at the Ohio River's precise midpoint, located on a hill overlooking Cincinnati's downtown riverfront, highlighting the area's symbolic importance to the project.

The city's elites wanted to reestablish a river trade that placed Cincinnati at the center of the remade Ohio River transportation network. They spearheaded efforts to redevelop the city's riverfront, with the goal of building modern waterfront terminals, warehouse facilities, and links with railroads for transshipping. In particular, they were concerned with access to bulk commodities, primarily coal and steel, which were critical to the rapidly expanding industry and power plant needs in the city (Ross 1985). Julian Pollack, from the Cincinnati Rail-Water Transfer Company, gave one of the more extensive OVIA convention speeches on terminals in 1924, urging other OVIA members to develop their own modern facilities (OVIA 1924, 36). He provided practical recommendations around the importance of rail connections, the need to tailor terminal design to the specific commodity that the operator planned to receive, and how to evaluate demand from tributary areas. Throughout his speech, Pollack used examples from his own enterprise, which was a facility for iron and steel on the Cincinnati riverfront using mechanical cranes and integrating connections with rail and motor truck lines.[6]

Initially OVIA members had argued that the lock and dam system would revitalize riverfronts as active places of employment and social life, claiming that through the project "the glories of past days will be revived" (OVIA 1895, 22). A major article in the *Cincinnati Enquirer*, printed to accompany the 1909 OVIA convention being hosted in the city, included a drawing of how the city's riverfront would look once the lock and dam system was completed, imagining a bustling hive of activity harkening back to the river as the city's "storefront."

But, as more attention focused on the river as a space for freight transportation, this vision began to shift among OVIA members. According to Congressman Swagar Sherley, from Louisville, the "condition of the rivers in the past

A comprehensive review of the work of the Ohio Valley Improvement Association---Questions of importance to be decided at the convention to be held in Cincinnati this week.

FIGURE 1.2. The Cincinnati riverfront as the city's "storefront," a hub of social and commercial activity. Drawing by Carll B. Williams, appearing in the October 10, 1909, Sunday-morning edition of the *Cincinnati Enquirer.*

has not justified the expenditure of money sufficient to bring about modern conditions, but we are rapidly approaching the time when these things must be taken into consideration; when the old mule with the cart will cease to haul river freight up a high levee and then deliver it over to a customer or to a railroad train" (OVIA 1908, 125).

Discussions of the need for modern terminals were concurrently about reshaping and replacing waterfront labor in the Ohio Valley. Rather than the boisterous docks filled with unruly Black and Irish workers that many associated with the riverfront, OVIA members envisioned these new river terminals as efficient transportation spaces largely devoid of people. OVIA advertisements explicitly contrasted modern methods with the traditional cargo methods that had featured intensive human and animal labor. OVIA members intended for this terminal infrastructure to become itself an advertisement for the modern river, as mechanization and stricter control over the workforce replaced the chaotic riverfront scenes of the past. Much as historian Ari Kelman (2006) documents for New Orleans, the creation of modern marine terminals and improved warehouse facilities across the Ohio Valley facilitated more corporate and private control over riverfront space, impeding regular public contact with the river.

In Cincinnati, river merchants used the new Ohio River to finally reduce their dependence on roustabouts and other undesirable river workers. The mechanization of river terminals threw the mostly Black and Irish dock hands out of work. Low-income riverfront workers in Cincinnati lacked significant union representation and were largely unable to resist efforts by employers to reorganize the labor process. Increasing racial segregation in the late nineteenth and early twentieth centuries further weakened riverfront labor strength, making Black and white dock workers less likely to cooperate. Only in a few cities like New Orleans were waterfront workers actually able to form cross-racial labor movements that could effectively push back on employer desire to streamline and mechanize dock work (Arnesen 1994).

The transformation was stark. In the late 1920s, *Cincinnati Times-Star* journalist Frank Grayson wrote about his experience heading down the riverfront to revisit the once-bustling docks. He remembered, in expressly racialized terms:

> I had gone there with the expectation of experiencing again the wild scenes of excitement and animation that formerly attended the business of loading and trimming a boat. I fully expected to see a long line of roustabouts "conjoining" and hear their untrained but melodious voices lifted in some improvised chantey as an inspiration to the proper execution of their work, but not a peep out of any of them. They went about their business with systematic regularity and we did not hear a solitary word uttered in that line which functioned hither and yon with the precision of a well-oiled machine. (Grayson 1929, 76)

As the Ohio River lock and dam project moved toward completion, Cincinnati's remaining river workers labored under a new regime of efficiency and discipline.

Cincinnati river merchants' calls for modern terminals was also about targeting these workers' riverfront neighborhoods for destruction. The Charles H. Moore Oil Company made these trends evident with its plans to displace the Black community of Rat Row in 1904, portrayed as a natural outcome of "the march of progress of railroads and other big concerns to occupy the bottoms" (*Cincinnati Enquirer* 1904a, 5). The company temporarily spared Rat Row from demolition when it selected another site, but railroad businesses soon began purchasing individual properties in Rat Row for their own riverfront terminal needs. This began a long-term process of tearing apart the community piecemeal (*Cincinnati Enquirer* 1904b; Hahn 2004). Railroad companies pressured landlords to shut off water supplies and refuse to maintain their buildings, facilitating the displacement of Black residents. A proposal endorsed by the Cincinnati Chamber of Commerce in 1923 even considered destroying the central riverfront area, commonly known as the Central Bottoms by this time, and replacing it with an enormous intermodal rail and river terminal.

These changes affected many other workers along the riverfront. By the 1880s, many of the upscale brothels had already moved out of the riverfront area (Findsen 1997). This process accelerated in the early twentieth century as more brothels, dance halls, and bars shut down or moved, with the last central riverfront "watering hole" closing in 1925 (Wilkinson 2008). Men and women with jobs in these establishments had to look elsewhere in the city for employment. Shantyboat communities also felt these pressures. Many states had begun passing legislation to discourage shantyboats from settling on their shores. Kentucky "passed, more as a police regulation than as a means of revenue, an act levying a State tax of twenty-five dollars upon each craft of this character" (Thwaites 1897, 53). A major flood in 1913 finally destroyed Cincinnati's Shantytown, long a thorn in the side of city officials (Hedeen 1994, 105). During the 1910s and 1920s, newspaper references to shantyboats dropped as

FIGURE 1.3. The OVIA's comparison of new and old ways of loading freight (OVIA n.d.(a)). From the Rail-Water Cooperation pamphlet in the Inland Rivers Collection of the Public Library of Cincinnati and Hamilton County.

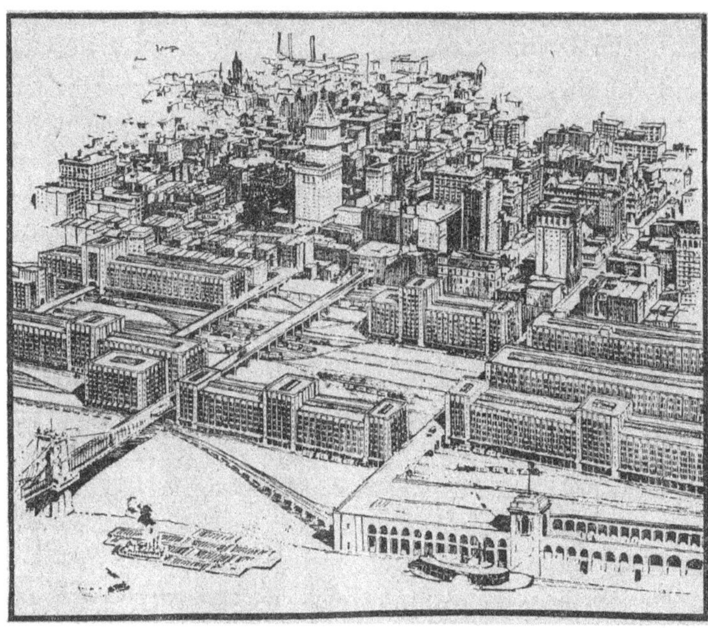

FIGURE 1.4. A proposal recommended replacing Cincinnati's entire central riverfront with a complex of rail terminals, barge terminals, and warehouses (*Cincinnati Enquirer* 1923, 3).

Cincinnati and many municipalities passed their own ordinances to permanently clear these residents out, citing criminal and sanitary concerns.[7]

As the Ohio River grew increasingly calm and predictable, it did not make the river more accessible or useful for the people who had long lived along its banks. Rather, with time, it became clear that the new Ohio River facilitated navigation to the exclusion of other uses. In Cincinnati, this transition is clear in looking at how the opening of the local lock and dam, the Fernbank Dam, transformed the way many Cincinnati residents interacted directly with the river. Since Cincinnati's founding, the riverfront had been an important location to bathe, draw water, and dispose of waste. While the growth of plumbing and private bathrooms limited some of these activities, in the early twentieth century the Ohio River still retained its role as a popular bathing area, with a number of private resort beaches on the Kentucky shore (Zimmerman 1972). A bend in the Ohio River just below the central riverfront helped create sandy beaches that were attractive for recreation during summer low water. Entrepreneurs had seized on the growing interest in public bathing to open the Queen City Beach, Primrose Beach and Canoe Harbor, Tacoma Beach, and a number of other destinations that drew thousands of weekly visitors throughout the summer months.

The USACE opened the Fernbank Dam in 1911, and many members of the OVIA executive council helped organize the massive celebrations across the city. Cincinnati residents took steamboat rides downriver to see the new construction and pass the afternoon picnicking or dancing. For their part, beachgoers celebrated the Ohio River's new behavior, since it meant that there was "hardly any current in the river, due to the raising of the Fernbank Dam, and the possibility of any danger's greatly alleviated" (*Cincinnati Enquirer* 1913, 47). Yet, with time, the lock and dam system eventually made the Ohio River less attractive for those who wanted to swim. The Fernbank Dam left many popular beaches permanently submerged, the remaining banks muddy, and the water stagnant. This forced the closure of popular private beach clubs, removing one of the few public spaces for white men and women to socialize (Zimmerman 1972; *Cincinnati Enquirer* 1958).

When the U.S. Army Corps of Engineers completed the lock and dam system in 1929, it shuttered the last remaining beaches. Fred Matre, the owner of the Primrose Beach and Canoe Harbor on the Kentucky shore, tried to sell his business in 1930, the year after the lock and dam system opened. The advertisement he placed in the paper describes facilities for up to a thousand bathers, but the ad spends much more time describing the more attractive and seemingly profitable canoe livery. Matre was still trying to sell the business in 1931. According to Rabbi Jack Skirball, who had studied at the Hebrew Union College in Cincinnati, speaking at the 1929 celebration of the opening of the lock and dam system, "We used to like to swim in the river, and thought of the picturesque beauty of the Ohio with its few boats. But now commerce has entered into it, and we think all the more of it for that reason" (OVIA 1929b, 166).

At the same time, with the river's velocity decreasing, it meant that the sewage dumped into the river from the city's homes and factories was also slower to move downstream, and some even accumulated as sludge sediments in front of the city. Although public officials had expressed apprehension about this issue before the Fernbank Dam even opened (*Cincinnati Enquirer* 1910), it was only after 1929 that the increasingly polluted river started to cause major health concerns across the Ohio Valley. By 1934 Cincinnati officials posted warnings against swimming in the Ohio River, and one Kentucky city decided to ban public bathing for health reasons (Cleary 1967). All of these changes removed even more people from the riverfront, discouraging the remaining bathers and families that drew water directly from the river.

Due to these changes, Cincinnati's riverfront area slipped from public view in the first decades of the twentieth century. The city's busy riverfront had been one of the archetypal urban spaces within the country, such that the world's oldest surviving urban landscape photograph is a panoramic daguerreotype of the Cincinnati waterfront taken in 1848. By the early twentieth century, the decline of river life had undermined this symbolic relationship between the river and the rest of the city. No longer was a bustling riverfront an important part of urban life, as transportation and commerce moved to railroads and the city center withdrew from the decaying waterfront. The decline of Cincinnati's riverfront also meant that pictures of the riverfront became scarcer. Publishers and illustrators instead used pictures of skyscrapers, rail terminals, and aerial views to represent the city. Perhaps most starkly, depictions of Cincinnati's riverfront were largely absent from prominent booster publications of the time. Texts like Charles Frederic Goss's *Cincinnati: The Queen City Vol. 1* (1912), the *Official Plan of the City of Cincinnati* (1925), and the *Cincinnati Municipal and Industrial Exposition 1788–1935* guide (1935) all forewent classic images of Cincinnati framed by its riverfront. This shift indicated a new way of understanding urban life in Cincinnati that had little reference to the river.[8]

Artists and other cultural chroniclers of the time noted these multifold social, economic, and visual changes in Cincinnati and elsewhere along the Ohio and Mississippi Rivers, heralded as the passing of an age. Writers such as Ben Lucien Burman, Harlan Hubbard, and Frederick Way Jr. produced elegiac laments about the end of river society, the passing of life on sternwheelers and shantyboats. Cincinnati artists including E. T. Hurley and Herman Wessel produced paintings and etchings featuring a charming but outdated river life. For many, the inauguration of the lock and dam system in 1929 was the final act of the old river. The *Cincinnati Times-Star* took the opportunity to publish *Thrills of the Historic Ohio River*, a collection of old news articles and human-interest stories from a now decidedly bygone era. The preface describes how, in compiling the book, the author Frank Grayson had "caught Old Man River, given him a shave, and turned him over to posterity" (Grayson 1929, xvii). A decade later, a group out of Marietta, Ohio, founded the Sons and Daughters of Pioneer Rivermen in 1939, an organization dedicated to sustaining this rapidly vanishing river life.

Conclusion

After inaugurating the last lock and dam on the Ohio River, Cincinnati's OVIA officers returned home from their celebratory cruise on Monday, October 28, 1929. They must have felt triumphant after decades of hard work, eager to turn to the opportunities that would be afforded to them and the city by the new

Ohio River. Unfortunately for Cincinnati's river merchants, their arrival also came one day before Black Tuesday and the start of the U.S. stock market crisis. Over the coming years the Great Depression seriously impeded Cincinnati river merchants' plans for a revitalized commercial riverfront, putting on hold plans for terminal facilities and redevelopment projects. While they had accomplished many of their goals in weakening Cincinnati's riverfront communities, especially in the downtown area, the lack of activity on the river meant they were unable to fully realize their own vision for this riparian environment in the near term.

However, the OVIA and USACE succeeded in their long-term goal to remake the country's inland waterways, producing a robust river transportation system sustained by government funding. By 1929 the river was moving 21.9 million tons of cargo per year; in 1957 the total was 81.5 million tons (Landon 1961), and in 2008 it totaled 230.8 million tons (USACE 2017). Together, the OVIA, USACE, and Ohio River remade the river as a space first and foremost responsive to the needs of navigation. They repositioned the riverfront as a depersonalized system of efficient transport and industry, with the Ohio River enabling local industries to cheaply receive raw materials, draw their water supply (after filtration), and occasionally ship their goods. Simultaneously, they consolidated navigation's central role in U.S. waterways management policy, preserving its prominent status in a wide range of issues moving forward.

In the United States, river navigation had long had enormous importance. In 1824 the U.S. Supreme Court decided the case of *Gibbons v. Ogden*, denying New York the right to issue a license to Aaron Ogden to operate a monopoly steamboat route within the state's borders. The ruling determined that the federal government had the obligation to ensure free navigation of U.S. rivers based on the Commerce Clause of the U.S. Constitution. This case is well known as the basis for a range of federal interventions in the U.S. economy and social life, with the Supreme Court subsequently interpreting the Commerce Clause widely to include both trade and more abstract issues like the exchange of ideas (Johnson 2010).

Gibbons v. Ogden also set the basic parameters for the federal regulation of all water rights across the country, establishing a legal precedent referred to as "navigable servitude," meaning that the federal government has absolute rights over any navigable stream "for purposes related to navigation and commerce, regardless of ownership and without compensation" (Pisarski 1996, 313). Rivers found to be navigable had to be automatically ceded to the state where they were found, with the land underwater at the normal high water mark required to be held in trust for the public (Frey 1974). Thus, any navigable rivers in the country constituted a commons, free to be used by U.S. citizens for commerce (Pisarski 1996). Numerous judicial cases have refined the definition of navigability, considering what constitutes commerce (whitewater rafting tours? floating logs? individual recreation?) and what could be considered physically nonnavigable (rapids? a river that dries up during a drought?). In almost all these cases, U.S. courts have robustly defended a public right to navigability (Pisarski 1996). Individuals, private organizations, and local governments cannot obstruct or deviate navigable streams without receiving a permit from the federal government.[9]

For most of the nineteenth century, navigability existed as the exclusive basis for federal interventions in regulating water (O'Neill 2006). By the early twentieth century, this status seemed at risk when the U.S. Congress authorized the creation of the Bureau of Reclamation (formed in 1902) to aid the development of arid western lands through irrigation and then later passed the Flood Control Act of 1917 for the Mississippi River and Sacramento River, significantly expanding the scope of government intervention in waterways management (Pisani 1992; O'Neill 2006). Despite this enlargement of the federal government's water usage authority, the OVIA and other navigation lobbies pushed back on the encroachment of other water management interests. In insisting on the completion of the Ohio River lock and dam system as solely a navigation project, the OVIA established the river's primary purpose as a transportation artery, in spite of conservationist objections. The OVIA, as the most powerful waterways lobby of its time, played a critical role in preserving navigation as the fundamental legal framework determining water management priorities, leaving "federal navigational servitude [as] paramount to all other interests in navigable waters" (Pisarski 1996, 316). As a result, navigable servitude has continued to feature prominently in numerous legal cases, invoked in situations ranging from pipeline construction to power generation to flood control planning. Moreover, as a result, inland waterways in the United States are evaluated first as spaces of navigation. Other uses, such as for drinking water or environmental considerations, are secondary to this central principle of navigability. Had conservationists prevailed with their multipurpose water management goals in the early twentieth century, waterway usage decision-making could look very different today.

Instead, the USACE remains the primary governmental agency overseeing the Ohio River, while many of the businesses involved in the OVIA are still active along the river, either in the river trade or in new industries. The OVIA continued as an independent body until 1983, when it merged with DINAMO, a group in Pittsburgh focused on updating the Ohio River lock and dam system. The leadership of DINAMO eventually launched the Waterways Council, Inc. in 2003, the leading national navigation-focused infrastructure lobby in the United States. The federal government replaced almost the entire Ohio River lock and dam system not once, but twice: first as part of a modernization project in the 1950s, and then again starting in the 1980s. While these new dams did not use the Chanoine design, instead relying on immovable dam structures, the welding of practical and technical knowledge remained central to the success of lobbying for upgrades.

The most recent Ohio River lock and dam project ended with the completion of the Olmsted Lock and Dam, near the junction with the Mississippi River. Operational launch took place in 2018, though final stages of the work lasted for years. The Olmsted project, begun in 1988, took more than three decades of work and cost more than $3 billion, making it the country's longest and most expensive civil infrastructure project ever (Glass 2017). With the operational launch of the Olmsted Lock and Dam, the USACE began destroying in 2022 the very last locks and dams from the original OVIA efforts, Number 52 (opened in 1928) and Number 53 (the very last, opened in 1929), almost a century after their construction.

CHAPTER 2

The Cincinnati Central Bottoms and Flood Control, 1925–1970

Suddenly, the Ohio River was everywhere. On January 18, 1937, the river reached flood stage. Initially observers had expected Cincinnati to see a normal winter flood, little cause for alarm. But then the rain kept coming and coming. As the waters surged, W. C. Devereaux—Cincinnati's chief meteorologist from the local U.S. Weather Bureau office—revised the anticipated crest height five times in twenty-four hours. Floodwaters reached places previously thought completely safe. Then they kept rising. After almost three weeks of widespread destruction, the Ohio River finally left flood stage on February 5.

The flood had crested almost nine feet above the previous high from 1884. This "thousand-year" event was the "worst river flood in American history" (Welky 2011, 6), tearing through countless communities and displacing hundreds of thousands of Ohio Valley residents. The devastation was particularly bad in Cincinnati, where flooding disrupted water supplies, electricity, and public transportation, paralyzing daily life. Five inches of snow and a bone-chilling cold accompanied the flooding. Left reeling, the city had never seen devastation on this scale.

Once the waters receded, there was an immediate outcry for improved flood protections. Along the Cincinnati riverfront, the U.S. Army Corps of Engineers, local business groups, politicians, and the City Planning Commission (CPC) all put forward their own flood protection plans. In the following years, these groups engaged in a heated debate over how and to what extent the city should protect its riverfront, particularly for the area in front of downtown. It was only with the opening of the Fort Washington Way riverfront bypass in 1961—which incorporated a levee structure along its southern face—that the local government finally settled the issue.

Disagreements over how to best understand and relate to the Ohio River shaped this discussion over the viability of a floodwall for the Central Bottoms district, as the central riverfront area in Cincinnati was known in the first half of the twentieth century. Residents of the Central Bottoms, urban planners, business owners, city officials, and engineers operated under different assumptions about what the flood of 1937 meant for the city. For each, the implications of "being flooded" were tied closely to the agency of the Ohio River, but these groups also had their own perception of the river's personality. Some wanted to cooperate with the Ohio River, others considered this idea impossible, and many riverfront residents thought it best to adapt to the moods of the river. Their struggle over the future of the Central Bottoms eventually hinged on the emerging power of Cincinnati's professional elites, who were pushing new approaches for urban governance and development in the city. The outcome of this fight pushed the Cincinnati riverfront in a new direction, forcing river merchants and the commercial sector that had long dominated the area to accommodate new interests.

While many studies have emphasized an increasing belief in the divisions between nature and society (Scott 1998; Kaika 2005), this chapter opens a new way of thinking about the role of nature in the city, one that highlights more flexibility in cooperating with nonhuman actors than is generally recognized. Professional elites in Cincinnati pushed for the city to work closely with the Ohio River as an ally. At the same time, this openness to the idea of cooperating with nonhuman actors did not necessarily translate into harmonious coexistence. In Cincinnati, the Ohio River, after avoiding the constraints a floodwall would have posed, used its freedom to slowly eat away at the buildings in the Central Bottoms neighborhood, a historic community that contained small-scale factories as well as low-cost housing for its Black and white low-income residents. Recounting this history expands our understanding of how local elite class formations can design policies and infrastructures that amplify the activities of nonhuman actors that further their own agendas.

Flooding as a Way of Life

Flooding was nothing new in Cincinnati. Major floods had wrought significant damages many times before. In Cincinnati's early years, the central riverfront had been the core of the city, a commercial district oriented toward the river, filled with shops, public offices, and other important social sites. But, due to its proximity to the Ohio River, the area regularly flooded, sometimes twice a year, contributing to mounting dissatisfaction with life along the riverfront. The city center eventually shifted out of the floodplain in the postbellum period. Many of the city's most important businesses and wealthiest residents followed. In turn, the central riverfront lost its prestige, gaining a reputation as home to numerous illicit activities, racial intermixing, and labor unrest (Ross 1985; Taylor 2004).

Sections of the central riverfront including Gas Alley, Rat Row, and Sausage Row were particularly notorious, synonymous for middle-class and upper-class white Cincinnatians with disreputable populations, such as roustabouts, shantyboat residents, entertainment workers, and prostitutes—both white and Black. Cincinnati's elites pointed to the regular flooding of the area to reinforce this view of the central riverfront as seedy and dangerous. Local papers repeatedly referenced how "dirty" or "muddy" water inundated "the denizens of Rat and Sausage Rows" (*Cincinnati Enquirer* 1884, 4). Racist and classist elite perceptions of riverfront residents were also evident in descriptions of floods as a "bath" for the area's poor tenants. During periods of high water, local journalists frequently made observations such as "The second big rise in the river has given the inhabitants of Rat row another bath" (*Cincinnati Enquirer* 1890, 1) and "Shanty boats that have perched high and dry along the shore for years were treated yesterday to their first bath since 1892" (*Cincinnati Enquirer* 1897b, 10). The central riverfront remained the area of most concern for local elites, but other sections of the riverfront slowly saw their reputations decline as well. To the east of downtown, the Fulton district was once a bustling hub of shipyards and other river-oriented employment. As the dry docks and associated industries shut down, these areas experienced sharply reduced economic activity, and well-to-do residents began to move out.

Despite this growing unease with the central riverfront, the area retained a strong attraction for some businesses. Small-scale industries took advantage of the neighborhood's cheap rents, plentiful water, and convenient location. In fact, many of these riverfront factory owners believed that their businesses could not prosper anywhere else in the city. Meanwhile, river and rail companies sited their new terminals throughout the riverfront, continuing the area's commercial focus. This bustling environment of wholesalers and warehousing facilities brought together buyers and sellers from Cincinnati and farther abroad.

The riverfront businesses regularly affected by flooding incorporated its damages and delays into their financial forecasts and accounting. According to an official municipal planning document, "Because the highest floods are rare and because the average floods have become so much a matter of course to that part of the community involved, the city has adjusted itself as to the real estate values and rents in the flooded zone and to the slowing down of business during the flood periods, so that the losses are largely discounted or otherwise provided for" (CPC 1925, 151). Even given the long history of local flooding, Cincinnati residents had only intermittently called for urban flood control measures prior to 1937 (Hedeen 1994). A public clamor for improved protection followed significant floods in 1907 and 1913, but these demands subsided not long after the floodwaters. Residents accepted flooding as a fact of life, annoying and even dangerous, but also unavoidable.

Moreover, Cincinnati had another major river priority at the beginning of the twentieth century. Many local business elites and politicians were deeply involved in the Ohio Valley Improvement Association, and therefore preoccupied by reviving the navigation potential of the Ohio River. In November 1916 a rumor spread across Cincinnati that the U.S. Army Corps of Engineers actually opposed the Ohio River lock and dam navigation improvements, sparking considerable concern in the city:

> The rumor that Secretary of War Baker is opposed to the further canalization of the Ohio River, a report which he denied vigorously yesterday, may have arisen, it was suggested to-day, from intimations that have become current concerning the attitude the corps of army engineers will take toward Federal aid for flood control in the Ohio Valley states. . . . It is understood, and has been published, that the army engineers cannot see that navigation will be benefited by flood control of these tributaries. . . . It is thought that the reported attitude of the engineers toward Federal aid on the Ohio tributaries may have been misconstrued to refer to the [navigation system] improvement program on the Ohio River itself. (*Cincinnati Enquirer* 1916, 16)

When it became clear that the USACE leadership only disapproved of a proposal for flood control reservoirs, relief among Cincinnati commercial and industrial elites was immediate. This was typical of Cincinnati in the first decades of the twentieth century: navigation as the dominant issue while other river concerns such as flood control took a back seat.

Yet, groups in other parts of the country had already spent decades lobbying the federal government for increased flood protection funding and technical assistance (O'Neill 2006). In the nineteenth century, federal politicians and bureaucrats largely opposed flood prevention in the belief that the U.S. Constitution only authorized the national government to fund navigation improvements on the country's waterways; nothing else. Another impediment was the belief that these projects would only have localized effects, benefiting primarily riparian landowners by opening new sections of their land for development and by increasing the value of their floodplain properties. In the absence of federal support, many states and districts organized their own flood control works, even as they continued to lobby for federal support.[1]

Sustained pressure by groups from the South and California finally led to the first national legislation authorizing direct federal funding for flood control works on the Mississippi River and Sacramento River in 1917 (O'Neill 2006). With this authorizing legislation, flood control joined navigation and irrigation as the only water management projects the federal government had authorized itself to oversee. Just prior to the major 1937 Ohio River flood, the Flood Control Act of 1936 expanded this federal jurisdiction for flood protection to encompass all of the country's navigable rivers and designated the U.S. Army Corps of Engineers as the agency responsible for managing these projects.

Flood Protection Proposals in a Reform-Minded Cincinnati

Despite these shifts on the national level, in the early twentieth century, Cincinnati continued to favor pursuing navigational improvements for the Ohio River over any consideration of flood protection efforts. Cincinnati elites, led by local river merchants at the helm of the Ohio Valley Improvement Association, remained united around the goal of creating a lock and dam system that would enable year-round navigation on the river. Meanwhile, other Ohio Valley cities had taken the opportunity to begin pursuing flood protection plans. In nearby Dayton, Ohio, the Miami Conservancy District built the country's first watershed reservoir flood prevention system following the devastating flood of 1913. Watershed reservoirs use dams to trap floodwaters closer to tributary headwaters before they can threaten downstream areas. Locals viewed the Miami Conservancy District as a major success (Welky 2011). These regional efforts slowly began to draw the attention of public officials in Cincinnati, and when "another Ohio Valley municipality guaranteed flood immunity to industries that might relocate to that city, Cincinnati's city planners were spurred to action" (Hedeen 1994, 152).

The most prominent flood protection proposal during this period was delineated in *The Official Plan of the City of Cincinnati*, adopted May 28, 1925. The 1925 *Official Plan* decried the short-sightedness of inaction, stating that "many individuals [in Cincinnati] believe that the community is not justified in expending large sums in flood protection works. Such persons measure only the individual cost and do not appreciate, or perhaps care, for the cost to the whole community involved in the slowing down of industry and business. Were these losses capitalized, it would probably be found in Cincinnati, as it has generally been found elsewhere, that adequate measures are cheapest in the long run" (CPC 1925, 151).

In response, the 1925 *Official Plan* proposed a "dyke in front of the principal business district" (CPC 1925, 152). The dyke (or levee) would hew to the river, approximately 140 feet wide and 30 feet high, with occasional concrete floodwalls if necessary. Large gates were planned along streets and railroads to allow continued access between the riverfront and city. The more than three-mile-long levee would stretch between the two hills bookending the lowland core of the city—Mount Adams to the east and Price Hill to the west. This would effectively seal off the entire basin containing the city center from flood threats. Pumping stations could move sewage over the dykes, preventing excessive runoff from building up behind the barrier in emergencies. A thoroughfare or esplanade could also be placed atop the levee, which the plan proposed should be completed by the 1930s or 1940s.

The 1925 *Official Plan*—the first comprehensive urban plan adopted by a city council in the United States—marked a dramatic shift in Cincinnati politics. The local Republican machine led by George B. Cox—also known as Boss Cox—had finally begun to falter. After three decades dominating local government, Boss Cox died in 1916, eulogized by the *New York Times* as "one of the last of the old-time personal bosses" (*New York Times* 1916, 38). Key lieutenants, particularly Rudolph Hynicka, took up the reins of Boss Cox's political machine. Hynicka shaped city politics over the next decade, even after he moved to New York City to run his theater business. He made concessions to progressive elements of the Republican Party in recognition of growing critiques, but also maintained many aspects of the Boss Cox machine.

In the early 1920s, agitation grew for more dramatic changes that would remake municipal governance in Cincinnati. Wealthy urban elites who identified themselves as professionals led this charge for reform. Emboldened by their increasing importance in city life, this growing group demanded a larger role in determining Cincinnati's future (Tucker 1967). Professions emerged in the nineteenth century as a new elevated status for workers who developed skills through formal training or certification. Many professions, such as public health experts and engineers, helped reshape the governance of the booming industrial cities. Their specialized expertise helped manage urban diseases, infrastructure, factory production, and countless other aspects of the industrial city critical to organizing rapidly changing urban life (Joyce 2003).

In Cincinnati, professional workers gained political prominence with the proliferation of local corporations in the early twentieth century. While industrialization had come to dominate Cincinnati's economy by the end of the nineteenth century, many firms sought a competitive edge by shifting to corporate business models and bringing on more professional staff. Local industrial giants like Procter & Gamble, a consumer goods producer, added more middle management staff and business process specialists to drive its continued growth. In addition, more segments of the workforce independently professionalized, such as with the formation of realtor associations, which introduced standardized practices like commission rates, ethics codes, and redlining.

Many of these new professionals were younger white men, frequently living in the suburbs found at the edge of Cincinnati proper or just outside its borders. Cincinnati had slowly been annexing many of these surrounding suburban communities, so that the number of professionals residing within city limits grew substantially. The majority of these professionals were eager to use their individual expertise to improve the city. Professionals were also notorious "joiners" and boosters, looking for places they could connect with other professionals and contribute to their communities. Sinclair Lewis captured this boisterous energy in *Babbitt*, his 1922 novel on middle-class professional life that was modeled in large part on Cincinnati (Lewis 1922). According to George Babbitt, the eponymous realtor at the heart of the story, "What is it distinguishes a profession from a mere trade, business, or occupation? What is it? Why, it's the public service and the skill, the trained skill, and the knowledge and, uh, all that, whereas a fellow that merely goes out for the jack, he never considers the—public service and trained skill and so on" (157). In this view, being a professional was not just about gaining specific expertise, but about the desire to be of service to one's community.

This enthusiasm found an outlet in the creation of numerous civic groups in Cincinnati. Civic groups led by urban professionals had been gaining prominence in Cincinnati since the late nineteenth century. Organizations such as the Young Men's Business Club, Optimist Club, and Better Housing League tackled topics such as housing, public health, educational standards, the deleterious effects of industrial employment, and a host of other issues (Miller 1980; Kornbluh 1986; Tucker 1967). These groups led reform campaigns and often achieved important successes. However, despite occasional compromises, the local Republican machine frequently blunted their efforts to reform municipal government. The leadership of Cincinnati's Republican machine included many local business elites who were sympathetic to progressive goals but loath to disrupt the Republican advantage in local politics by pushing for too much change. As a result, most reforms, especially those aimed at restructuring local government to challenge machine politics, faltered in the early twentieth century (Tucker 1967). By 1920 though, a new wave of reform organizations driven by young professionals began to gain significant traction with their proposals to remake municipal government.

Three of the most prominent groups with this focus were the Cincinnatus Association, the Charter Committee, and the United City Planning Committee. The Cincinnatus Association was a "good government" group of professional elites advancing "projects important to the people of Cincinnati through the effort of its members and the formation of intelligent public opinion" (Tucker 1967, 73). Cincinnatus Association members formed committees to investigate issues facing the city, make recommendations about improvements, and then led their own campaigns in support of their platforms, publishing their findings in the local press and pressuring municipal officials to adopt their suggestions (Tucker 1967). The Charter Committee began as a committee of Cincinnatus Association members interested in electoral reform. The group then grew into its own organization with a mission of completely rewriting the city charter to foster more efficient and transparent governance. Their proposals included changes like replacing ward-level elections for the city council with citywide proportional representation, as well as the appointment of professionals such as a city manager to oversee much more of the city's day-to-day operations (Burnham 1992a). The United City Planning Committee launched in 1915 with a focus on the creation of the urban plan for the city. The reform enthusiasm of the 1920s brought new momentum to their work, and they raised enough donations to pay for the entire 1925 *Official Plan* without municipal funds.

These groups had a shared interest in the emerging discipline of urban planning as a means of improving the governance of Cincinnati. Urban planning focused on the systematic organization of land usage for cities, using new quantitative methods to determine the best purpose for different areas across the city and laying out tools for local government to support these developmental goals. Maintaining segregation—by race and class as well as by types of land uses—became a core tenant of the field, as did a commitment to new forms of urban development that incorporated green spaces, low population density, and modern architectural design.

Cincinnati became a leader in embracing the field. Urban planning advocates across the country hailed the adoption of the 1925 *Official Plan* by Cincinnati's city council. The Charter Committee also succeeded in its campaign to reform the city charter in 1924. One of the new charter's key contributions was the creation of the powerful City Planning Commission, which could weigh in on all development-related decisions of the city council. Lead reformer Murray Seasongood, who became mayor of Cincinnati in 1925, gleefully declared that the city "has become an exemplar among American cities and we are constantly having requests for information from various sections of the country" (Tucker 1967, 142–43).

The city's professional reformers celebrated these landmark accomplishments, seeing urban planning as a way to address the "urban problems" that concerned them while also protecting their own interests in the city (Silver 1997). Cincinnati's new municipal charter had been designed to provide more representation to the newer immigrant, religious, and racial communities in Cincinnati, and ensure their voices factored into public debates (Burnham 1992a). Yet, even as these "good governance" activists promoted a more open political system, they also retained a "perception of political conflict as irrational, a skepticism about the competence of the average citizen, and a faith in the reforming power of technical expertise and managerial skill" (Fairfield 1994, 179). The reorganization of Cincinnati's municipal government placed professional experts in prominent positions and frequently relied on technocratic rather than democratic decision-making processes (Fairfield 1994). The Great Depression further reinforced these elites' faith in urban planning, as mistrust for market-driven policies grew in tandem with rising calls for solutions administered by government experts (Davis 1991; Welky 2011).

In parallel to these political changes, the city's intense focus on navigation had finally begun to slacken. The Ohio Valley Improvement Association (OVIA), long dominated by Cincinnati elites driven to complete the Ohio River lock and dam navigation system, finally achieved its original objective in October 1929. After the completion of the project, and the subsequent commercial crisis brought on by the Great Depression, the OVIA broadened its objectives, expanding its membership, and considered projects outside the scope of navigation for the first time. At the OVIA's meeting in 1930, the Cincinnati city planning engineer at the time pushed for the group to move beyond navigation concerns to also consider issues like beautification and flood control: "The canalization of the river was certainly not the ultimate purpose of this Association, for if it were you would not be meeting here today [after the 1929 inauguration of the lock and down system]. You all should be accustomed to thinking in terms of the future and I trust that you will not lose sight of the fact that the future development of the banks of the Ohio River is in your hands" (OVIA 1930, 49).

In response to these shifting currents, in 1934 the organization's leadership revised its mission: "Where formerly the subject of navigation and operations immediately related thereto were dominant, it was felt that the relevant projects of the land must now be considered. These involve flood and drought control, domestic water supply, stream pollution, forestation, soil erosion, and kindred matters" (OVIA 1934, foreword).[2] Even before the major flood of 1937, flood control had already thus emerged as a major new concern in Cincinnati. New Deal funding opened up the possibility for the construction of numerous flood prevention measures, including levees, flood reservoirs, and emergency drainage basins (O'Neill 2006). Meanwhile, Cincinnati's urban planning experts explored how to increase flood protection measures for the city, with the willingness of professional elites to throw their weight behind these efforts. As a result, Cincinnati seemed to be well on the path toward embracing and implementing flood control measures in the 1930s.

A Flood Crisis

Coming in the midst of increasing interest in flood control both locally and nationally, the Ohio River flood of January and February 1937 brought unprecedented damage. The flood lasted nearly three weeks and crested in Cincinnati at 79.99 feet on January 26, 1937, almost nine feet above the 1884 record of 71.1 feet.[3] Numerous survivor accounts register residents' panic as the waters crept up to places they had never known the river to go before (Welky 2011). Many residents had moved all their possessions to the second floor of their houses to safeguard them—as they did with most large floods—but were forced to return to retrieve what they could when the river continued rising. One local resident remembered how his father borrowed a small barge to return to their home on a salvage mission, floating back above their submerged street: "My dad had a two-by-four and a hatchet. As we came down the street and wires got in our way, he'd pop them with the hatchet. We got to the second floor of the house and he took the hatchet and knocked the window out" (*Insurance Journal* 2007).

Cincinnati's infrastructure could not cope with the devastating flood. Rising waters forced the suspension of streetcar service, limiting transit options. Isolated riverfront neighborhoods in Cincinnati such as the East End faced food shortages as store owners pulled out and "transportation [was] virtually nil" (*Cincinnati Enquirer* 1937b, 18). On top of this, downed telephone lines cut off communication to whole neighborhoods, as phone companies desperately sought to restore emergency communications. The flood also shut down power stations located near the waterfront, requiring the city to route in energy from nearby Dayton, which was largely shielded from the flooding by its flood prevention reservoir system. Finally, backed-up sewers spewed wastewater into the streets, turning floodwaters into a noxious brew. When these floodwaters poured into the city's waterworks facilities, it contaminated drinking water for local residents. As a last resort, local companies began bottling drinking water from their own wells to supply the city.

Meanwhile, uprooted gas and oil tanks leaked into flooded areas. Downed electrical wires, many cut by residents attempting to escape in boats, sparked massive fires on the water, making rescue efforts in the freezing winter weather even more chaotic. A fervent nighttime battle with one of the city's largest ever fires developed in the neighborhood of Northside, covering "three and one-half square miles due to the scattering of blazing oil on the flood waters of Millcreek." Fighting the blaze, "firemen slipped and sloshed through ankle-deep snow, stood up to waists in flood waters, and ventured into the flame-bound area in boats" (*Cincinnati Enquirer* 1937a, 1). For forty-six hours, more than five hundred firefighters worked to control the flames in the Mill Creek Valley.

The devastation across the city was enormous and unnerving. Years later, George Stimson, a journalist for the *Cincinnati Times-Star*, recounted venturing out in a canoe, witnessing surreal scenes along the riverfront. As he floated along, "Somewhere in an empty, flooded building, a lonely telephone was ringing," while nearby in "the snow on the top of nearly submerged shed roofs were the footprints of rats" (Stimson 1964, 98). Visiting the Central Bottoms in front of downtown, he found a foreign landscape:

> Empty, deserted, a ghost city, was the impression of Cincinnati's frontage on the Ohio. The water had submerged many waterfront one-story buildings. The old structures, harking back to the halcyon days when the River was Cincinnati's means of livelihood, felt the lapping waters on their limestone and sandstone walls well into the second floors. Everywhere the water poked long fingers into alleys and streets, reaching up toward the higher ground of the business district. Oddly, the only sign of life was a cluster of houseboats, moored close to a warehouse, swinging this way and that with the current, fathoms above what had been, a week before, a busy waterfront thoroughfare. It was a strange sight and one long remembered. (Stimson 1964, 99)

At the flood's highest point, water covered one-sixth of the city (Stradling 2003, 113).

The Ohio River finally left its flood stage in Cincinnati on February 5, 1937. The receding waters left behind a city in shock, with locals in disbelief about what had just happened. As the flood level dropped, it slowly revealed the extent of the wreckage. Many buildings had been torn apart by the floodwater and the debris it carried, while a few had floated away entirely. Those structures that escaped more serious destruction were left coated with a layer of slime, and returning occupants found a thick deposit of mud waiting on their floors. Eight Cincinnatians lost their lives, and economic damages reached tens of millions of dollars. Since many local residents no longer spent much time near the Ohio River, the flood served as a wake-up call that Old Man River still had a role to play in the city. After the initial shock, Cincinnatians felt bewildered to find that the river could still have such a profound impact on their lives.

As the city began to pivot to picking up the pieces, many residents were almost as concerned about what came next as they had been about the flood itself. Coming at the depths of the Great Depression, the 1937 flood left numerous families facing almost certain financial ruin. Cincinnati's economy had weathered the Great Depression relatively well up to that point with a diverse industrial base that actually saw increasing demand for some locally produced goods such as inexpensive soap brands and preassembled radios (Stradling 2003). Even so, too many Cincinnatians were already in vulnerable positions, and the flood only served to exacerbate their precarity.

In response, middle- and upper-class white women and men led efforts to provide relief to those most affected by the catastrophe, drawing on resources provided by the federal government and private citizens (Welky 2011; Cook 2007). The mayor and city manager appointed a Citizen's Rehabilitation Committee to coordinate recovery efforts spearheaded by local and federal government agencies as well as private aid organizations such as the Red Cross. The Ohio National Guard arrived to assist as well. The result was an effective and rapid deployment of resources to areas of need, addressing urgent deprivation as well as support for finding food and shelter in the coming weeks, though these services were understaffed for Black neighborhoods (Cook 2007).

Preparing for the Next Flood

In parallel to the efforts to get the city back on its feet in the aftermath of the flood, a flurry of civic groups and government officials quickly pivoted to the longer-term question of how to best protect the city from the next such flood. The city government's emergency Citizen's Rehabilitation Committee established a subcommittee, the Flood Control and Future Planning Committee, on February 11, 1937, to consider responses available to the city. Simultaneously, the city government, primarily through the city manager's office, began coordinating with the U.S. Army Corps of Engineers to design proposals to protect the Cincinnati waterfront. The City Planning Commission , a semiautonomous municipal agency, also began developing recommendations, requesting a report outlining considerations for any flood control works from one of the consultants who had created the 1925 *Official Plan* (Goodrich 1937).[4] Outside of city government, the Cincinnatus Association, which remained a very active association of business and professional elites, formed its own Flood Protection Committee. The Cincinnatus Association flood committee produced its first three reports on March 9, 1937, covering soil conservation, the federal flood reservoir system, and dyking the city (Tucker 1967). Dominated by men, these groups sprang into action to first investigate and then attempt to guide future flood control activities. These efforts led to quite different proposals and saw many of these groups eventually coming into conflict with one another.

Provisions in the 1936 Flood Control Act set the stage for these disputes. The act designated the USACE as the agency responsible for designing flood control works and committed to providing federal funds to cover the cost of flood protection works. Municipalities had to purchase properties in the path of the flood control works, reconstruct affected utilities, and maintain the infrastructure after the project's completion. These requirements represented a considerable expense to be borne by municipalities, which they often met by creating special tax assessment districts affecting the neighborhoods that would benefit most from flood control. The need to take responsibility for these expenses also opened significant avenues for local interests to influence the creation of public works affecting their rivers. Municipalities could effectively "opt in" to USACE flood protection plans by agreeing to provide local matching funds and the necessary land titles, which gave them leverage to suggest modifications to the USACE designs (O'Neill 2006). In this regard, many actors could seek to influence the process, providing input on the scope, timeline, and goals of a flood control project. This helped produce the postflood context in Cincinnati, with the rapid proliferation of different groups providing their own flood control suggestions.

A consensus rapidly emerged among the city's industrial and government elites that the Mill Creek Valley should be protected from the Ohio River's potential backflow. During the flood, the Ohio River had reversed this tributary's current, forcing it back into a heavily industrialized section of the city that also contained populous residential neighborhoods, so that the "inundated lower Mill Creek basin appeared to be a lake . . . which had taken eight days to fill" (Hedeen 1994, 154–55). This backflow flooded areas of the city previously thought to be safe, and the heavy concentration of industry in the Mill Creek Valley created major losses for local corporations.

After the flood receded, the city's elites turned their attention to protecting this important industrial neighborhood. The editor of the *Cincinnati Post* pointed out, "In this valley are situated factories which represent perhaps 75 percent of the city's capital investment in industry, and which employ 65 percent of its industrial workers. It is truly the city's 'meal ticket'" (Hedeen 1994, 156). Louis Coffin, the director of foreign sales for the U.S. Playing Card Company and a member of the Cincinnatus Association, rallied corporate and government support to build a barrier dam near the mouth of Mill Creek. In normal conditions, a massive gate built into the barrier dam would be open and the creek would flow out into the Ohio River naturally. In times of high water on the Ohio River, sealing the gate would protect the Mill Creek factories and neighborhoods from backflow. When the barrier dam closed, massive pumps would carry Mill Creek's water over the barrier to discharge into the Ohio River (Hedeen 1994). With Coffin acting as a "one-man lobby for his project" (Tucker 1967, 175), and advocacy from companies with large factories in the Mill Creek Valley—such as Procter & Gamble's famous Ivorydale facility—the barrier dam plan gained almost immediate support. After construction was interrupted by World War II, the USACE finally completed the Mill Creek Barrier Dam in 1948; it quickly prevented an estimated $2 million in damages from a spring rise during April 1948 (*Cincinnati Enquirer* 1948a).

Less straightforward was the discussion around what to do with the Central Bottoms, the area of the riverfront located directly in front of downtown. Many members of the public assumed that the city would pursue the objectives outlined in the 1925 *Official Plan*: building a riverfront levee starting at the base of Mount Adams, just east of downtown, which would then connect with the flood control works in front of Mill Creek. As late as February 1936, City Planning Commission staff engineer Myron Downs gave a presentation before the Lower Cincinnati Business Men's Association on the "Feasibility of the construction of a dyke, or dykes, along the Cincinnati riverfront to hold back flood waters, particularly to protect commercial and industrial properties in the lower 'bottoms district'" including "illustrating the duration and effect of Cincinnati's five highest floods on commercial and industrial properties in the downtown area of the city" (*Cincinnati Enquirer* 1936, 10). At this 1936 presentation, Downs urged the Lower Cincinnati Business Men's Association to support the levee plan as it was laid out in the 1925 *Official Plan*.

After the 1937 flood, city and federal government offices moved slowly toward the construction of a floodwall for the Central Bottoms. The Lower Cincinnati Business Men's Association, which drew its membership heavily from the smaller-scale factory owners and wholesalers located in the Central Bottoms area, came out in favor of a floodwall, arguing that it would increase the value of their properties. They and other local groups believed that it would be best to follow the plan that had already been "in existence for a number of years" (*Cincinnati Enquirer* 1937c, 16). After the completion of the Ohio River lock and dam system, many businesses had invested in improvements to their facilities and wanted to see the area protected. Moreover, after their recent experiences, many city residents were willing to support flood protection at whatever cost. On November 2, 1937, voters passed a $5 million bond issue to fund the construction of flood protection works for the city, with 70.5 percent in favor (*Cincinnati Enquirer* 1937f).

When City Manager Clarence Dykstra, who had taken control of the city during the flooding emergency, left for a post in Wisconsin later in 1937, the city successfully reenlisted Colonel Clarence Sherrill to fill the city manager position beginning on June 14, 1937. Sherrill had been Cincinnati's first city manager, from 1926 to 1930, and it was thought that as a former USACE officer who had overseen improvements along the Mississippi River, he would be able to guide the city through the upcoming public works process. Shortly after being selected, he declared flood control "one of the city's foremost problems" (*Cincinnati Enquirer* 1937d, 3).

Sherrill was also closely connected with maritime interests in Cincinnati. After originally leaving the city manager position in 1930, he had become an executive at the Kroger Grocery and Baking Co., interacting regularly with riverfront wholesalers and barge freight companies as part of his work. He was active in the Ohio Valley Improvement Association and closely aligned with its river merchant and industrial leadership, as well as its close USACE partners (OVIA 1930; OVIA 1934). These groups eagerly wanted to see a floodwall built in the Central Bottoms, protecting the area's concentration of marine terminals, warehouses, and rail linkages. The combination of support from municipal government, the USACE, riverfront business owners, and the broader public represented a formidable array of interests aligned behind the creation of a central riverfront floodwall.

Yet, opposition to dyking the Central Bottoms soon began to mount among the committees that had sprung up in the aftermath of the flood. From the Cincinnatus Association, Herbert Schroth's report at the March 9, 1937, meeting gained attention for portraying a system of dykes in Cincinnati as an absurdity. Schroth (1937) argued that the project would create a "Dyked City of the Hills." In his view, Cincinnati's hilly topography meant there was only ever a small proportion of land in the floodplain and that the system of dykes offered a "false security" (22). Schroth also argued that a dyke would at best save structures that were already "dilapidated" (16). While not so strident in its critiques, the Flood Control and Future Planning Committee of the Citizen's Rehabilitation Committee recommended a self-liquidating agency to purchase and tear down riverfront property, followed by using fill to build up the vacant land out of the floodplain and selling the new lots at a profit for commercial use. Meanwhile, the City Planning Commission, in its December 30, 1937, report *The Cincinnati Waterfront: Its Problems and Recommended Future Utilization*, rejected the recommendations from the 1925 *Official Plan* for dykes or floodwalls along the Central Bottoms, worrying that a floodwall would create "protected slums" (15). Others, while acknowledging that disasters like the 1937 flood provided bad press, with scenes of misfortune and urban vulnerability, also portrayed the infrastructure itself as a negative advertisement. One critic described existing flood works in Huntington, West Virginia, as a "penitentiary wall" and "hideously ugly" (Marting 1939, 1), a constant reminder of looming danger. Other business elites in the city eventually joined this opposition to the central riverfront floodwall, including the Cincinnati Chamber of Commerce and the Cincinnati Engineers Club.

Many opponents of the proposed floodwall came from the professional class. This elite group had grown in importance during the Great Depression. Corporations in Cincinnati that had been able to adapt to the new economic conditions relied on their professional staff to help them navigate changing demand. In one well-known example, Neil McElroy, part of the advertising team at Procter & Gamble, wrote a memo credited with launching the modern practice of brand management, helping the company successfully reposition its products for more cost-conscious consumers (Low and Fullerton 1994). Politically, professionals that had driven Cincinnati's governmental reform remained entrenched in City Hall. Former Cincinnatus Association member and realtor Russell Wilson served as mayor from 1930 to 1937, consolidating many reform efforts from the 1920s. Professionals active in the Cincinnatus Association were also a critical source of support. The group's Flood Protection Committee vocally opposed the floodwall plans. Schroth's leadership was particularly surprising given that he was a civil engineer who worked for the Charles V. Maescher & Co. general contracting firm, which specialized in concrete construction and could easily have stood to benefit from the building of a massive concrete floodwall in the Central Bottoms.

Despite the diverse group of critics they faced, those supporting a floodwall for the Central Bottoms, including Sherrill and members of the Lower Cincinnati Business Men's Association, increasingly saw Alfred Bettman as their primary antagonist. Bettman was the chair of the City Planning Commission (CPC) and a nationally recognized land use planning attorney. For decades, Bettman had been a key figure in the field of urban planning, helping to shape the field. He had argued the government's case in the 1926 hearing of *Village of Euclid v. Ambler Realty Co.* before the U.S. Supreme Court, which upheld the new practice of municipal zoning laws. Through Bettman's efforts, Cincinnati had become one of the leading proponents of urban planning. Bettman had also taken an active role in efforts to organize the preliminary city planning commission in 1918 (Burnham 1992b). In his role as CPC chair, he was well positioned to coordinate efforts to oppose the construction of the floodwall in the Central Bottoms area.

In the years following the 1937 flood, disagreements over whether to build a floodwall for the Central Bottoms became increasingly bitter. Sherrill, with the support of river merchants and small-scale industrialists, sought to push through floodwall construction as quickly as possible, while Bettman and other professional elites obstructed their progress. The tensions between these elite groups pivoted around differing visions for the future of the central riverfront area.

How Much Flood Control

At first look, the desire not to build a floodwall along the Central Bottoms appears perplexing. Many of the other cities along the Ohio River took the opportunities presented by the 1936, 1937, and 1938 Flood Control Acts to build floodwalls or levees, including Covington and Newport, the two Northern Kentucky cities directly across the Ohio River from Cincinnati (Bauer 1988). Simultaneously, efforts ramped up across the Ohio Valley to build flood control reservoirs at the headwaters of the Ohio River's tributaries. This surging interest in flood control arose in tandem with a boom in infrastructure construction across the country, the majority linked to work relief efforts during the Great Depression. Seemingly daily, the federal government launched massive new projects to reshape the country. Reflecting this ethos, Senator Will Whittington, architect of the 1938 Flood Control Act, declared, "I want to live in a constructive age. . . . I want the age in which I live to build" (Welky 2011, 279).

For many, these projects were an obvious outcome of the ascendancy of science and its mastery over nature. Engineering advances and scientific planning provided a newfound capacity to make nature manageable and useful, so that instead "of being fearful and threatening, nature became tame and serviceable" (Kaika 2005, 107).[5] These new infrastructural systems constrained, purified, and circulated an explicitly nonsocial nature, that is, a nature understood as outside of everyday life. Infrastructure also made city dwellers less tolerant of the vagaries of nature, leading them to expect to exist "outside the reach of nature's processes" (107).

Natural disasters like earthquakes, droughts, hurricanes, and flooding posed notable threats to this new order. Whereas in the past such disasters had been seen as an inevitable part of life, urban residents now believed infrastructure could minimize the effects of these unpredictable events. In many cases, governments used the crises brought on by specific disasters to justify new infrastructure projects that would purportedly prevent future crises (Graham 2010). Shortly after the Ohio River flood in 1937, Major H. H. Pohl, assistant to the division engineer of the Ohio River Division of the USACE, stated, "It may be that the people of the Ohio Valley are now learning what the inhabitants of the Mississippi Valley learned [after their flood] in 1927, that is, that the best way to secure flood protection is to have a good flood" (Pohl 1937, 589).

Given this context, one would expect the 1937 flood to provide the final impetus toward the construction of a Central Bottoms floodwall. Most residents assumed that the city would build the dyke and floodwall proposed in the 1925 *Official Plan*. Initial postflood events bore this out, with the city residents voting to authorize the $5 million in flood works bonds and the USACE drafting a plan to protect the complete downtown riverfront area.

An analysis of the 1937 flood using an assemblage perspective helps explain the problems encountered by the expected Central Bottoms floodwall infrastructure. In this case, assemblage is useful in terms of tracking relationships across different elite groups in Cincinnati as well as the claims they made relative to understanding and incorporating the Ohio River's desires. A major actor in the floodwall debate, the Ohio River had recently undergone significant transformations with the creation of a lock and dam system that maintained a navigable depth on the river year round, finalized in 1929. In the past, the Ohio River had had highly variable depths throughout each season, with high flood crests in the spring and fall but also summer drops that occasionally were so shallow that people could walk across the river. In place of this, the new lock and dam system maintained a minimum navigable depth of nine feet throughout the year and also shifted perceptions of the Ohio River and the riverfront as a more predictable space. This attracted interest of local professional elites, who began to dream about how things could be different along the riverfront with this friendlier Ohio River. The first hints of this shift were captured in the 1925 *Official Plan*, which named the central riverfront "Cincinnati's greatest asset" and called for it to be redeveloped with parks.

The 1937 flood definitively disrupted views of a more orderly Ohio River. In order to understand these shifts though, it is first important to clarify how the flood transformed understanding of the Ohio River and life on the riverfront, particularly in the Central Bottoms. To begin, this requires moving away from a linear flood disaster narrative, one where a crisis begins and ends, to be followed by a community decision on a course of action as a response. Instead, experiences of flooding can vary markedly in terms of their physical, legal, social, and psychological ramifications (Walker et al. 2011). Foregrounding assemblage attends to these multiple experiences, without prioritizing one as more relevant or revealing.

Leading up to and in the aftermath of the 1937 flood, numerous spatial experiences overlapped in the Central Bottoms. Residents, workers, local business owners, city planners, and engineers each had their own perceptions of the Central Bottoms, whether it was home, an inefficient commercial zone, a site of vice and racial intermixing, or a necessary part of the local economy. Each individual's view on the Central Bottoms considerably influenced whether they found flooding intolerable or a part of everyday life.

A core matter in question after the 1937 flood was the definition of "being flooded." As the geographer Gordon Walker and his colleagues detail in their study of a June 2007 flood in Hull, England, "being flooded" versus "not being flooded" fails to neatly correspond with the high-water mark from the body of water that overflowed its normal boundaries (Walker et al. 2011). Rather, "being flooded" involves a confluence of numerous actors and interlinked experiences unfolding over a long period. Responses can shift with time, such as with individuals who previously accepted flooding as a normal occurrence later changing their minds to instead fear rising water, a transition that could be tied to new building materials and technologies, understandings of cleanliness, or other factors (Whatmore 2013, 43).

In Cincinnati, commercial interests in the Central Bottoms in the first few decades of the twentieth century were initially opposed to a redefinition of "being flooded" as an unacceptable state. They accepted flooding as a necessary trade-off that came from their proximity to the water. Businesses benefited from access to rail and marine transportation routes, the cheap labor that congregated near the riverfront, and the lower property values they believed the floods brought. The release of the 1925 *Official Plan* marked a shift in this discussion. City officials and business elites began to argue that "being flooded," even if only affecting some individuals, was inefficient and avoidable, leading to unnecessary damages and a loss of profit due to interruption of trade for the city as a whole.

Many small industries and warehouse distributors in the Central Bottoms slowly came to support a levee for the area, such as those who were active in the Lower Cincinnati Business Men's Association. Many had invested in expanding their facilities with the expectation of a surge in commercial activity with the opening of the lock and dam system. They became closely aligned with federal and municipal officials who were eager to push forward a floodwall plan. Still, others, including many owners of rail and marine terminals, persisted in their dislike of a levee or floodwall on the central riverfront, believing it would separate them from river transportation and impede their businesses. W. W. Marting, a marine terminal operator at the Ohio River Company, complained that his coal shipping business "would be cut off from the use of our property at the slightest threat of a flood because the steps necessary to close these [floodwall] gateways could not be left until the last moment" (Marting 1939, 1). A vice president of the Hatfield Campbell Creek Coal Co. similarly argued "that a flood wall . . . would not permit the city to get more benefit of river transportation that she is entitled to" (Hatfield 1939, 1). At the same time, the Great Depression beginning shortly after the completion of the Ohio River navigation lock and dam system in 1929 had forestalled any massive growth in river trade. This outcome did not totally diminish the importance of these river merchants' complaints—especially those coming from powerful coal and wholesale merchants—but it did mean that river merchants were not the overwhelming dominant interest on the riverfront that they had hoped to be.

For their part, Central Bottoms residents were only fleetingly considered when planning the future of the neighborhood (CPC 1946). This population's numbers had been declining but still reached close to 2,900 individuals in the 1940 census. Central Bottoms residents had long adapted to seasonal flooding, with most of their apartments located on the second or third floors of their buildings in order to avoid instances of rising water. Similar "bottoms" neighborhoods were found throughout the United States, most located in the floodplains near rivers and occupied by low-income individuals and families. Bottoms communities, such as those in Frankfort, Kentucky; Detroit, Michigan; and Kansas City, Missouri, shared many similarities with Cincinnati's Central Bottoms. The urban public perceived them as predominantly Black neighborhoods—even when they were home to a mix of ethnic and racial communities—and as places of "violence, poverty, corruption, dirt, saloons, pool halls, whiskey, cockfights, disease, murders, gambling, bootlegging, prostitution, slums, and crime" (Boyd 2011, 1).

These representations ignored the many other activities that took place in these areas. Cincinnatians from other neighborhoods frequented the Central Bottoms to purchase produce (including their Christmas trees during the holiday season) and to fish (*Cincinnati Enquirer* 2008). Numerous Black and white residents worked in the area's warehouses and small factories. Even though the mechanization of terminal facilities threw many roustabout residents out of work, the remaining riverfront workers and boat hands also mingled along the riverbanks (Souther 1957).

The professional groups organizing against the Central Bottoms floodwall represented a new perspective. Prior to the 1937 flood, many had been in favor of a floodwall as the accepted course of action. In large part, professionals had appreciated this infrastructure solution to controlling the Ohio River, recognizing and applauding the specialist skills their engineering peers required in undertaking such a daunting project. Yet, a combination of changing environmental and social conditions brought new perspectives to the fore. Whereas Cincinnati's major floods in 1907 and 1913 (and earlier) had failed to cause serious reevaluations of contemporary conditions and policies regarding flood control policy, the unprecedented height of the 1937 flood spurred consternation among professional elites and the desire to chart new potential paths forward.

The fight over the Central Bottoms floodwall represented the first time in decades that another elite group besides merchants and small-scale industrialists had shown a major interest in the riverfront. These professional elites did not have a defined strategy for how to redevelop the Central Bottoms, but through evaluations of how other cities in the United States and Europe had treated their riverfronts, they decided that the area would be a critical asset for Cincinnati's future growth. Proposed uses for the area diverged greatly—from civic to recreational to transportation—but shared the conviction that the existing riverfront businesses should have a reduced role along the central riverfront moving forward.

In line with this mindset, professional groups immediately after the 1937 flood began to spend an enormous amount of time on fact-finding and investigation, forming numerous temporary committees to study conditions, and activating their networks to understand other groups' plans.[6] These committees examined the existence and behavior of other actors, both human and nonhuman, collecting data on topics such as water flow, population density, damages, property values, and land usages. Through their investigations, these groups sought to reconfigure the local understanding of "being flooded," shifting what was and was not acceptable as well as pushing forward their own proposals for the Central Bottoms.

The Cincinnatus Association Flood Protection Committee, which eventually became the focal point for drumming up support for the construction of the Mill Creek Barrier Dam, typified this approach. The committee set information gathering as one of its primary objectives after the 1937 flood. Louis Coffin, working with industries in the Mill Creek Valley, gathered information on the water table, potential stream deviation options, and other environmental factors. The Cincinnatus Association group also sought to understand how other groups were framing the problem and pursuing solutions, so that it could best promote its preferred option. A letter conveying the outcome of a telephone call between Cincinnatus Association member Ralph A. Kreimer, a local attorney who had long been involved in reform movements in the city, and USACE district engineer Lieutenant Colonel Elliot provides a clear example of this mentality. Kreimer is careful to probe Elliot for information about how the Cincinnatus Association could provide its own input to the USACE plans without offending the district engineer:

> (The Colonel was speaking rapidly and at some length. I had the impulse to ask him whether in stating that the alternate plans, modified plans or new plans would have consideration, he meant that consideration would end before the plan or plans are submitted. But I did not like to make too obvious what I was driving at, or to antagonize him by appearing to pin him down when he was in a cordial mood, so I finally got in this question):
>
> Question. "Well I understand then that about the end of February [1938] your plans will be ready and that while they will be definite in shape, there will be some flexibility about them."
>
> Answer. "*I suppose so*; but the purpose is to push construction as soon as possible." (Kreimer 1937, 2, emphasis in original)

Kreimer concluded his letter by asking his Cincinnatus Association colleagues, including Louis Coffin and Herbert Schroth, how they should proceed with their flood control investigation, "Please let me have the reaction of yourself and Messrs. Coffin and Schroth on how we might best smoke-out where, when, and by whom the 'consideration' of alternate or modified plans is to be given" (Kreimer 1937, 2). This term "smoke-out" became a catchphrase of the group, with Kreimer even adopting "Yours for a smoke-out" as his sign-off.

Numerous other professional groups across the city were undertaking their own parallel investigations, trying to ascertain what response the conditions called for as more information became available about the key human and nonhuman actors involved in the decision-making process. In this, they were evaluating and seeking to redefine local meanings of "being flooded" in Cincinnati, rearranging the relationships between local actors to their favor, and searching for new partners to tactfully influence core decision-making in the city. The Ohio River ultimately became the focus of these efforts. In particular, efforts to define how the river behaved and its relationship to urban blight emerged as the key point of contention in discussions around whether to build the Central Bottoms floodwall.

Respecting the Ohio River

Specialists from the City Planning Commission, with the support of professional business elites in groups including the Cincinnatus Association, proposed a new relationship to the river. Built on an idea of respecting the river rather than trying to control it, this viewpoint had dramatic implications for both riverfront infrastructure plans and the Central Bottoms neighborhood. Through their emphasis of cooperating with the Ohio River, these elites in Cincinnati sought to work with the river to support the cause of white supremacy in the city, which had long seen the Black and white residents in the Central Bottoms as undesirable and, increasingly, as dangerous sources of urban blight.

The March 9, 1937, report by Herbert Schroth of the Cincinnatus Association provided a first indication of a new perspective. Discussing what Cincinnati would look like with a levee system, he satirized this possible future as the "Dyked City of the Hills," rejecting any underlying attempt to control the river through levees or floodwalls. According to Schroth, rivers were impressively destructive in their own right, and this could be exacerbated by efforts to manage their flow. Thus, Schroth claimed, "professional opinion is showing a decided trend toward theory of letting rivers have their just due, and to quit confining them" (Schroth 1937, 20). The best response would be to find ways to remove people from the floodplain, out of harm's way.

Alfred Bettman used his position as CPC chair to push a similar perspective.

Arguing that urban planning had only recently begun to study flooding, Bettman compiled resources concerning floodplain zoning (Bettman 1939a), including references to "getting out of the river's way" so that it could "have a little more elbow room" (Anonymous 1937). This approach was built on ideas put forward by the planner Lewis Mumford, who argued that instead of dominating nature, the planning practitioner should "accommodate the land," being guided by "its features, not our wishes" (Welky 2011, 43).[7] Bettman also corresponded extensively about the issue with his colleague, well-known urban planner Ladislas Segoe (who had also worked on the city's 1925 *Official Plan*), discussing the possibilities of using riverfront zoning to force people to leave zones threatened by flooding.

Bettman saw the 1937 flood as an opportunity to reshape the riverfront, but not from a flood control perspective. In a memo to Myron Downs, the CPC staff engineer, Bettman discussed how he wanted to approach the Ohio River not in terms of "the problem of flood prevention or flood problems, but in terms of the problem of the replanning for a long period of time of the [riverfront] district of the city, with the flood question itself being treated as the occasion for doing some replanning and as one of the major factors in the process of the replanning" (Bettman 1937a, 2).

For Bettman, the 1937 flood was the Ohio River acting as it should. The flooding pointed out preexisting deficiencies in the neighborhood, with its undesirable mix of residences and industries, general slum conditions, and inefficient commercial arrangements. Bettman wanted to clear out the Central Bottoms and start anew. A report commissioned by the CPC shortly after the flooding recommended considering the 1937 flood in a similar light to the 1906 San Francisco earthquake and the 1904 Baltimore fire, urging Bettman to take advantage of the opportunity presented by a disaster to do replanning that these other cities had let slip (Goodrich 1937). To this end, Bettman pushed CPC staff engineer Myron Downs to come up with alternative uses for the area that the commission could publicize, helping to chart a new course for the neighborhood.

Schroth and Bettman did not see "being flooded" as a fact of life along the riverfront, as many long-time Central Bottoms residents did, but they resisted efforts to completely control the Ohio River with a floodwall, as the U.S. Army Corps of Engineers and many city officials believed was the obvious response to the 1937 flood. Instead, they pushed for a position respecting the river's power to flood and using zoning to guide the efficient use of the riverbanks area. According to Bettman, "Students of the problems created by floods have pointed out that flood protection works are not necessarily the only or best solution, but that in many places along rivers it is wiser to convert the flood areas to uses which would not entail serious damages and impairment from floods" (Bettman 1938a, 2).

A review of Bettman's personal correspondence makes clear that he favored removing residents from the floodplain along the Ohio River, even though he was careful to not be seen as wanting to "evacuate" people from their homes no matter what, as a letter he penned to the *Cincinnati Enquirer* editors on April 9, 1938, clarifies; in it, he called such claims "a complete fallacy" (Bettman 1938b). Yet, in communicating with the CPC members and the city council, he recommended zoning plans that would only permit the construction of new industrial and commercial buildings in the riverfront area elevated out of harm's way or specially designed to be minimally impacted by flooding. Calling these riverfront areas a "sub-standard environment" for residential occupation (Bettman 1938c, 3; see also Bettman 1937b), he pushed for the eventual exclusion of residential buildings. He believed, "For the development of the city, the general direction of the policy should be toward the development of the higher levels for residential uses and toward the gradual use of river-edge areas for purposes which are not so harmed by floods as are residential uses" (1938c, 3).

The River, Property Taxes, and Urban Blight

At the same time, a corollary debate developed around the Ohio River and its relationship to urban blight. For both federal and local government officials, property values mattered greatly in discussions around whether to build flood protection projects. The U.S. Army Corps of Engineer used cost-benefit analysis as a fundamental first step in determining whether a project should even be undertaken. USACE staff calculated the outcomes for each flood protection plan based on the cost of construction versus the sum of the property values and expected damages to be prevented by a proposed flood control measure. Ideally, the property values protected and damages prevented should well exceed the project cost (O'Neill 2006). Meanwhile, local governments' views on property values often played a key role in determining whether to support a USACE flood control project, since they typically created tax assessment districts to cover part of the ongoing maintenance costs required as contributions to the project. If a district had low tax capacity, it made it much more difficult to gain backing for a project since other municipal funds would have to be tapped to maintain the infrastructure.

These dynamics played out when the USACE developed a flood protection plan encompassing Cincinnati's small neighborhood of California, about eight miles upstream from the city core. A low-income white community lacking many basic improvements like electricity or paved roads, California did include a waterworks pumping station, increasing its importance for protection. Lieutenant Colonel Elliot, the USACE district engineer, announced in February 1938 that the U.S. Congress would make funds available for the works at California. The city government needed to make a commitment to the work before July 1, 1938, or the offer would expire. City Manager Sherrill urged the city to authorize its portion of the project, even if the tax assessments gathered from California were unlikely to approach the costs of municipal contributions (Sherrill 1938a).

The CPC report on the Cincinnati waterfront from December 1937 argued against any flood protection works for the "sparsely settled suburb of California," due to low property values in the affected areas and continued likelihood of flooding (CPC 1937, 30). In fact, the CPC recommended city funds be used to buy out homeowners in California and relocate them, turning the area into industrial zoning or parkland. Sherrill countered by showing that evacuating California would incur even higher costs, while also presenting an opinion by the assistant city solicitor that the $5 million in funds raised by the municipal flood protection bond approved by Cincinnati residents could not be applied to relocate citizens away from the floodplain (Sherrill 1938b). Besides these issues, Sherrill reminded everyone that even if the city did not accept the federal project, it would still have to protect the waterworks pumping station without any outside financial support, since federal flood protection funds could not be used to protect a singular site, such as a factory or government waterworks.

On April 18, 1938, the CPC officially declined to endorse the California proposal, which meant the city council required a two-thirds majority to ignore its recommendation and authorize the project anyway. The council passed the California flood works measure by a margin of 5–4 on April 27, insufficient to overturn the CPC decision (*Cincinnati Enquirer* 1938).[8] Despite an effort in 1939 by Sherrill and others to revive the California plans, the city council did not provide support to build a floodwall protecting the neighborhood (*Cincinnati Enquirer* 1939c).

Support for the floodwall in the neighborhood of California faltered significantly when the CPC reported that the tax assessment on the neighborhood would likely cover only a miniscule portion of the local cost share, with 25 percent of neighborhood households already tax delinquent (CPC 1938, 2). Still, in cases of low property values, most local officials and corps engineers expected that flood protection would improve property values and tax capacity in districts protected by flood control projects, meaning that even in troublesome places like the Central Bottoms there was an expectation that rebounding property values would eventually help cover project costs.

As the floodwall discussion advanced in Cincinnati, the debate between Sherrill and Bettman increasingly began to revolve around the relationship between Ohio River flooding and urban blight. Sherrill and his allies assumed that the risk of flooding had caused property values to decline, and flood protection would reverse this trend, making tax assessment districts more sustainable. In a letter to Bettman, Henry A. Potthoff, vice president of the well-known Robert A. Cline real estate firm, argued, "If this portion of the city has gradually gone down and land values have been reduced to such an extent as has been said, the only reason for it is the flood hazard" (Potthoff 1939, 1). Even before 1937 many riverfront business owners in groups including the Lower Cincinnati Business Men's Association, traditionally resigned to the occurrence of flooding, had been won over to the necessity of a floodwall because they believed it would aid their investments, making property in the central riverfront more valuable. Glenn Adams, president of the Lower Cincinnati Business Men's Association, opined, "If given some protection against floods, this area—by reason of its location—could be enormously valuable as an asset of the city's business life" (Citizens' Rehabilitation Committee 1937, 1).

Those arguing against the Central Bottoms floodwall sought to undermine this certainty. Schroth's report described the floodwall as a "spectacular experiment in tax valuation enhancement" (1937, 16), or, as Florence Stuart Kreimer—wife of Cincinnatus Association member Ralph A. Kreimer and also an active participant in local reform movements—put it in a letter to Bettman about the California floodwall, "My family, for one, does not want to pay out any tax money to maintain fictions (I use the word in what I understand to be its legal sense)—whether they be pleasant fictions about the undoubtedly splendid Engineer Corps of the Army, or fictions about valuations, or about assessments" (Kreimer 1939, 4).

Bettman and Downs argued that the Ohio River's flooding did not represent the root cause of property devaluation in the Central Bottoms. They repositioned urban blight as an issue much more complex than Sherrill and others had made it out to be. In the early twentieth century, sociologists from the University of Chicago had introduced "blighting" as a metaphor from ecology in order to make intelligible the decline of specific urban areas (Pritchett 2003). Subsequently, urban planners such as Bettman had adopted blight as an issue their training had prepared them to handle, using the danger of urban blight to position zoning regulations and other specialist planning techniques as the kind of expert knowledge required to manage the urban landscape. In this view, the blighting of the Central Bottoms was due to a multitude of factors, such as the type of housing stock, transportation linkages, neighborhood demographics, and mix of industrial, residential, and commercial usages. The causes of urban blight went well beyond an issue that could be resolved by flood control measures. As proof, Bettman pointed out that waterfront districts were similarly declining in cities that did not experience flooding, such as Cleveland (CPC 1939).

This is not to say that Bettman and other opponents of the Central Bottoms floodwall rejected any flood control measures at all. In fact, they were very supportive of the Mill Creek Barrier Dam, which protected the western half of the urban core, including the major factories and more respectable residential neighborhoods that were found there. Rather, they believed flood control should only be built for areas not already suffering from "urban blight." Bettman and the CPC staff undercut the belief that the construction of a floodwall would benefit property values, casting it as an uncertain outcome. Instead, they argued that flood prevention measures could not remedy the fall in riverfront property values. Only the professional expertise of urban planning offered a certain outcome in the long term. According to Ladislas Segoe, the prominent planner who worked closely with Bettman, the issue was not just about the needs of Central Bottoms residents, but rather, "The planner's job is to answer first the planning questions: What is the best use for this district? . . . By best use, I do not mean best for the property holders in the district alone or in the immediate future only, but, of course, for the long-range development and redevelopment of the whole community" (Segoe 1939, 2).

In Bettman's opinion, the current occupants of the riverfront did not merit the time and resources required by a public works project, casting them outside of the "public" represented within his urban planning vision. Moreover, from the vantage of these urban planning critiques, the floodwall would only serve to limit the city's future development options for the area and cut Cincinnati off from one of its most distinctive features, the Ohio River.

As the Central Bottoms floodwall debate advanced, City Manager Sherrill clashed with Downs and Bettman frequently over their portrayal of property in the Central Bottoms area, disagreeing with their total valuations for the area as well as the assertion that the floodwall would not increase the value of individual properties. Still, property holders along the riverfront heard with concern that declining land values in the Central Bottoms were not tied directly to flooding, but to a range of factors obscure to the normal citizen. Bettman told them that without proper oversight, the city could produce spatial arrangements adverse to residents and property owners. The CPC's 1937 report, *The Cincinnati Waterfront: Its Problems and Recommended Future Utilization*, cited the problem of "slow, uncontrolled growth since the days of the first settlement of Cincinnati" (2) as a key reason for the "blighted riverfront" (15), an intractable problem that would only drag down property owners in the area. The message hit home with many landlords in the area. As one exasperated property owner confirmed at a public hearing on the Central Bottoms floodwall: "All south of Pearl Street is not worth reclaiming. I own real estate there and it costs more than it produces" (*Cincinnati Enquirer* 1937e, 4).[9]

Through these arguments, Bettman and the CPC staff successfully shifted the discussion from a focus on the engineering-driven problem of river management in 1937 to an urban planning problem of urban blight. Writing on the California issue, Bettman laid out this rationale succinctly:

> So far as I have seen or heard, nobody has as yet sought or claimed to support the flood wall method on the ground of its lower economic costs and greater social benefits. The advocates point out the wall will keep the water away. Well of course that is so. It is always possible to work out a structural plan for keeping out any element or matter, air, water or anything else, from a given area. If the problem were as simple as that, we would not need to trouble ourselves about planning or about money or costs or about anything except mere structural engineering; and on a purely structural engineering problem we know we can rely upon the Army and City Engineers. (Bettman 1938a, 2)

He continued by clarifying that "In the planning problem there is involved not merely the negative question of what to do about the water, but also the constructive question of what to do with the land and what to do for the people" (3).

Bettman and the floodwall critics thus undercut engineering proposals, portraying them as only a solution to flooding, whereas urban planning proposals provided solutions to the fundamental problem of blight. Without oversight from urban planners, Bettman argued that redevelopment strategies were likely to make the same mistakes of the past, having unintended consequences in the short and long terms. Bettman and Downs, along with Charles Taft II, their ally on the city council, argued that even if property values somehow increased in the Central Bottoms as the result of building a floodwall, it would drive out the current tenants who relied on the cheap rents to eke out profits from their small factories and warehouse operations. Ultimately, only an urban planner could provide the vision necessary to guide redevelopment that unlocked an area's highest and best use, integrated into a comprehensive city plan.

Deciding on the Central Bottoms Floodwall

After the setback in building a floodwall to protect the California neighborhood, Sherrill presented the U.S. Army Corps of Engineers' plans for Cincinnati's central riverfront area to the city council on March 8, 1939. He again called for the council to act urgently, requesting a quick decision in order to include the project in an upcoming congressional flood appropriations bill (Sherrill 1939). The USACE presented the council with two options. Plan I included both a barrier dam for Mill Creek and the floodwall for the Central Bottoms area. Plan II featured only the barrier dam without the Central Bottoms floodwall. Outside of City Hall, the Cincinnatus Association lobbied for Plan II, and on March 14, 1939, the group "'unanimously' repudiated the proposal of a dike along the 'Bottoms'" (Tucker 1967, 175). Still, after a recommendation to proceed by the CPC's board, the council approved Plan I on March 20, 1939, setting in motion the construction of a floodwall in front of the entire downtown area of Cincinnati.

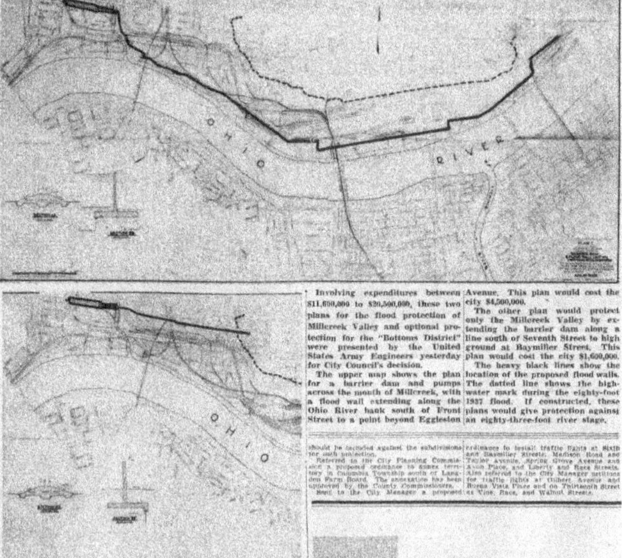

Involving expenditures between $11,600,000 to $20,500,000, these two plans for the flood protection of Millcreek Valley and optional protection for the "Bottoms District" were presented by the United States Army Engineers yesterday for City Council's decision.

The upper map shows the plan for a barrier dam and pumps across the mouth of Millcreek, with a flood wall extending along the Ohio River bank south of Front Street to a point beyond Eggleston Avenue. This plan would cost the city $4,500,000.

The other plan would protect only the Millcreek Valley by extending the barrier dam along a line south of Seventh Street to high ground at Baymiller Street. This plan would cost the city $1,600,000.

The heavy black lines show the location of the proposed flood walls. The dotted line shows the high-water mark during the eighty-foot 1937 flood. If constructed, these plans would give protection against an eighty-three-foot river stage.

should be included against the subdivisions for such protection.

Referred to the City Planning Commission a proposed ordinance to annex territory in Columbia Township south of Langdon Farm Road. The annexation has been approved by the County Commissioners.

Sent to the City Manager a proposed ordinance to install traffic lights at Sixth and Baymiller Streets, Madison Road and Taylor Avenue, Spring Grove Avenue and Avon Place, and Liberty and Race Streets. Also referred to the City Manager petitions for traffic lights at Gilbert Avenue and Buena Vista Place and on Thirteenth Street at Vine, Race, and Walnut Streets.

FIGURE 2.1. Plan I above, and the smaller-scale Plan II below (*Cincinnati Enquirer* 1939b, 3). Image courtesy of the *Cincinnati Enquirer.*

However, the issue remained unsettled. In the months after the March city council decision, two council members, Charles Taft II and Wiley Craig, proposed modifications to Plan I. Taft, son of former U.S. president William Taft, strongly opposed the floodwall measure and had been one of two votes against the Plan I proposal in March 1939. Taft was a long-time Cincinnatus Association member and carried the groups' criticisms to City Hall. Looking to disrupt Sherrill's momentum, Taft put forward a third plan incorporating a floodwall cutoff that would have enabled the city to first complete the Mill Creek Barrier Dam section (along a slightly new route compared to the previous proposal) and then consider the Central Bottoms floodwall later, after more studies had been completed. Meanwhile, Craig, an independent politician with a background in engineering, suggested a plan to combine a Sixth Street viaduct with the Mill Creek Barrier Dam.

CPC chairman Alfred Bettman, who had vigorously opposed Plan I, seized the opportunity for the CPC to review the new modified plans. He believed approval of the new modifications would rescind the CPC's approval of Plan I, reopening the possibility to prevent the Central Bottoms floodwall from being built. Due to health-related absences, the CPC's vote on June 20, 1939, for a combination of the Craig and Taft plans ended 3–3, leaving the process in limbo (Bettman 1939b).

Meanwhile, the city council, particularly council member Craig, increasingly saw City Manager Colonel C. O. Sherrill as overstepping his authority in pursuit of federal construction funds. Though Sherrill was brought on because of his engineering experience, critics began to claim that he had become too "enamoured with the idea of constructing large-scale public works projects" (Burnham 1992b, 247). For instance, Sherrill delayed signing a city contract to build flood control works specifically protecting the California pumping station, holding out hope that a levee would be authorized for the entire neighborhood of California. He also resisted any suggested changes to the USACE plans, loyal to the agency that he had previously served with.

Finally, on September 11, 1939, the CPC considered the Taft plan by itself (without the Craig proposal, which was deferred) in the presence of all the CPC members.[10] The modification was approved by a vote of 4–3, recommending the construction of the Mill Creek Barrier Dam and leaving the Central Bottoms floodwall for later consideration. At this CPC hearing, Sherrill (a member of the CPC due to his position as city manager) read a letter from USACE district engineer Elliot stating that "the later extension of the protection line to Pearl and Martin Streets [if the Taft option was pursued], would not, in my opinion, be economically feasible. Consequently, I would be unable to recommend it to the department" (*Cincinnati Enquirer* 1939d, 3). The letter effectively signaled that the Central Bottoms floodwall was unlikely to be built if the city pursued Taft's plan. Keen to keep alive the possibility of the Central Bottoms floodwall, Sherrill and his ally council member Albert Cash (also a representative on the CPC) delayed a final council vote on the Taft proposal, arguing that the CPC resolution requested further study of the suggested Central Bottoms plans (*Cincinnati Enquirer* 1939f).

These debates, closely tracked by local newspapers, enthralled the Cincinnati public. Supporters and opponents of the floodwall jockeyed for position throughout the fall of 1939, with a *Cincinnati Enquirer* editorial comparing it to the "more serious battles in Europe," just as "fickle" in its fortunes (*Cincinnati Enquirer* 1939e, 6). In November 1939 the CPC published its *Preliminary Report: A Redevelopment Plan for the Central River Front*, providing an overview and comparison of the different possible approaches to the Central Bottoms area, including options with the floodwall, but also proposing alternatives for the area including a bypass freeway, parks, and a civic stadium. In its conclusion, reviewing the different possibilities, the report recommended that no Central Bottoms floodwall be constructed and the central riverfront area be dedicated to civic purposes. In December the USACE, now under district engineer Major Fred Bass (after Elliot had been transferred to a new position), offered a modification to its proposal more closely following the Taft plan, and asked the city council to determine shortly what course of action it would choose, whether to request the Central Bottoms floodwall or decline to support it. The council turned the issue around by requesting an opinion from the USACE chief of engineers about the advisability of the Central Bottoms floodwall project in late December 1939 (*Cincinnati Enquirer* 1939g).

Reporting back to the city council in January 1940, the USACE announced a lower cost for the Taft plan than originally expected. The CPC reaffirmed its support of the Taft plan in a meeting on January 15, 1940. Finally, in an unexpected decision, on January 26, 1940, exactly three years after the crest of the 1937 flood, the Cincinnati City Council voted to reverse its earlier decision and only pursue the Mill Creek Barrier Dam (*Cincinnati Enquirer* 1940). Sherrill and other advocates for the Central Bottoms floodwall had been defeated. Besides effectively ending the potential for a Central Bottoms floodwall, this decision made clear the interest among professional elites in the area. It also broke the grip that small-scale riverfront businesses had maintained on the area since the nineteenth century.

Nature in the Central Bottoms

The ways that Bettman and others positioned the Ohio River in this debate expands an understanding of nature in the city. As outlined earlier, many technical experts saw nature in the first half of the twentieth century as antagonistic to city life and needing to be controlled (Kaika 2005). Nature was a capricious and uncooperative threat, one external to human society. Ohio Valley residents during the first decades of the twentieth century had begun to see flooding as an expression of this bothersome nature, "a constant threat even though (or rather because) damaging events happened irregularly and unpredictably" (Lübken 2012, 131).

Surprisingly, after the flood of 1937 in Cincinnati, Bettman, Schroth, and others sought to redefine this relationship with the Ohio River, claiming that the river had existed long before Cincinnati, and that any damages from flooding "can all be traced to the location of valuable property or some vital unit or part of an important public service of facility, within the path of the flood" (CPC 1937). Rather than viewing flooding as the object of control, they argued that the river needed to be respected and given its "just due." In fact, they treated the river as a useful partner instead of a threat, showing willingness to collaborate with nature in the development of the urban landscape. For his part, Bettman approached the 1937 flood as an opportunity to shape redevelopment opportunities in the Central Bottoms, working in tandem with an independent river that had its own essential role in shaping the landscape.

The dimensions of this human and nonhuman partnership become clear in examining its central objective: erasing urban blight. Bettman wanted to enlist the Ohio River in order to clear out the blighted Central Bottoms area along the riverfront. He believed the Central Bottoms neighborhood to be irredeemable and a threat to spread blight to adjacent neighborhoods. Fortuitously, flooding would destroy the neighborhood and its blight—not through a single, catastrophic flood event, but rather through the cumulative effects of prolonged exposure to flooding, with each rise further undermining the area's viability. As the flooding Ohio River surged over its banks, it would eat into riverfront buildings' foundations, rot their structural wood, and loosen bricks, contributing to the deterioration of the Central Bottoms' environment. Paradoxically, the Ohio River would help solve the Central Bottoms blight problem by making it worse. This approach recognized the Ohio River as a primary force in a highly symbolic location with the city, the site of the original

Cincinnati settlement. Bettman believed that moving forward, people occupying the Central Bottoms would have to defer to the river instead of attempting to dominate it.

Understanding the significance of this partnership requires an expanded perspective on the relationship between scientific expertise and nature. Scientific and professional expertise played a critical role in the separation of nature from society, since experts consistently portrayed nature as unalterably different from human society and vice versa (Latour 1993; Mitchell 2002). Political theorist Timothy Mitchell claims that experts based their authority on efforts to divide the world into "what seemed nature on one side, and human calculation and expertise on the other" (2002, 36). Experts, through the study of natural forces using scientific methods, asserted that they had determined the laws that govern the world while also providing the means to manipulate these forces for human benefit.

In the case of the Central Bottoms floodwall, CPC staff and the Cincinnatus Association justified their plans for the Central Bottoms in terms of a refined understanding of nature. Through deployment of their professional and scientific expertise, these professional groups argued that the Ohio River should be understood not as nature writ large but as a distinct nonhuman actor whose needs did not differ radically from the desires of human society. Rather than a polarity with the Ohio River as part of nature on one side and Cincinnati as part of human society on the other, this approach called for selectively reincorporating nonhuman actors as part of the urban landscape. Only professional expertise could determine what these acceptable nonhuman actors wanted and how to best engage them over the long term, navigating their role in the city.

In the end, Bettman put aside the bigger question of controlling nature and focused on the fact that the Ohio River wanted the same things he wanted, as seen through the behavior of flooding. Together Bettman and the Ohio River could remake the Central Bottoms into a more productive urban space. As used by the Central Bottoms floodwall critics, this argument opened up a new view on urban nature. Bettman, Schroth, and others saw the Ohio River as a nonhuman actor that could potentially share their goals within a framework of capitalist development. This is important because popular understandings of nature as either passive and bucolic (Marx 1964; Williams 1973) or wild and uncooperative (Tsing 2005; Braun 2006) ignore these contexts where professional elites engage with a nonhuman actor like the Ohio River in order to achieve their goals. An assemblage perspective is particularly crucial to understanding this unique partnership, since it encourages a view of nature that recognizes that its agency is both multiple and open-ended. In Cincinnati, where the river and urban planning experts worked together to redevelop the Central Bottoms and displace its mixed-race residents and small-scale industrial tenants, nature is neither inert nor restricted to being uncooperative. Bettman felt confident that the Ohio River agreed with him that the Central Bottoms was an undesirable neighborhood and that over time the river would help fix the problems he had identified in the area. Bettman, Schroth, and others embraced and empowered the river's agency as a tool for redevelopment, which gained them increasing support among professional elites in the city.

Thus, in Cincinnati, city officials used the 1937 flood as an opportunity to recontextualize the nature-society relationship, based on an argument that urban planners like Bettman were the ones who were actually working with and respecting nature, in many ways arguing that providing a river its "elbow room" was more apt for the time than any talk of "Old Man River." This is fundamentally different from the combination of practical and technical knowledge described in the previous chapter, where U.S. Army Corps of Engineers experts relied on the knowledge of the unschooled rivermen to guide their collaboration with Old Man River. Here, the professional experts have moved to the center of the equation, directly claiming to best speak for the Ohio River. Meanwhile, the Ohio River went where Bettman and other urban planning experts had asked it to, sending its destructive floodwaters into poorer neighborhoods while staying outside the Mill Creek Barrier Dam and the industrial district that it protected. Recast in this light, the liveliness of the river then became a justification for and a participant in the disinvestment in and displacement of the Central Bottoms' low-income Black and white residents and workers.

In the bureaucratic debates around Cincinnati's floodwall, there is little evidence that any of the elite governmental, scientific, and professional leaders fundamentally doubted a separation of nature and society. Bettman, for one, believed strongly in the capacity of scientific expertise to resolve tricky natural processes like flooding. Yet, the understanding of the Ohio River as a cooperative urban nonhuman actor, and specifically its inclusion in flood preparedness planning at the time, blurs the way we understand these categories, opening up new possibilities for how the division of nature and society can be used to govern the city.

Individuals pushing for the redevelopment of the riverfront strategically used the vitality of the Ohio River to undermine assumptions about the necessity of a floodwall and what riverfront infrastructure could look like. Thus, nature during this era of high modernism was far from being reduced to only an inert collection of resources, a nonsocial nature (Scott 1998). Rather, experts from the era were much more willing to recognize and embrace the productive capacity of nature if particular nonhuman actors' behaviors aligned with elite interests around redevelopment and white supremacy. The Central Bottoms' deep links to representations of Blackness in Cincinnati made it undesirable. The Ohio River would fix that. The result is a picture of capitalist urban development in the United States more flexible and creative than commonly acknowledged, open to collaborating with partners that many would view as antithetical to their strategies. This alliance between the Ohio River and local professionals slowly unfolded in the decades after the 1937 flood, in parallel with the latter figuring out what they actually wanted to happen on the central riverfront area.

The Ohio River and Urban Renewal

Once the Central Bottoms floodwall finally fell to defeat, it left a massive unresolved question for city elites: what should be done with the neighborhood? Floodwall critics had urged business leaders, the city council, and the public to consider what other uses the Central Bottoms could serve, and to see the floodwall as foreclosing many of those options. They argued that constructing a floodwall would cut downtown Cincinnati off from a primary asset in the river. As Mayor James Stewart put it when reluctantly voting against the floodwall, "The bottoms flood wall would preclude plans for future development of the river front" (*Cincinnati Enquirer* 1940, 9). However, there was little consensus around what to do with this riverfront asset—whether it should be used for aesthetic, industrial, civic, commercial, or recreational ends, or some combination thereof.

Bettman and his ally Taft defeated the Central Bottoms floodwall, but they were unable to move forward with their own vision for the riverfront. The *Preliminary Report: A Redevelopment Plan for the Central River Front*, published by the CPC in 1939, included recommendations for civic buildings, a stadium, parks, parking lots, and a bypass highway. The 1948 *Metropolitan Master Plan*—the final project Bettman worked on for Cincinnati, completed under the direction of his son after Bettman's death in 1945—further developed many of these proposals, settling on a recommendation for a futuristic collection of riverfront buildings, including a monumental civic center, built on platforms raised out of the floodplain. The plan intended to remove an unsightly neighborhood and push back on negative images of the city. The plan also called for an east-west highway to be built between the Central Bottoms and the Central Business District, allowing for easy entry into downtown and for improved connections between different sections of the city. Through these plans, the CPC argued that the Central Bottoms could move on from its lackluster status as "a relic of bygone days" and be transformed into "an area of great value, utility and inspiration (CPC 1948, 144).

City officials wanted to reconfigure downtown to respond to rapidly changing residential patterns within the city. Accelerated suburbanization in the postwar years had moved Cincinnatians farther from the urban core. As many middle-class families moved out of the city proper, waves of low-income Black and white migrants from Appalachia and the upland South replaced them (Stradling 2003). This urban exodus was accompanied by a growing belief across the country that cities' urban cores had become dangerous, unhealthy, and obsolete. In this context, Cincinnati's urban elites wanted to preserve the downtown district as accessible and desirable to suburban commuters for shopping and office space. They supported urban renewal proposals to destroy "blighted" Black neighborhoods including the Central Bottoms and the adjacent West End and replace them with massive highways, so that white office workers and shoppers could still make their way downtown conveniently and quickly. According to a *Riverfront Redevelopment* report produced by the CPC in 1946, the Central Bottoms had "a depreciating effect on the whole downtown business area, tending to prevent it from attaining its full stature as a regional trade center" (CPC 1946, 21).

Meanwhile, in the absence of a concrete plan for the Central Bottoms, the floodwall debate surprisingly lingered on as well. Even though Bettman and others had fought so hard to defeat the Central Bottoms floodwall, the CPC made an effort after the fact to make it seem like the deterioration of the neighborhood itself held responsibility for the final decision not to build a floodwall. The CPC's report on the riverfront from 1946 claimed that the decision to abandon the area came after "studies by the U.S. Engineers concluded that damages to the Downtown Riverfront by recurring floods are not sufficient to justify Federal participation in the construction of flood control works" (CPC 1946, 46). While reference is also made to the city council's original passage of a flood protection plan encompassing both Mill Creek Valley and the Central Bottoms, there is no mention of the council's vote in January 1940 reversing this decision. Instead, emphasis is on the "assessed valuations" (14) produced by the USACE and the city engineer, which showed that the property values and potential prevention of damages from flooding in the Central Bottoms did not warrant floodwall protection.

Politicians and civic groups looking to make a name for themselves continued to raise the issue. In 1951 the city council convened the Central Riverfront Advisory Committee with representatives from ten local organizations to review the issue once again. The council had recently requested that the USACE revisit flood protection for the Central Bottoms, and in parallel the Central Riverfront Advisory Committee gathered input from fifteen experts to consider changes to the 1948 *Metropolitan Master Plan* relative to the riverfront. In its final report, the group urged that the bypass highway be prioritized, but decided to make no recommendations regarding a floodwall or best land usage for the Central Bottoms (Central Riverfront Advisory Committee 1951).

In the 1950s, newly authorized Federal Aid Highway Act funds enabled Cincinnati municipal officials to finally build the city's long-desired bypass highway in front of the Central Business District. Named Fort Washington Way after the military fortification built on the site shortly after the city's founding, the bypass was completed in 1961, running along Third Street across the northern edge of the Central Bottoms. As part of construction, engineers had incorporated a levee within the Fort Washington Way structure, finally deciding where and how flood protection would feature on the riverfront. Placed well back from the waterline, this levee would protect the Central Business District from extreme cases of high water, but left the majority of the Central Bottoms exposed.

Although a final plan for the Central Bottoms remained elusive, several proposals emerged in this postwar era. In addition to the 1948 *Metropolitan Master Plan* for Cincinnati, in 1962 the Cincinnatus Association proposed a competition to imagine a brand-new riverfront monument in the Central Bottoms—meant to rival St. Louis's Gateway Arch—which would be called the Symbolon. The association established a panel of experts to determine a winner for the Symbolon competition. After receiving sixty-two submissions, the judges declared on October 19, 1962, that none of the proposals had shown sufficient merit and the project would not move forward (Tucker 1967).

Flooding remained a fundamental aspect of Central Bottoms life. The warehouses, small factories, wholesalers, and low-income residents in the area continued to experience flooding, with major floods of more than sixty feet in 1945, 1948, 1955, 1962, and 1964 (flood stage for Cincinnati is anything above fifty-two feet). Even with an outward appearance of stagnation in the Central Bottoms, changes began to take place that would play a vital role in finally enabling redevelopment of the area.

The decay of the Central Bottoms building stock represented a core issue. As a riverfront neighborhood regularly affected by flooding, renovations had been a central aspect of life in the area. Whenever the river crept up into the

Central Bottoms, it left damaged and dirty buildings in its wake, requiring immediate repairs ranging from cleanups to more significant overhauling. Residents and property owners existed in a constant cycle of ruin, repair, and renewal. However, the decline in property values made securing loans more difficult and repairs less worth the investment. In the postwar period, damage from flooding thus went untreated, pushing buildings further into what the City Planning Commission described as a "trend of obsolescence" (CPC 1945, 1). As hoped, the unfettered river made living in the Central Bottoms increasingly untenable. CPC staff engineer Myron Downs succinctly predicted this cycle in a letter to Bettman from 1939, stating that "Unquestionably, time and depreciation of buildings will remove many of those now living at flood stage" (Downs 1939, 1).

After the 1937 flood, these new property logics began eating away at the Central Bottoms even when the neighborhood's physical appearance appeared largely unchanged.[11] The buildings looked the same as they had before, and flooding continued to occur much as it had throughout the history of the city, but the way Bettman and others had empowered the river's agency made more and more difficult the cleanup that in the past would have been a matter of course.

Neighborhood residents who had been through cycles of floods and repairs for decades were now entangled in new property relationships of mortgages and building inspections that defined flooding as unacceptable. Long term, these new property relations limited the resources that wholesale merchants, factory owners, landlords, and residents could access to renew their neighborhood. A similar process was taking place in the adjacent sections of the West End neighborhood, the city's largest Black community at the time. The part of the West End closest to the riverfront, which featured a mix of factories and residences similar to the Central Bottoms, had also been left outside of the Mill Creek Barrier Dam by city officials and the USACE. With no floodwall to contain it, the Ohio River took an increasing toll on this southernmost strip of the West End with each new flood season (Cook 2007). The loss of control over home and environment in the Central Bottoms and the West End must have significantly undermined residents' feeling of well-being and personal security in the area.

Early on, several property owners in the Central Bottoms had begun to tear down the buildings on their sites and convert their land into parking lots, catering to the suburban drivers coming downtown for work or shopping. By the time engineers began planning the Fort Washington Way bypass, noticeable gaps had appeared in the once-congested neighborhood. Meanwhile, developers waited to see what plan the city would eventually support. As a result, only seven new structures were built in the Central Bottoms during the 1950s, all of them warehouses (Mitchell 1998, 304). And by 1960 only an estimated 120 persons still lived in the area, a massive decrease from the 2,900 residents recorded in 1940 (CPC 1961, 6). Flooding contributed to these transitions, but so did several other factors, such as increasingly negative views of urban life, creditors being less willing to lend in the city core, and economic restructuring that shifted river traffic away from the central riverfront.

Federal urban renewal efforts to demolish what were perceived as blighted and decayed neighborhoods provided additional energy to this process. To access federal funding, the City of Cincinnati developed an urban renewal plan for the Central Bottoms in the 1960s, calling for parks, modernized light industry, and a redesigned streetscape. The Cincinnatus Association, while dismayed by the failure of the Symbolon monument project, was quick to point out that its competition had driven interest in these urban renewal efforts. Shortly after the competition in 1962, a $6.6 million bond referendum passed for the purchase and demolition of riverfront properties. The contrast of the Central Bottoms against ambitious new urban renewal plans served to further portray the neighborhood as stuck in the past. According to a chronicler of the Cincinnatus Association, plans like the Symbolon only made more obvious the "accumulated filth of a century of floods" in the Central Bottoms (Tucker 1967, 201).

In preparing the urban renewal application materials, city officials entered Central Bottoms homes and businesses to conduct building assessment surveys, documenting the state of each building and the type of occupation. It is telling that the justification for the Central Bottoms urban renewal project focused on the neighborhood's inadequate construction and physical decay, rather than signs of "blight," which the federal Department of Housing and Urban Development operationally defined as behavioral instead of physical deterioration.[12] A February 1965 application for a federal loan by Cincinnati's Department of Urban Development listed 258 Central Bottoms properties to be purchased as part of the city's plan. Of these, 186 were listed as having "major defects," including "buckling walls, cracks caused by differential settlement, dangerously sagging or eroded joists or other structural elements, seriously chipped columns, etc." (Cincinnati Department of Urban Development 1965, 3), capturing in detail the effect of Ohio River flooding on the neighborhood. The application considered only eleven of the 258 buildings to have a "blighting" influence according to Department of Housing and Urban Development standards, but described the rest as physically substandard or inadequate to modern industrial needs. The urban renewal process made the river's work more legible, charting its progress in public documents. The proposal forms and progress reports submitted to the federal government helped transfer these depictions of ruin onto maps, property values, and city plans, tracking the course of chronic disinvestment and flood-driven destruction on the Central Bottoms.

Still, for many years the ultimate fate of the Central Bottoms and downtown redevelopment appeared to be an intractable problem, a "political football" according to Eugene Ruehlmann, mayor of Cincinnati from 1967 to 1971 (Walker 1988, 43). Yet, the combined effects of river flooding, blight rhetoric, and urban renewal created the conditions for a redevelopment plan to coalesce rapidly and seemingly from nowhere. In 1966 a whirlwind process led to plans for a riverfront stadium that would be shared by the city's professional baseball and American football teams (Cowan 2005). A powerful nexus of political leaders and business interests supported the new plan for the stadium to be located in the Central Bottoms.

Unsurprisingly though, the plan had last-minute complications involving the river. The owner of the baseball team, Bill DeWitt, greatly opposed a riverfront location because of his concerns over flooding, even as he was also dissatisfied with the team's current location in the nearby "blighted" West End neighborhood. DeWitt's fear of flooding, even as the first step in the Central Bottoms' redevelopment finally loomed, showed the continued power of the idiosyncratic assemblage of "being flooded" in the Central Bottoms, with flooding as both ally and adversary. Even as local elites had cooperated with the Ohio River to destroy the Central Bottoms neighborhood, the recurrence of flooding left many people skeptical of the riverfront area. DeWitt finally had to be convinced to sell the team to a specially formed group of business elites before a lease could be signed on the new stadium (Walker 1988).

During 1967 and 1968 city officials removed the last Central Bottoms residents and factories in preparation for stadium construction. Many of the remaining residents moved to the East End and other riverfront neighborhoods (Halperin 1998), while many industries fought relocation in a series of delaying actions before being moved to the city's suburban fringe (Wadsworth 1967). Of the former businesses in the Central Bottoms, only the wholesale companies successfully lobbied to remain in the area, in new buildings city planners deemed acceptably flood resistant. By 1970 the completed Riverfront Stadium opened, built on a giant concrete platform raised out of the floodplain, inaugurating a new period for the riverfront. Professional elites were finally, definitively rid of the Central Bottoms.[13]

Conclusion

Recent research by anthropologist Roberto Barrios in New Orleans has shown how "various social actors mobilize a disaster to air moral grievances, to further their preferred development agendas, or to reassert their political power" (Barrios 2017, 155). In Cincinnati after the 1937 flood, these included both human and nonhuman actors who had widely different perceptions of how the riverfront should be used. Ultimately, urban planners and professional elites succeeded in advancing their vision for the Central Bottoms, overcoming critiques from small business owners in the area and the engineers who favored massive construction projects. They won by arguing that the Ohio River needed to be respected and that their plan would not limit future use of the central riverfront. The deployment of professional expertise, focus on redevelopment potential, and partnership with the Ohio River charted a new path forward for dealing with flood disasters after 1937. These changes also signaled the end of the Central Bottoms neighborhood, although the process took decades to complete.

Much disaster-related research has focused on the social production of vulnerability in urban settings. Critically, the investigation of vulnerability treats disasters as events that are the result of long-term decision-making processes that expose specific populations, usually lower income, to more dangerous contexts, while also pushing back against a view of disasters as unpredictable and with unexpected consequences (Oliver-Smith 1999). While wealthy communities can be sited in at-risk locations as well, they typically have individual and government-provided resources to mitigate their vulnerability. Meanwhile, lower-income communities suffer more sustained consequences (Bolin and Stanford 1999). A similar process unfolded in the Central Bottoms after the 1937 flood when professional elites denied residents the resources or the right to restore their neighborhood.

Considering vulnerability as part of determining what "being flooded" means also requires recognizing that communities are not thrust into these dangerous contexts unknowingly. Occupants may consider their home or place of business as safe or manageable, even while recognizing their exposure to things like flooding. Moreover, the social production of vulnerability is experienced unevenly—one person may consider themself vulnerable while another does not. Relations of power shape these discrepancies, creating uneven spatialities at the intersection of vulnerability and "being flooded." Exploiting these uneven spatialities in Cincinnati, urban planners and developers pointed to flooding and what they perceived as the spread of urban blight to justify disinvestment. The new relationship Bettman and his allies sought with the Ohio River distorted and displaced the previous relationships endemic to the Central Bottoms, where residents had lived collaboratively with the Ohio River. Bettman and many others had argued that Central Bottoms residents were unacceptably vulnerable to flooding, even if these same residents did not think so. As Bettman's redefinition of vulnerability and the Ohio River's desires gained acceptance, it helped legitimize the slow destruction of the neighborhood.

In many ways, these experiences in Cincinnati, and in similar river cities such as Pittsburgh and St. Louis, presaged situations faced along many urban waterfronts today. With climate change leading to rising sea levels and more powerful storm surges, numerous urban waterfronts are increasingly subject to flooding. Scientists and other specialists are designing new infrastructures to protect these communities from the threat of flooding. In tandem, as numerous people are moving back to the city, urban developers are eager to redevelop deindustrializing and low-income neighborhoods on the waterfront. As a result, numerous cities are already seeing developers taking advantage of climate change and new regulatory environments to transform urban waterfronts into upper-class enclaves, with fantastically expensive condominiums and houses that incorporate the latest flood-resilient technologies (Gandy 2014; Robbins 2016). These developers, and the government officials and environmental experts that support them, are arguing that they are working with the changing conditions of the oceans or rivers, rather than opposing climate change, in order to reduce vulnerability. From this professional analysis emerges a racial and class geography of flood protection and flood exposure that explains why increasingly the wealthy are the only ones who can afford to occupy areas that are vulnerable to flooding, ensconced in costly climate-proofed buildings.

While some see waterfront retreat as at times a necessary step in the face of increased chances for disaster (Koslov 2016), the experience from the Central Bottoms shows that the dynamics of flooding need to be analyzed carefully in terms of how vulnerability is being defined, and for whom. It is important to challenge ideas of climate change and vulnerability that, in the name of scientific expertise, ignore existing communities' understandings of how to relate to local nonhuman actors and their means of navigating risk. This is critically important in the United States, where many of the communities that experts and developers are determining to be unacceptably exposed to flooding are also communities of color and/or low incomes. Experts push forward plans to destroy these waterfront neighborhoods, ignoring local protests to the contrary as uninformed or unrealistic. As anthropologist Sarah Vaughn writes, "Technoscientific culture and popular culture . . . hierarchize some citizens as possessing more expertise about floods than others because of their race" (Vaughn 2012, 361). Unless these dangers are taken seriously, the history from the Central Bottoms shows that the Ohio River and other bodies of water will readily collaborate with white supremacy and capitalism to undermine waterfront communities that elites have targeted for redevelopment.

CHAPTER 3

Stream Pollution and Riverfront Recreation, 1934–1988

In 1977, during the clearing of a steel scrapyard on the Cincinnati central riverfront, workers uncovered "the ruins of a large stone structure and a series of many deep tunnels" (Ahlering 1983, 46). The large structure puzzled the project planners, who were working on Sawyer Point, the city's dazzling new riverfront park. Learning of the find, the Miami Purchase Association (precursor to the Cincinnati Preservation Association) stepped in to investigate. Their research determined that the building and tunnels were part of the Front Street pumping station, the city's first waterworks (Ahlering 1983). The city had closed the downtown facility in 1907 due to concerns about increased pollution from local sewage discharges affecting the city's drinking water. The city shuttered the Front Street facility because it had just completed construction on a new waterworks further upstream in the neighborhood of California, which would purify most of the city's water supply. Seven decades later, by the time the city purchased the scrapyard site from American Compressed Steel and was clearing it of decades of scrap waste, the Front Street waterworks had been long forgotten.

The Sawyer Point Park project team, collaborating with partners at the Cincinnatus Association and Riverfront Advisory Council, chose to incorporate these rediscovered ruins as the backdrop to an outdoor amphitheater for the new park. This symbolic reclamation of Cincinnati's first waterworks reinforced the project's development goals. Through deft public relations work, the project planners seized the opportunity to show that they were cleaning up the landscape, connecting the new park to a healthier environment that would also encourage economic growth.

In doing so, they built directly on previous efforts led by sanitary engineers and industry elites in Cincinnati to reshape public perceptions of pollution on the Ohio River and Cincinnati waterfront. Through two organizations, the

Cincinnati Committee on Stream Pollution (CSP) and the Ohio River Valley Water Sanitation Commission (ORSANCO), a midcentury antipollution movement in Cincinnati transformed water pollution from being seen as a necessary outcome of industrial expansion to instead a dangerous inhibitor of growth, impacting both the economy and public health. The active participation of industry in the process preserved a role for industry to provide input on pollution regulations and limit their impact on factory conditions, but it also led to a new belief in the importance of access to clean water. Industry, which had previously shown little concern about the availability of clean water, began to feel that pollution could threaten their operations. The Ohio River largely cooperated with these shifts, becoming an active participant in ORSANCO's clean waters work while also still receiving the discharge of chemicals and other pollutants that enabled businesses to cheaply dispose of their waste.

The CSP and ORSANCO's efforts did little to change expectations for the Cincinnati riverfront. A visitor to the riverfront in the 1970s would find a strange assortment of land uses, including a massive new multipurpose stadium, wholesale warehouses, and industrial tenants that used the area as a dumping ground. In order to make the area more appealing to the public, city elites had for decades sought to build parks in the area, with little success. Taking a cue from the CSP and ORSANCO, city elites used environmental language to argue that the riverfront represented an important area in the fight against pollution and that building parks would spur private investment and economic growth. These efforts shaped new perceptions of pollution, cleanliness, and profitability for the Ohio Valley region in ways that did not track neatly with actual impacts on community health.

The Sanitary City and Its Limits

Popular understandings of pollution in Cincinnati had already undergone numerous changes since its founding. The second half of the nineteenth century witnessed particularly dramatic transformations. Scientific breakthroughs from bacteriologists, building on discoveries by Louis Pasteur and Robert Koch, began identifying germs as the cause of disease, replacing a belief that miasmas—noxious fumes or "bad air" created by decaying organic waste—caused illness (Melosi 2008). This germ theory of disease focused on organic waste and highlighted the crucial role of water in transmitting bacteria and thus spreading contagions in urban centers. In this context, health experts pushed fresh water as a fundamental prerequisite for public health, a "universal cleaning agent" (Barles 2012, 96) that could help prevent disease. In response, Cincinnati and many other cities in the United States and Europe became preoccupied with securing a constant supply of fresh water for their residents, as well as ensuring the prompt removal of dirty water (Gandy 2014). This meant building water filtration facilities and water supply pipelines that brought fresh potable water directly to households, as well as sewage systems to take wastewater away. In 1850, Cincinnati sent its waterworks engineer to Europe and, based on his observations, began developing a centralized, planned sewer system.

The city's burgeoning sewage system still deposited waste directly into the Ohio River, the source of the city's water supply (Giglierano 1977). While Cincinnati's sanitary engineers recognized that this liquid waste could cause disease, they also believed that the Ohio River's water could dilute the waste sufficiently through natural purification, arguing that "when fecal matter is mixed with water, it is no longer harmful due to chemical change" (Giglierano 1977, 230). They also trusted that new technologies of filtration and chlorination would protect the city's waterworks from any remaining germs (Hedeen 1994). As a result, the Ohio River served as Cincinnati's primary source of drinking water as well as its ultimate sewer, used to carry waste downstream and away from the city.

The increased emphasis on sanitation coincided with the arrival of a new wave of immigrants from Central and Eastern Europe, as well as white and Black populations relocating from the upland South. These recent arrivals settled in the urban core, while wealthier white residents began to move outward to the rapidly expanding suburbs located in the surrounding hills. Many urban elites grew alarmed about living conditions throughout the urban core, as these new arrivals moved into rapidly decaying tenements. Feeling these neighborhoods were "unhealthy and unwholesome", many elites advocated for both housing and sanitation reforms to clean up the area (Fairbanks 1988, 13). The proximity of many of these tenements to "foul-smelling, polluted" bodies of water such as Mill Creek, as well as Duck Creek, the Miami and Erie Canal, and, increasingly, the Ohio River, only strengthened elite concerns about the area (15). The Cincinnati Health Department led efforts to educate these new urban residents about how to practice cleanliness and avoid epidemics like cholera and typhoid.

This confluence of factors in the nineteenth century across the United States and Europe is often referred to as the "sanitary city." The conceptual framework of the sanitary city connects emergent bacteriological epistemologies with growing concern about public health as part of urban governance (Joyce 2003; Melosi 2008). In the sanitary city, reducing pollution levels emerged for the first time as a major concern of municipal politics and reforms efforts, particularly in terms of proper disposal of organic wastes such as fecal matter and food waste. Simultaneously, municipal officials showed an increased preoccupation with urban living arrangements and cleanliness. Cincinnati's sanitation engineers used new metrics like bacteria counts and dissolved oxygen levels to quantify the success of diluting organic waste in the river and progress toward limiting sources of potential disease outbreaks (Melosi 2008). Meanwhile, public health officials began to more proactively investigate and regulate residential living conditions.

By the early twentieth century, Cincinnati's local government had initiated a major sewer expansion in the city. Local citizens welcomed these upgrades and additional services, as many were struggling to deal with their liquid wastes, particularly as more residences incorporated private bathrooms rather than shared cesspools. As with many other growing cities, the expansion of Cincinnati's sewer system improved sanitary conditions in the home and the workplace, but at the cost of further degrading urban waterways. New concerns arose about the growing quantity of sewage poured directly into the river. Sewage discharges just upstream from the city center led the city's waterworks department to close the Front Street pumping station in 1907, shortly after opening the new facility farther upstream in the neighborhood of California.

Cincinnati sanitary engineers also successfully lobbied the U.S. Public Health Service to locate its first Field Investigation Station in Cincinnati in order to conduct research on stream pollution. This pollution laboratory opened in 1913 and began studies to monitor seasonal bacteria fluctuations in the Ohio River. Despite these initial measures to address rising pollution, the general public still had limited interest in Ohio River stream pollution, which was largely seen as minimal or intractable (Giglierano 1977).

Elsewhere, other municipal governments experimented with ways to minimize organic waste instead of dumping it directly into local waterways. Activated sludge treatment facilities concentrated waste for processing, rendering it less dangerous to public health, before releasing it into waterways. Research on many other waste treatment or diversion options, such as interceptor sewers and fertilizing techniques, also advanced throughout the early twentieth century (Barles 2012; Deligne 2012; Melosi 2008). Still, cities felt little commitment to treating sewage prior to dumping it in public waterways. According to historian Martin Melosi, the bacteriological theory of disease was "insufficient, in and of itself, to produce a major commitment to [sewage] treatment" (Melosi 2008, 106), primarily because of the belief that sewage could be safely diluted in waterways and that waterworks filtration science would contain any remaining threats.

The sanitary city represented a cityscape primarily preoccupied by internal dynamics, with little interest in the effects of pollution on other urban centers or a natural environment located outside the city. Instead, in the sanitary city, engineers and the public largely understood the pollution produced by urban residents as having localized impacts (Melosi 2008). Pollution created in Cincinnati could have negative impacts within Cincinnati itself, but was unlikely to affect other areas. Rivers occupied a unique position within this viewpoint, given their ability to cross regions and create upstream-downstream relationships between communities (Harper 2005). However, even in terms of the elevated levels of pollution found on rivers crosscutting highly industrialized regions like the Ohio Valley, U.S. sanitary engineers still largely believed that water's capacity to dilute pollution limited its regional impacts.

In a well-known case from the period, the state of Missouri brought suit against Illinois and the Sanitary District of Chicago, charging that the opening of the Chicago Drainage Canal in 1900 would bring fecal pollution to the Mississippi River and impact local drinking water. After years of competing sanitary tests overseen by the litigants, the U.S. Supreme Court dismissed the case in 1906 because of a lack of evidence, instead citing anecdotes that the water actually appeared to be cleaner than before due to increased volume (Paavola 2006). In the rare cases when cities did end up constructing sewage treatment plants, they were largely intended to have a local effect by lowering the strain on nearby waterworks filtration facilities (Andreen 2003, 167).

While urban sanitary engineers were deeply concerned about the bacteriological threat posed by organic wastes, they were much less interested in the study of inorganic wastes from industries. The rapid growth of Ohio Valley cities in the nineteenth century was closely tied to industrial manufacturing, many of which were sited along waterways to have both access to water and to dispose of industrial by-products. In Cincinnati, factories were concentrated along the central riverfront area as well as in Mill Creek Valley, the city's industrial heart. The enormous number of factories along the Ohio River and its tributaries led to massive amounts of waste disposal. Of these, sanitary engineers only monitored factories with organic by-products, such as the tanning and meatpacking industries.

Even if local authorities had been more inclined to regulate this factory waste disposal, industrialists wielded incredible economic and political power at the municipal level during the late nineteenth and early twentieth centuries. In this context, it was highly unlikely that city health departments would target industrial pollution, and some even went so far as to argue that chemical discharges represented a boon by helping to kill harmful bacteria in the water (Tarr 1985; Colten and Skinner 1995). Cincinnati was no different in this sense, as industrialists represented the dominant force in the city and region, making direct attacks on their operations an unlikely proposition.

The insular nature of the sanitary city and its narrow focus on bacterial pollution proved untenable in the long run. Even as city officials assured the public that advances in sanitation engineering had eliminated potential threats, a number of drinking water crises forced Cincinnati residents to grapple with the implications of regional stream pollution. In the first decades of the twentieth century, increasing industrial pollution and changing hydrodynamics in the Ohio River produced a series of new dangers to public health.

As early as 1908 a group of sanitary engineers, politicians, and business leaders from across the Ohio Valley began to discuss the need for a regional approach to pollution problems, rather than just a city or state-based one. At their first meeting, held in Wheeling, West Virginia, in May 1909, the group firmly rejected the reliance on water filtration systems alone, arguing "that the interests of the public health may not be sufficiently safeguarded by the installation and operation of water purification plants when the source of supply is a highly sewage polluted water" (OVIA 1935, 25). Despite two further meetings, one later in 1909 and another in 1911, little resulted from this first regional initiative.

The issues identified by this group came to a head in 1923, when increasing levels of phenolic acid originating from the industrial production of steel and coke fuel in the Pittsburgh area began to affect drinking water across the Ohio Valley. Whereas much focus up to that point had been on organic waste, phenolic acid presented a chemical pollutant that the waterworks filtration systems in use at the time had no way of eliminating or reducing. Phenolic acid did not pose an apparent public health concern but did cause an unpleasant odor and taste in drinking water that the filtration systems could not mask.

In response, a group of sanitary engineers, most working in their state public health departments, created the Ohio River Interstate Stream Conservancy Agreement in 1924. Through coordinated outreach to industries across the region, the conservancy agreement succeeded in finding a profitable reuse for phenol by-products, reducing the presence of phenol in the Ohio River. Following its phenolic acid campaign, the group continued to meet to exchange information, but took no action on other regional pollutants (Cleary 1967, 23).

In addition to the threat of inorganic industrial pollutants that could travel long distances, the public perception of pollution in Cincinnati began to change with the completion of the system of locks and dams on the Ohio River in 1929. The canalization of the river had important hydrological consequences. Instead of the river's flow being widely variable and dynamic, the river became much slower and deeper, interrupted at numerous points by the navigational dams. Whereas regular spring and autumn flooding previously had scoured the riverbed, now thick deposits of silt and human waste, called sludge, accumulated at low-velocity sections of the river, particularly near the navigation dams. According to F. Clark Dugan, chief engineer of the Kentucky State Department of Health, speaking to a group of stream pollution activists in Cincinnati in 1935, "The installation of navigation dams has caused many of the rivers to become a series of pools or impounded lakes which results in the more rapid settling out of suspended matter with an increasing growth of microscopic organisms or algae which, in their turn, produce objectionable tastes and odors, and in many instances these tastes and odors are beyond the power of the water filtration plant to eliminate" (Cincinnati CSP 1935, 5).

To study the effect of the recently completed navigational dam system on the Ohio River, the U.S. Public Health Service Field Investigation Station in Cincinnati launched a new project to monitor the river during 1929 and 1930. The station's researchers found much higher levels of organic waste compared to the previous study they had done on the river, conducted from 1914 to 1916. As a result of the higher concentration of sewage, in times of low water the Ohio River became a place of "unpleasant odors, [with] bubbling gases of decomposition" (Cincinnati CSP 1938, 2). Severe droughts in 1930 and 1934 exacerbated these issues, concentrating pollution and leading to gastroenteritis outbreaks affecting thousands of individuals across the Ohio Valley. Moreover, major floods, such as the flood in 1937, tore up long-accumulating sludge banks, rapidly releasing a heavy waste load. These spikes in the levels of organic pollution exacerbated numerous flooding crises, mixing the floodwaters with freshly released contaminants.

Not only were these threats new, but they were caused by activities in faraway locations, making them more difficult to account for. The technologies and policies of the U.S. sanitary city, which relied extensively on localized water filtration and state health boards, were ill-equipped to deal with nonlocal sources of pollution. These issues forced sanitation engineers in the Ohio Valley to look outside their own cities for the first time. The wider public also began to express concern about the quality of drinking water.

Cincinnati Industry and a New Pollution Control Proposal

Recognizing the regional scale of these issues, new groups formed in Cincinnati to investigate solutions to stream pollution that would embrace the entire Ohio Valley. To this new wave of waterways activists, the self-contained sanitary city no longer served as the appropriate frame of reference. According to Kentucky chief engineer Dugan, the solution to this new problem could not be achieved "by one city, or one state, but [by] all the cities and all the states, working together" (Cincinnati CSP 1935, 7). The Cincinnatus Association, which by the 1930s brought together one hundred of the most powerful business leaders in the city to study and advocate around pressing local issues, established a stream pollution committee that published six reports during 1935, covering local and regional pollution impact, public health considerations, and relevant state regulations.

Two reports by civil engineer Herbert Schroth (who would later feature prominently in the floodwall debates after the 1937 flood) were widely circulated to cities throughout the Ohio Valley. Prompted by these reports, the *Cincinnati Enquirer* ran dozens of editorials about water pollution, including front-page stories eight days in a row in May 1935, overlapping with the American Water Works Association convention simultaneously being hosted by Cincinnati (Tucker 1967). In addition, the Cincinnatus Association convinced the Ohio Valley Improvement Association, the powerful lobbying group focused on securing federal support for improving the Ohio River, to make stream pollution a special focus of its 1935 convention, bringing further interest to the topic.

The *Cincinnati Enquirer*'s general manager, William Wiley, became preoccupied by the issue. Wiley was also president of the Cincinnati Chamber of Commerce, and he used that platform to organize and host the Cincinnati Committee on Stream Pollution (CSP) in 1935, bringing together representatives from a range of groups interested in water quality.[1] The inaugural group elected Hudson Biery as its first director. According to the organization's own history, Biery had become involved in antipollution efforts after taking part in a 1934 "Clean-up and Beautify Week" effort organized by the Cincinnati Chamber of Commerce (Cleary 1967). At the committee's last meeting, the project coordinator posed a general query about whether anything else needed cleaning up in the city, and Biery passionately urged the group to tackle the dirty Ohio River. His plea set off hours of debate and excitement among the group, it generated so much public enthusiasm that it (supposedly) spontaneously sparked the formation of the Cincinnati Committee on Stream Pollution.

Biery himself presents a more methodical and calculated history of the group's origin, describing the Cincinnati CSP as "a group of interested citizens: it started in the Health Department of the Chamber of Commerce, rather with the Health Committee of that organization. Two years ago [in 1933] we had brought to our attention the question of stream pollution. We began to do a little under-cover work, to see how much public support could be brought together on the solution of the problem. It soon became apparent that there was great public interest in the subject" (NRC 1935, 15–16).

In its activities, the Cincinnati CSP brought together a wide range of parties interested in water pollution, such as "sanitary engineers, industrial leaders, railroad men, representatives of large civic associations, with membership as high as 50,000, Department of Health Officials, recreation officials, an array of distinguished counsel giving their attention unselfishly, construction engineers, bank officials, the President of the Real Estate Boards, Life Insurance executives, etc." (NRC 1935, 15–16). According to Biery, the CSP represented the manifestation of shared interests across all of these sectors and professional backgrounds. Despite this impressive coalition, local industry represented the primary driver behind the creation and advancement of the committee.

By 1935 Cincinnati's industrial sector was fed up. From industry's perspective, the New Deal—the programs put in motion by President Franklin D. Roosevelt to combat the Great Depression—had gone too far in regulating businesses and market structures, putting undue strain on their capacity to survive and grow. Increased worker protections, production quotas, the creation of government-sponsored enterprises, social security contributions, reconfigured tax codes, and many other measures implemented by Roosevelt's administration infuriated business leaders, even if the political climate made it difficult to resist them. According to Morris Edwards, the Cincinnati Chamber of Commerce's executive vice president, "the period has produced much legislation hostile to business and industry, not only in the form of vast extension of government regulation of the everyday operations of business, but quite as hurtfully in the form of tax burdens so heavy as to make serious inroads on the working capital of business enterprises" (Edwards 1939, 18).

Across the country, the industrial sector began to launch counterattacks in the second half of the 1930s. The proposed regulation of pollution featured among its top targets. Industrial pollution had for a long time garnered relatively little attention from public officials, but this context had begun to shift in the 1920s with the emergence of new groups like the Izaak Walton League, recreationists who were fierce critics of the impact of chemical waste by-products discharged by factories into waterways. This new generation of conservationists blamed industry and chemical pollutants in streams for loss of wildlife and recreational opportunities. In the 1930s new pollution control proposals began to circulate that would make the federal government responsible for regulating both residential waste and industrial waste discharges. These new proposals for federal-level pollution supervision were much stricter and broader than the existing state and local-level requirements they would replace.

Cincinnati industry eyed these proposals nervously and with resentment. Industrial leaders were bothered by the exclusion of industrial perspectives in the process. If enacted, they believed these regulations would add burdensome costs to their production processes, making a difficult economic climate even less manageable. Morris Edwards decried this "drastic legislation which showed little understanding of industry's problems" (Edwards 1939, 18). The Cincinnati Chamber of Commerce was determined to be heard on the matter and began formulating its response.

Cincinnati at the time was already a leading center of efforts to provide industry with more say in how chemical pollution would be regulated. In 1930 Dr. Robert Kehoe had launched the Kettering Laboratory of Applied Physiology, hosted at the University of Cincinnati. The laboratory became one of the first research centers dedicated to investigating the effects of industrial toxins. It quickly gained a reputation for being friendly to industry, particularly in terms of investigating occupational health dangers. Kehoe's approach—known as the "Kehoe paradigm"—argued that industrial contaminants should only be regulated if an "actual hazard" could be proven via data. Kehoe also believed that any potential health threats should be evaluated relative to the economic benefit derived from the industrial production process. Rather than taking a preventative stance, the Kehoe paradigm shifted the burden of proof to opponents of a given industrial chemical by-product. Pioneered in a review of the dangers of adding lead to gasoline, industry widely embraced this perspective. Putting the Kehoe paradigm into practice, industry began to take the lead on exploring the dangers of potential chemical pollutants by funding places such as the Kettering Laboratory and their own corporate research staff (Ross and Amter 2010).

As frustration grew with the New Deal, the Cincinnati Chamber of Commerce and local industry sought to prevent the rise of a competing industrial pollution paradigm that would be much more prohibitive in managing potential health risks posed by chemical pollutants. The Cincinnati CSP under Biery's leadership became their vehicle of resistance. Edwards described the committee's aims as "to formulate and obtain passage of legislation which would help to abate stream pollution, and would assure a pure source of water supply to river cities such as Cincinnati, but would do it without placing impossible burdens and requirements upon industries and municipalities" (Edwards 1939, 18).

At the Cincinnati CSP's inaugural meeting, the founding participants represented a broad swath of interests—but industrial representatives played an outsized role, including representation from the asbestos, lumber, cement, and consumer goods sectors (*Cincinnati Enquirer* 1935). Many of these representatives, such as local asbestos executive George D. Crabbs, were outspoken critics of New Deal policies (*Cincinnati Post* 1938b). As committee chairman, Hudson Biery, who also was an executive at the Cincinnati Street Railway Company and a long-time local booster, led efforts to organize industry while keeping the wider coalition on track and engaged.

Under Biery's leadership, the Cincinnati CSP focused on exploring local, regional, and national solutions to Ohio River pollution problems. The committee's first actions involved correspondence with a number of agencies, sanitation engineers, and other civic groups across the country to investigate the approaches being taken in other cities and states. After these preliminary consultations, the CSP settled on a dual approach. On one track, it would pursue an interstate compact incorporating many or all of the states in the Ohio Valley. On a parallel track, it would lobby for federal legislation to encourage research and financial support for state-led initiatives tackling pollution (OVIA 1935, 39).

The first approach, the interstate compact, would bind member states to standardized pollution controls and enable a coordinated response regarding interstate streams. It would also preserve state control over pollution enforcement, rather than shifting responsibility to federal agencies. Since these types of interstate compacts required preliminary approval by the U.S. Congress before they could be negotiated by the states, the Cincinnati CSP pushed for permission to move forward this effort, which it quickly succeeded in getting in June 1936 (Cleary 1967).

The compact itself still had to be negotiated and required enabling legislation to be approved by each participating state's legislature, a daunting task. The Cincinnati CSP solicited delegates from each of the Ohio Valley states to negotiate the actual treaty, hosting the first treaty convention in November 1936 (Conference of Delegates Appointed by Governors of Ohio Valley States 1936). The delegates used a draft agreement provided by the CSP as a base to start their work. The Ohio River flood of 1937 temporarily diverted attention from water pollution, but delegate meetings resumed in 1938, until the treaty's finalization that October. Industrialists were surprisingly active in the technical meetings, but they also counted on enthusiastic participation among municipal and state-level sanitation officials, who stood to lose a great deal of influence from increasing federal control over pollution regulation.

Second, in tandem with these regional efforts, the Cincinnati CSP and its allies decided to push for federal legislation that would support these regional and state-level efforts. According to Biery, members of President Roosevelt's administration told him, "At Washington we are a little discouraged about present efforts on legislation to further these things[,] and if your local committee out in the country can formulate some definite suggestions that originate in the field, they may have a good chance to go through in Washington" (OVIA 1935, 39–40). Working closely with Senator Alben Barkley and Representatives Fred Vinson and Brent Spence, all from Kentucky, the CSP advanced proposals in the Senate and House that called for federal stream pollution research and grants to support the construction of treatment facilities (Cleary 1967). This approach would increase federal support for local pollution control efforts but in no way increased federal responsibility or policing powers to regulate stream pollution.

The Izaak Walton League and Stopping Industrial Pollution

In its efforts to promote an interstate compact alongside federal grants for treatment facilities and pollution research, the Cincinnati Committee on Stream Pollution came into direct opposition to the Izaak Walton League, the group of recreational enthusiasts and conservationists who were some of the era's strongest critics of stream pollution (Paavola 2006). In 1922 fishermen and other outdoors enthusiasts formed the league in Chicago to push for the interests of anglers, including the preservation of wild land and an end to waterways pollution. The league's initial objectives tied the work closely to fishing, but from there the work quickly grew.

Izaak Walton activists drew attention to the massive die-offs of fish and other wildlife affected by pollution, primarily from industrial contamination (Scarpino 1985). According to the Izaak Walton League, more leisure time had the public seeking out new recreational opportunities, but pollution was forcing these recreationists into more and more remote locations to find pristine streams and unspoiled woods. By curbing pollution, the government would satisfy public demand for healthy recreation, while also providing financial opportunities in the growing tourism industry.

The Izaak Walton League represented a new wave of more combative recreation advocates compared to the older, more elitist conservation groups such as the Sierra Club and National Association of Audubon Societies (Gottlieb 1993). By 1927 the league had already grown enormously, reaching 200,000 members in 2,900 chapters across the country, becoming the country's first mass membership conservation group (Paavola 2006).[2] Membership was drawn primarily from the rapidly expanding professional class, which meant that even though the Izaak Walton League was strident in its attacks on polluters, it also had to be mindful of not going too far in discounting industry's economic contributions (Casner 1999a, 540).

The Izaak Walton League had first focused its efforts on localized campaigns—with several notable victories including the creation of the Upper Mississippi River National Wildlife and Fish Refuge—but a lack of overall progress had it shift to more national efforts. This transition accelerated under Kenneth Reid, a Pennsylvania Fish Commissioner elected as the league's national director in 1936 (Casner 1999a). Reid ran his family business, which produced mining equipment, but he found much more fulfillment once he became active in antipollution efforts. After joining the Izaak Walton League, Reid led successful campaigns in West Virginia and Pennsylvania and began quickly moving up the organization's management structure.

Under Reid, the Izaak Walton League staked out an antipollution position that differed sharply from the Cincinnati CSP. While the latter pushed for federal legislation that preserved the police power of individual states to regulate pollution, the Izaak Walton League wanted complete federal control over water pollution and the power to regulate all waste discharges (Casner 1999a). Working closely with Senator Augustine Lonergan from Connecticut and, later, Representative Karl Mundt from South Dakota, the league argued that the states had been given the opportunity to regulate pollution for a long time and had produced inadequate results. And whereas the CSP pursued water quality standards that still permitted some waste discharges into waterways—maintaining a diminished role for waterways' natural dilution of pollutants—the Izaak Walton League wanted complete sewage treatment throughout the country, with no pollution discharges of any kind permitted without treatment (Paavola 2006). This brought the organization into close cooperation with federal technocrats, including from the U.S. Public Health Service and other departments connected to sanitation and waterways management.

Throughout the second half of the 1930s and into 1940s, the Izaak Walton

League and Cincinnati CSP promoted their competing proposals for federal legislation, each pushing their vision in Congress and in newspapers across the country. The capacity of state and interstate groups to control pollution—and the role of industry in determining pollution control measures—stood at the crux of their disagreement. Both sides agreed that industry had long prevented any kind of effective regulation of pollution, exploiting the interstices between state and federal government to preserve weak oversight. An Izaak Walton League officer in Pennsylvania described the situation from his experience:

> During the 1935 session of our [Pennsylvania] legislature, a manufacturer's representative appeared at a committee hearing and said in effect: "We are in sympathy with the lofty purpose of this bill, but its adoption would place Pennsylvania industry at an unfair competitive disadvantage. If drastic pollution legislation is to be fair, it must be national in scope to provide for uniformity." This argument helped defeat pending legislation of that time, but there was an interesting sequel. This same individual checked his bags and appeared at a later hearing before the Commerce Committee of the United State Senate and said, in effect: "We are in sympathy with the lofty purpose of this proposed legislation, but it is just none of the business of the federal government how Pennsylvania conducts its pollution problem." (Cleary 1967, 42–43)

Izaak Walton League activists saw state laws as a mishmash of regulatory exemptions and loopholes. Cincinnati served as a clear example of these defects.

The Ohio legislature had passed the Bense Act in 1908, regulating sewage discharge in the state and requiring most cities to begin working on sewage treatment plans. Yet, the legislators exempted communities whose sewers emptied into interstate streams, such as Cincinnati along the Ohio River. The Ohio legislature intended this exception to prevent more relaxed regulations in a neighboring state like Kentucky from creating a competitive disadvantage for communities in Ohio. Moreover, if a factory in Cincinnati discharged waste by-products into the Ohio River, the Ohio health board would not be able to regulate this waste, since it was being sent into Kentucky territory, which contains all of the Ohio River to its low-water mark, while the Kentucky health board had no jurisdiction to bring action against an industry located in Ohio (Cincinnati CSP 1935, 10).

Differing regulations across state lines discouraged the enforcement of any sewage treatment requirements, either officially, as with the Bense Act in Ohio, or through a lack of effective policing. Even the Ohio River Interstate Stream Conservancy Agreement, which state sanitation boards had formed to reduce phenol pollution back in 1924, still had to rely on the goodwill of industry and local governments for interstate issues, since it was only an informal arrangement to coordinate efforts at the state level rather than a binding agreement (OVIA 1935, 27). Without policing mechanisms, legislators created numerous exemptions for their jurisdictions, emphasizing that if cities located upstream—such as Pittsburgh—did not treat their sewage, then Ohio had little incentive to institute changes that benefited downstream communities (Cleary 1967). While Dayton, Columbus, and other interior Ohio cities began to consider treatment facilities, Cincinnati did nothing to limit the amount of sewage dumped into the Ohio River. According to the Izaak Walton League, these kinds of exemptions were proof that states were too invested in their own industrial growth to effectively regulate pollution, and only the federal government would be able to undertake the disinterested enforcement necessary (Paavola 2006).

The Cincinnati CSP countered that its proposal for an interstate compact remedied these issues, without the necessity of adding another layer of federal bureaucracy. According to Biery, "Most people believe federal control in this country has gone far enough and that some powers should be retained by the states. More can be accomplished through cooperation than through coercion. . . . Some people want the federal government to do everything for them and we have had a rapid extension of federal control in the past few years. We do not want the federal government to change our linen and clean our back yards" (Biery 1940, 8).

After ratification by each of the participating states' legislatures, the interstate compact would standardize regulations across the region, as well as providing interstate police power to take action against polluters who failed to meet enforcement standards. These measures would close loopholes and exemptions that industry in the Ohio Valley had taken advantage of to avoid regulation. The Cincinnati CSP argued that a formal interstate compact resolved these jurisdictional issues and could be more effective operating through existing bodies that understood the context better and could work with local actors to improve sewage treatment standards (Cleary 1967). Under the CSP's proposed interstate compact, the Ohio River and other streams that acted as state borders, as well as streams that began in one state but passed through at least one other state, would all be under common jurisdiction.

For the Izaak Walton League, Reid argued that interstate compacts would fall into the same nonenforcement pressures that already plagued pollution control by the states, just amplified to a larger scale (Casner 1999a, 544). In his view, the Ohio Valley interstate compact was a more formalized version of the existing regional agreements that saw state health boards, industry, and municipal officials prioritize economic growth while only slowly working to mitigate pollution levels. Labeled by historian Terence Kehoe (1997) as "co-operative pragmatism," this approach did just enough to keep major pollution crises from occurring, while still enabling industry to focus most of its energies on profitability. According to Reid, "In theory compacts sound fine; in practice they just don't materialise, but as a legal means of putting off the day of reckoning in pollution control, the interstate compact probably has no equal" (Paavola 2006, 455).

The Izaak Walton League decried one of the Cincinnati CSP's core proposals. At the heart of the CSP's interstate structure was a plan to form industrial committees covering major chemical sectors, such as mining, distilleries, and steel production. Comprised of industrial actors, these committees would help establish regulations for the discharge of the inorganic pollutants by their sectors. The CSP argued that these groups would best know how to modify and adapt existing production processes. Biery believed in the capacity of industrial firms to find profitable alternate uses for their own polluting discharges, arguing that the reuse of many by-products could be worked out through encouraging new lines of thinking:

> I remember it was only a few years ago that if you walked behind any of the canning factories in southern Indiana you would find a beautiful crimson stream of tomato juice flowing into the nearest creek or the nearest river, possibly a foot deep and four or five feet wide. If you had passed a law forbidding the companies to dump that stuff into the streams you would have put them out of business. That is not what you did. Some scientist explained to those fellows that people ought to drink tomato juice. You drank it for breakfast and liked it. They do not dump that stuff into the streams now. They are producing tomato juice and working the rest of it up into catsup. I do not know if you can reclaim any of the sulphuric acid that comes out of the mines, but through this process of live and let live, and calm analysis, I think this whole difficulty can be licked. (OVIA 1935, 42)[3]

To the Izaak Walton League and others calling for centralized pollution control, the Cincinnati CSP's proposal that committees comprised of industrial representatives would set contamination standards for their own industries represented a clear conflict of interest. Reid argued that anything these groups came up with would be far inferior to technical standards determined by unbiased scientists employed by federal agencies (Paavola 2006). Analyzing the cumulative effect of these flaws with the Cincinnati Committee on Stream Pollution's approach, Reid argued that any positive effects from interstate compacts would only be felt when "you and I may have long white whiskers and be drinking water imported water from Canada" (Casner 1999a, 544).

Pollution Abatement or Pollution Control

The Cincinnati Committee on Stream Pollution worked with treaty delegates from each of the states to negotiate a final draft of the interstate compact in 1938. State legislatures across the Ohio Valley region then began considering adoption of the treaty over the following years. The work advanced slowly. World War II pushed water pollution concerns into the background, since most government officials viewed water pollution control measures as irrelevant considerations in the face of the country's military industrial needs. Despite this setback, the Cincinnati CSP kept pushing the issue, and states gradually began adopting the enabling legislation for the interstate compact treaty. In December 1944 the delegates reconvened to consider the results of an exhaustive study on Ohio Valley pollution conducted over 1941 and 1942 by the U.S. Public Health Service and U.S. Army Corps of Engineers, as well as to pressure the remaining nonsignatories, Pennsylvania and Virginia, to join the compact. The convention, hosted in Pittsburgh, succeeded in getting Pennsylvania to take up and pass enabling legislation in April 1945 (ORSANCO 1949b). The last holdout was Virginia, which West Virginia had stipulated must join before it would make its own participation final. Virginia's legislature eventually indicated it was willing to join the compact, but it still needed to organize a pollution-control board before ratification, since the compact listed this as a prerequisite to joining (Dixon and Thompson 1955).

At the same time, the Cincinnati CSP and its allies advanced its federal pollution bill in the U.S. Congress, which restricted the federal government's role to research and to providing grants or loans for waste treatment facilities, reserving enforcement powers for the states. President Roosevelt proved ambiguous about the measure, though his capacity to shape domestic water policy was already waning by the late 1930s, as the public elected fewer New Deal Democrats (Shanley 1988). Meanwhile, the CSP-backed bill introduced by Senator Barkley had gathered an extensive list of powerful supporters from both technical and industrial backgrounds, including "state Departments of Public Health, the American Public Health Association, the Surgeon General, the Head of the U.S. Public Health Service, and the Water Planning Committee of the National Resources Committee . . . the National Association of Manufacturers, the U.S. Chamber of Commerce (and a number of local and state affiliates), the American Coal Association, the American Mining Congress, the Association of Independent Petroleum Producers, and representatives of the pulp and paper industries" (Shanley 1988, 324–25). The U.S. Congress eventually approved a first version of the Cincinnati CSP's federal pollution bill in 1938, but Roosevelt then vetoed it based on a budgetary concern (Cincinnati CSP 1938, 4) and because it failed to support his recently created National Resources Committee (Welky 2011, 278).

Much like negotiations for the Ohio Valley compact, federal water pollution legislation did not gain traction again until after the war. As war production slowed down, Biery and Reid continued to push their respective positions within the U.S. Congress. Reid reported to his conservation and wildlife peers in 1947 that for "10 years, that cat-and-dog fight has gone on [between the Izaak Walton League and the Cincinnati CSP]" but that he and Biery were finally working on a compromise bill (North American Wildlife Conference 1947, 149–50). However, even though the Izaak Walton League continued to grow in popularity—especially as more recreational opportunities became attainable for a larger segment of the population—pro-business forces also gained ground across the country. In the postwar period, many households were eager to spend, sparking a broad new wave of mass consumerism. Industrial output boomed, and housing production and other sectors reorganized to meet demand. Industry had gained hard-fought victories against New Deal proposals in the late 1930s and during the war, and its leaders were eager to roll back further regulations. After years of economic recession and war, few wanted to slow down this industrial boom.

In Cincinnati, a pro-industry politics had begun to consolidate late in the New Deal. In 1938 Republicans retook control of the city council and mayor's office after more than a decade of governance by the Charterites, the third-party political group that had led efforts to rework the municipal charter in the 1920s. Though they had to initially make deals with labor interests to regain control over municipal politics (*Cincinnati Post* 1938a), the Republicans maintained municipal dominance throughout World War II, overseeing a massive expansion of Cincinnati's industrial production to support the war effort. In the immediate postwar period, many factories devoted to military industries retooled for new markets, such as the opening of the General Electric Aviation plant in Evendale, which became a major airplane engine manufacturer and one of the city's largest employers (Stradling 2003, 134–36). In the postwar years, commitment only grew among Cincinnati's industrial elites to dictate the terms of pollution control and prevent federal intervention.

These shifts doomed compromise efforts between Biery and Reid. With economic growth the country's number-one priority after years of recession and war, the U.S. Congress had little appetite for federal pollution regulations (Ross and Amter 2010). With fresh momentum, on June 30, 1948, Congress passed its first Federal Water Pollution Control Act. The new bill resembled previous bills backed by the Cincinnati CSP, retaining a dominant role for states in establishing and policing pollution regulations while foregoing any substantial role for the federal government beyond providing funding and leading research to encourage municipalities to build their own sewage treatment plants through local bond measures (Ross and Amter 2010, 106). Senators Alben Barkley and Robert A. Taft (one of the earliest members of the Cincinnati CSP) and Representatives Charles Elston and Brent Spence, all from Ohio or Kentucky, introduced the final bill before approval. In recognition of his key role in the process, President Harry S. Truman gave the pen used to sign the legislation into law to Biery (*Cincinnati Enquirer* 1948b). The bill also authorized the construction of a new $4 million stream sanitation laboratory in Cincinnati.

On the very same day, the governors of Illinois, Indiana, Kentucky, Ohio, Pennsylvania, Virginia, and West Virginia (as well as a representative of New York's governor) met in Cincinnati to sign the Ohio Valley interstate compact treaty. After more than a decade of lobbying politicians across the region, Biery and the Cincinnati CSP had achieved their goal. Once finalized, the interstate compact constituted a new administrative entity, the Ohio River Valley Water Sanitation Commission (ORSANCO), which would be based in Cincinnati and funded by all the treaty parties. Once the group completed signing the documents, attention shifted toward organizing next steps, immediately jumping into committee meetings and the practical considerations of setting up a brand-new organization (Gordon 1948; *Cincinnati Enquirer* 1948b).

Hudson Biery had also been pushing for sewage treatment improvements in Cincinnati. Arguing that Cincinnati needed to take the lead in tackling pollution, he pushed for the creation of sewage treatment plants for residential waste along the city's Ohio River frontage and its local tributaries. One of Biery's major objectives was the construction of a sewage treatment facility on the Little Miami River, a heavily polluted tributary of the Ohio River on the east side of the city. At times of high water, outflow from the Little Miami River actually moved upriver to reach the California waterwork, causing a contamination risk for the city's water supply. ORSANCO and federal pollution legislation provided additional impetus for the project, completed in 1953. Northern Kentucky opened a facility later that same year, while Cincinnati eventually opened additional plants on Mill Creek (1959) and Muddy Creek (1961). These efforts led to the slow improvement of water quality on the Ohio River in front of Cincinnati and Northern Kentucky.

Pollution Publicity in the Ohio Valley

A number of studies have portrayed these Cincinnati CSP-led efforts as a pollution control dead-end. Rather than requiring all pollution to go through sewage treatment before discharge, the CSP was able to consolidate a pollution abatement approach that called for the reduction (but not elimination) of the direct discharge of untreated pollutants. In this view, interstate compacts such as ORSANCO and the Federal Water Pollution Control Act effectively forestalled any real progress until the environmental movement achieved a breakthrough in the 1970s (Colten and Skinner 1995; Ross and Amter 2010; Brooks 2009). Largely glossing over the role of the Cincinnati CSP and other organizations, this perspective treats interstate compacts and the federal legislation these groups supported as a cynical alliance of industrial polluters (who were motivated to prevent effective pollution regulation) with state sanitation agencies (who were eager to avoid further extension of federal jurisdiction). In many ways, these analyses are accurate, capturing the economic and political arguments that underpinned the CSP's efforts.

Despite its relevance, this view privileges an overarching narrative of movement from polluted to healthy, evaluating progress in terms of progress between these two poles. An alternative is focusing on how approaches to pollution control instead shifted concepts of cleanliness over time, irrespective of the direct impacts on public health, as well as how actors moved in and out of assemblages around these concepts and how their involvement in these efforts transformed them. In this sense, it is equally important to evaluate the goals of the Cincinnati CSP and nascent ORSANCO in terms of how their activities rearranged understandings of pollution. Under ORSANCO, the percentage of households receiving sewage treatment went from 1 percent to 97 percent between 1948 and 1963 in the Ohio Valley (Paavola 2006), impacting millions of residents' sanitation concepts as well as their utility bills. Perhaps more importantly though, the CSP and ORSANCO reconfigured relationships to industrial pollution, including the way the business community perceived the impact of pollution on its operations. The publicity strategies the Cincinnati CSP and ORSANCO deployed, as well as how they overcame the parallel efforts of the Izaak Walton League, were critical to the success of their work.

Situated in the relatively understudied period between the nineteenth-century rise of the bacteriological theory of disease and the emergence of the environmental movement in the 1960s (Melosi 2008), both the Izaak Walton League and Cincinnati CSP developed in a period where the inadequacies of the sanitary city began to be exposed. In response, both of these groups called for increased recognition that water pollution problems impacted areas far larger than just the city where they originated. In the Ohio Valley, the phenolic crisis of 1924, the drought-related gastroenteritis outbreaks of 1930 and 1934, and growing awareness of the impact of acid mine drainage had underlined the importance of this perspective. To meet this moment, a new generation of stream activists had to search for new ways to convey to the public how pollution operated and its effects. They also had to expand the spatial boundaries of what pollution control looked like. Much as historian Robert Stolz (2014) documents in late nineteenth-century Japan, this transition is not just about automatic outcomes tied to rising levels of stream pollution, but also about having to reorient public understanding of how pollution functions and where it can come from. To get their messages across, both the Izaak Walton League and Cincinnati CSP realized that public relations would be a core component of their work, and they developed novel publicity strategies that enabled them to motivate large populations to change their perspectives on pollution.

The Izaak Walton League has long been recognized for its innovative public relations work. The group placed advertising expertise at the center of its work from the beginning. Of the league's inaugural fifty-four members in 1922, "twelve worked in advertising or sales, the largest single Occupational group represented" (Scarpino 1985, 119). Moreover, Will Dilg, the founder and first director of the organization, used his background as an advertising executive to develop the ambitious plan to rapidly grow the league and mobilize a massive national membership base. Dilg oversaw a messaging campaign that drove home a crisis of nature confronting the United States, delivered in a blitz of public events and through the launch of the group's attractive member magazine, *Outdoor America*. Roving Izaak Walton League organizers spread this message to both men and women, encouraging them to establish new chapters in cities across the country and driving the group's explosive growth (Scarpino 1985). Even though many Cincinnati CSP members saw the Izaak Walton League as unrealistic and radical in its approach to sewage treatment, they nonetheless admired the effectiveness of the Izaak Walton League's publicity campaigns (Conference of Delegates Appointed by Governors of Ohio Valley States 1944, 8).

In contrast, little critical attention has focused on the strategies developed by the Cincinnati CSP and ORSANCO for the Ohio Valley. The first chairman of both organizations Hudson Biery, played a key role in shifting public perceptions around pollution in the region. Similar to Will Dilg of the Izaak Walton League, Biery had a formidable advertising background. By the time he became involved in stream pollution issues, Biery had already built a successful career as the public relations director for the Cincinnati Street Railway Company. He had published extensively in the trade literature on advertising techniques, covering topics such as the effectiveness of visual language, which should ideally communicate with the "flash, the strength, and the simplicity of the sunflower" (Biery 1930, 69), and on the fact that messaging was often more important than the facts, arguing that "many of the most widely used products on the market are sold, not on their intrinsic merits, but by dint of persistent and well phrased advertising" (Biery 1932, 1108). Responsible for both paid advertisements and public service announcements on the Cincinnati Street Railway cars, he also recognized that the most important goal of publicity efforts was "the binding of public good will" (Biery 1930, 69). From the beginning, he drew on this advertising background to guide the Cincinnati CSP's work.

Public relations work already featured prominently in the creation of new sewage infrastructure, but it had primarily focused on projecting the modernity and cleanliness of treatment facilities and waterworks in order to overcome community concerns around odors or other effects (Murphy 1932; Radebaugh 1933). Instead, Biery set out to reshape public understanding of pollution as a potential hazard. In doing so, he brought his own shock tactics to the effort, outstripping even the Izaak Walton League's dire language. Using graphic bacteriological examples, he aggressively changed the narrative on dilution as an acceptable means of managing sewage, while also showing that pollution had wider impacts than previously thought.

One of his favorite slogans—"Let's take the dead horses out of the river!"—brought these points home concisely. Drawing on Public Health Service data, he would follow up this rallying cry by explaining that approximately 450 tons of human excrement were dumped into the Cincinnati section of the river every day, the equivalent of "dropping a dead horse into the Ohio River every two minutes, night and day, year in and year out" (Cincinnati CSP 1938, 3). His tactics horrified audiences who lacked a clear picture of how the water supply system worked, peppering his speeches with comments like: "It is barbaric to drink our own bodily wastes even if we do salve our self respect with scientific filtration and chlorination" (5). In 1938 after he completed an interview for local AM radio station WLW—a high-wattage signal reaching audiences across much of the eastern United States—censors felt forced to edit the broadcast considerably, fearing "a wave of public hysteria if all the harrowing details were known" (Biery 1940, 11).

Once launched in 1948, ORSANCO served as a platform to further spread this message among communities in the Ohio Valley. Fine-tuned by Biery's public relations background, ORSANCO developed a state-of-the-art strategy for motivating cities and towns in Ohio Valley to construct their own sewage treatment facilities. While Biery continued as ORSANCO's first chairman, Edward Cleary, the first ORSANCO director, wanted to perfect the organization as a vehicle for "the art of communication," making a case for improvements built on "emotional appeal" (Cleary 1967, 95). Biery and others handpicked Cleary for his extensive public relations work as editor of the *Engineering News-Record* (Cleary 1983).

According to an early ORSANCO report, the organization had adopted "the philosophy that persuasion with facts rather than compulsion by law was a speedier way to gain its objectives" (ORSANCO 1951, 3). In a typical event, ORSANCO treated the October 1953 opening of Cincinnati's Little Miami River sewage treatment plant as a major promotional opportunity, with the Cincinnati Chamber of Commerce subsidizing attendance by mayors from close to one hundred towns from across the Ohio Valley. At the "Clean Water Rally" accompanying the opening of the Cincinnati plant, ORSANCO gave each mayor a gold-plated shovel to break ground on similar facilities in their own communities (Cleary 1967).

ORSANCO developed two distinct types of publicity campaigns to encourage support for sewage treatment (Cleary 1967). The first was what leadership termed a "buck-shot" campaign targeting the general public across the Ohio Valley. This included publications, films, interviews, speeches, and exhibits developed for a regional audience. ORSANCO intended to saturate the entire region with information to increase public awareness of pollution issues, tackling "the problem of education—the development of understanding and a sense of common responsibility for the preservation of water resources" (ORSANCO 1950, 6). In response to these public awareness efforts, ORSANCO's staff received a concerned letter: "I have requested that my last remains be cremated and dispersed into the Ohio River at Pomeroy, Ohio. In view of your campaign to free the Ohio and its tributaries of stream pollution, I would like to know what liabilities would be incurred by my estate. Frankly, I do not feel this would be very harmful, but I do not want to cause any problems for my heirs. If there is a fine, could it be paid before the event takes place? Please advise me of your decision as I have not felt too healthy recently" (Feck 1963, 9).

A second option, the "rifle-shot" campaign, involved ORSANCO's support for the passage of specific sewage treatment plant bond issues in municipalities around the Ohio Valley. ORSANCO helped local organizations develop and implement a campaign strategy, as well as sending staff representatives and all the collateral materials needed to support passage of local bond issues: "fact sheets, speech outlines, suggested proclamations and resolutions, news releases, program outlines for radio and television presentations, slogan cards and other aids" (ORSANCO 1951, 17). ORSANCO provided any interested group with a complete ready-made campaign kit to support the construction of sewage treatment plants in their hometown. By 1966 a total of 1,399 communities in the Ohio Valley had sewage treatment plants, representing almost a billion dollars in investments (Cleary 1967, 124–26).

Throughout these publicity efforts, ORSANCO desired to constitute the entire Ohio River basin as a regional community brought together by experiences of pollution. In the context of a U.S. population that increasingly relied on advertising to make sense of the world and their shared place in it (Marchand 1985), these strategies found a ready audience. Biery focused on common waste practices across the region, expressing disgust that "all the cities along the river empty their sewers into the stream without any treatment. Cincinnati is just as guilty of this filthy practice as Pittsburgh or Wheeling or Louisville and the rest of the cities" (Biery 1940, 11). ORSANCO also focused on the unique scale of pollution in the heavily populated area: "Nowhere has community growth and industrial expansion brought a greater foulness to streams than in the Ohio Valley" (ORSANCO 1950, 5).

Studies going back to sociologist Émile Durkheim's *Elementary Forms on Religious Life* (1995 [1912]) and anthropologist Mary Douglas's *Purity and Danger* (1966) have emphasized pollution's central role in creating and sustaining community. Defining people, things, or places as polluted has been fundamental to "placing boundaries" (Douglas 1966, 68) that delimit the inside and outside of a community. The Cincinnati CSP and ORSANCO under Biery repeatedly emphasized pollution's role in defining community, lifting up the limits of the Ohio Valley watershed as a relevant boundary for constituting this community.

Across the United States and Europe in the first decades of the twentieth century, the watershed (also known as a drainage basin) gained popularity as a scientifically defined region for the technocratic administration of water, including flooding, irrigation, and hydropower (Molle 2009; Cioc 2002). Despite this, pollution control remained stubbornly resistant to appeals for watershed-based governance. In part this was due to resistance from industrialists and their investments in maintaining patchwork regulations across municipalities and states (Molle 2009; Cleary 1967). In addition, many scientists, bureaucrats, and members of the general public continued to believe in the first decades of the twentieth century that pollution's effects were localized, restricted to the local city or town.[4] Rather than making a purely scientific argument, the Cincinnati CSP and ORSANCO overcame doubts among industry and the general public about a watershed-based administrative structure by arguing that the Ohio River basin should be regarded as a community constituted by pollution, brought together by their shared dependence on the valley's waterways.

Biery and ORSANCO argued that no one location could handle the job of cleaning up waste in the Ohio River and its tributaries. The importance of a watershed-level approach, going beyond the municipal and state-level solutions of the past, fit naturally within a growing focus in the 1930s around "regionalism," the belief that rational planning at the regional level could overcome the Great Depression–era challenges faced by capitalist development and spur new prosperity (Molle 2009, 487).

Alfred Bettman, the chair of the City Planning Commission, along with fellow planner Ladislas Segoe, both pioneers in the planning field, lent their support to the Cincinnati CSP's claims, arguing that the Ohio Valley river basin was an important planning unit for water pollution control and a range of other issues. According to Segoe, "The people in the Valley are alive to their interdependence and to the need of regional collaboration in the solution of some of their most important problems" (Segoe 1937, 31). This aligned with contemporary industry-led arguments that regional interests were better positioned to confront local issues than were broad proposals emanating from the federal government (Jewell 2017).

The Cincinnati CSP and ORSANCO went beyond this regionalist perspective. They centered the Ohio River system as not only the setting for the region but also an active part of the Ohio Valley community. The Ohio River and its tributaries were the common "lifeline of our valley" (ORSANCO, n.d., 5), the feature that connected everyone in the area even if they did not realize it. The Ohio River wove together the Ohio Valley community; without the constant movement of its waters, the Ohio Valley would cease to exist as a meaningful region.

As the Cincinnati CSP mobilized the public to support this river basin approach, its most effective tactic was to demonstrate that polluted waters traveled great distances along waterways and retained their potential to affect far-flung locations. According to the CSP, the flow of waterways made connections stretching across hundreds of miles among many people who would have rarely thought their daily lives intersected. Biery was particularly fond of these examples, describing how "under [cold] conditions like this when the [Ohio] River is well refrigerated the raw sewage from Pittsburgh is carried downstream along with the ice and the ice cold water, almost as good as new" (Biery 1940, 3). Another of Biery's favorite campaign phrases facetiously complained that Cincinnatians "don't want to be reminded every time asparagus is served for supper in Pittsburgh" (Tucker 1967, 185).

Many individuals across the Ohio Valley found this argument compelling in making sense of their own experiences. A journalist who also served as a Chamber of Commerce executive in Marietta, Ohio, spoke of his conversion to the watershed approach in terms of this spatial connectivity. The residents of Marietta, on the banks of the Ohio River, were disturbed to learn that calcium chloride discharged from just one factory in Barberton, Ohio, close to Akron, had been clogging up their wells and making it more difficult to tap into their groundwater. According to this journalist, "It was here that the eye-popping fact began to emerge. . . . It is more than 200 miles from Barberton to Marietta. Yet, throughout this entire distance the waste material from this one factory has created for many municipalities and industries a problem" (Dixon and Thompson 1955, 61).

ORSANCO's messaging highlighted many such linkages across the Ohio Valley, urging cities and towns to understand themselves as part of one community, knitted together by their rivers. Within this framework, the Ohio River and its tributaries played a crucial role in creating a new regional assemblage of pollution and cleanliness defined by Ohio Valley residents' relationship with the Ohio River watershed, building a community awareness where previously one had not existed. These waterways linked people from across the region together, and it was the role of the Cincinnati CSP and ORSANCO to make them aware of this interconnection. In this sense, Biery and later ORSANCO positioned the Ohio Valley river basin as the obvious context for a new set of relationships based on the movements of organic and inorganic pollution.

In this Ohio Valley pollution assemblage, the waterways were not just a connective tissue but also an active participant. The postwar period represented a high-water mark for belief in the power of science and technical expertise to improve life through technologies that tamed nature. Beyond this view though, ORSANCO recognized and argued for a more powerful role for the Ohio River, specifically once it had been cleaned up. ORSANCO made a central part of its publicity work the message that clean water would lead to better outcomes among a diverse cast of water users.

In 1951 ORSANCO's community relations team synthesized this multistakeholder messaging through their new motto: "Clean Waters Protect Your

Health . . . Protect Your Job . . . Protect Your Happiness" (ORSANCO 1951, 17). In this sense, clean water's vitality became an essential asset across a range of daily activities. If regional waterways were clean, they would take care of the people of the Ohio Valley. If they were polluted, these waters would cause problems. Local residents had to tend to the Ohio River's health so that it could properly provide for them. Communities that failed to tackle their pollution risked falling behind significantly. This shift had major implications for how industry began to rethink its relation to stream pollution.

Clean Water as an Economic Elixir

Much historical analysis has focused on how industrial actors secured a major victory for their interests by working with state health boards and sanitation experts to develop this watershed-based approach to pollution control. Industry circumvented strict pollution control by framing its opposition as finding the best use for water resources, arguing that controlled waste disposal was compatible with uses such as navigation, recreation, and power generation (Ross and Amter 2010, 102). For proponents of this approach, ORSANCO's interstate compact exemplified an effective solution. As a core component of its structure, ORSANCO depended on its industrial pollution committees, composed of factory owners and other actors from each sector, to set the standards and policies for their own waste disposal practices (ORSANCO 1952).

For Cincinnati's industrial interests, the Federal Water Pollution Control Act of 1948 and the formation of ORSANCO certainly represented a net win. The Federal Water Pollution Control Act preempted national regulations that would have been imposed by distant technocratic functionaries less interested in responding to industrialists' needs (Colten and Skinner 1995). Any effort by business groups to avoid participation in these efforts met with a sharp rebuke. In one newspaper article about Ohio's mining industry seeking an exemption from state regulations, a clearly irate Biery urged the mining business owners to "get in line" and that by resisting regulations, they were assisting activists like the Izaak Walton League who wanted much more stringent pollution controls (*Cincinnati Enquirer* 1939a).

However, this analysis misses an important component of the Cincinnati CSP's approach, one that both helped legitimize the new Ohio Valley clean water messaging at the heart of ORSANCO and also had important consequences for how businesses and developers viewed the relationship between pollution and economic potential in the Ohio Valley. The communications strategy developed by Biery, and later ORSANCO, stressed that stream pollution affected industrial users as much as the rest of the Ohio Valley community, and that cleaning up stream pollution provided not just a boon to public health but also an economic benefit. According to ORSANCO's 1950 report, "Degradation of water quality by pollution is not simply an offense against social decency. In the Ohio valley, at least, pollution abatement is a dollars-and-cents investment in survival. If water is foul, people still must drink it and take the consequences. And industries, most of whom require vast quantities of water, can turn to no substitute material" (ORSANCO 1950, 6).

Whereas the Izaak Walton League almost exclusively focused on the negative effects that industrial pollution had on nature, the Cincinnati CSP and ORSANCO repeatedly chose to highlight the ways that industry itself was adversely impacted by pollution. Before a congressional committee, Biery carefully clarified that "water supplies, both domestic and industrial, suffer from the effects of these polluting substances" (Golden 1948), while elsewhere stating that pollution was "harming public health, handicapping industry, and destroying recreational assets of our nation" (Biery, n.d.). Seen from this perspective, rather than just being a polluter, industry was just as much a part of the Ohio River basin's new community, because just like everyone else, industry needed clean water, "and polluted streams cannot furnish the quality of water that industry must have" (ORSANCO 1950, 7).

The historian Nicholas Casner (1999b) has detailed in depth the social and legal roots of this growing belief that pollution affected industry in the Ohio Valley. It was long known in the region that the extremely acidic water leaking from active and abandoned Appalachian mines corroded any metal equipment it came in regular contact with, such as pumps and barge hulls. Acidic mine drainage particularly affected railroads since they needed massive amounts of water to run their steam-powered trains: the acidic water constantly damaged engine boilers. By 1927 the Pennsylvania Railroad had invested $30 million in a water delivery system including thirty-six reservoirs and 441 miles of pipe to ensure the availability of clean water along its rail lines. When coal-mining efforts threatened an important reservoir in the Pennsylvania Railroad's water supply system, the railroad sued the nearby mining companies, demanding an end to acidic water leaking into the water supply. After a lengthy court battle, the Pennsylvania Supreme Court ruled in favor of the Pennsylvania Railroad. This legal decision overturned decades of Pennsylvania precedent establishing the right of mines to produce acidic waste. Previously, the courts had overlooked any threat posed to public health by acid pollution in the belief that it was more important for coal mining to proceed without restrictions because of its contributions to local employment and the economy.

According to Casner, this landmark case represented an early "recognition that industry itself suffered from the consequences of contaminated water" (Casner 1999b, 197). This change can be regarded as an important step in moving from the opinion that pollution represented an inevitable by-product of industrial productivity to instead actually seeing it as a potential menace to economic growth. The Pennsylvania Railroad case failed to generate widespread recognition among industrialists that pollution posed a threat to their operations, but it did set the stage for the Cincinnati CSP and ORSANCO's later work.

Biery knew that changing the perceptions of industrialists would be challenging. Building on conservationist arguments about efficiency and waste (Hays 1959), he made convincing industrialists a major focus of the Cincinnati CSP's work, arguing that the group had to first "educate them and start a program that over a period of years can be worked out" (Biery 1935, 42). Progress came slowly, with Biery explaining in 1939 that "two years of intensive cultivation" of industry had only led to an uneasy truce regarding possible pollution regulations (Biery 1939, 28). Even after the launch of ORSANCO, the group's *Second Annual Report* stated, "Taken as a whole, industry has been tardy in grasping the significance of pollution abatement efforts. Part of this points up the fact that management has lost sight of the basic importance of water in production operations" (ORSANCO 1950, 34).

After World War II, a partnership with General Electric (GE) helped provide additional impetus and clout to Biery's industrial messaging. In GE, which had faced sustained criticism for its role in polluting the Housatonic River near Pittsfield, Massachusetts, Biery and later ORSANCO found a key ally in developing public education materials about the economic impact of pollution treatment. ORSANCO relied heavily on a documentary titled *Clean Waters*, produced by GE about the importance of antipollution measures for the country's waterways, which made a special point to focus on how pollution also affected industrial profitability as well as public health. ORSANCO's staff wore out several reels of *Clean Waters* by showing the film so frequently (Cleary 1967, 96). In addition, GE, which opened its Cincinnati-area aviation factory in 1948, made available H. Vance Crawford, a member of its public relations staff, who "spent nearly a year in Cincinnati, where he worked with the ORSANCO staff in developing exhibits and other promotional aids" (Cleary 1967, 97). Crawford and H. Peter Converse, a GE community relations specialist, helped ORSANCO develop their campaign materials and publicity strategy both for the public at large and to target specific industries (ORSANCO 1951, 20).

With this expanded support, the Cincinnati CSP and ORSANCO found increased success in convincing industrialists that pollution affected them as well and that it mattered what kind of river system they were partnering with for their production processes. ORSANCO's collection of different "industry-action" committees played a critical role in this effort, since a key activity for each committee member involved promoting "within the ranks of their specific industry an appreciation of the need to minimize pollution wastes" (ORSANCO 1951, 23). These committees created sector-specific studies that ORSANCO mass-produced and disseminated to factory owners throughout the Ohio Valley (ORSANCO 1951). By the time of the ORSANCO treaty signing in 1948, Pennsylvania governor James Duff, a conservationist, described how he was now finding that "one of the first questions new industries put in inquiring about a site is 'What is the analysis of the water?'" (*Cincinnati Enquirer* 1948b). Given this outreach and the role of its industrial-waste committees, ORSANCO led the way in engaging industry in its work. According to environmental researcher Jouni Paavola, of all the interstate compacts developed for pollution control, only ORSANCO had any significant "influence on industrial water pollution" (2006, 454).

FIGURE 3.1. Still from the film *Clean Waters.* Concurrent narration with this image: "Industrial plants needing a plentiful supply of clean water will not locate along polluted streams" (Wolff 1945).

Given Biery and ORSANCO's sustained outreach to industry, it is important to view how they, on the one hand, helped industry circumvent federal pollution control through an interstate compact approach that gave business leaders a powerful voice in establishing pollution control measures, and, on the other hand, spread new understandings of how stream pollution negatively affected industrial productivity within the region, moving factory owners to believe that too much pollution would impact their bottom lines. The engagement of technical experts and industrialists at the center of ORSANCO's approach was not a simple story of industry manipulating state-level sanitation engineers and health officials in order to continue discharging waste with limited oversight or consequences. Rather, ORSANCO moved to make industry feel dependent on the power of clean water. In the face of industrialists arguing "that pollution-abatement requirements are putting them at competitive disadvantage," ORSANCO flipped the equation to claim that these businesses stood "to gain competitive advantages from a stream clean-up program" and that "there is hardly an industry that would not be in a stronger profit-making position if it could get better water" (ORSANCO 1950, 34). Through sustained outreach, ORSANCO's publicity efforts transformed ideas of clean water in the Ohio Valley, helping to move public opinion from a belief that stream pollution was an inevitable side effect of industrial progress to a view that stream pollution actually impeded development and that clean water represented growth (Casner 1999b, 197).

ORSANCO's publicity efforts—focused on this messaging that linked together clean water, health, and economic development—helped forge a wide-ranging clean water consensus in the Ohio Valley. ORSANCO brought together factory owners, municipal officials, sanitation engineers, and the Ohio River itself, working in coordination to tie together public health and employment through the potency of clean water. If officials of the sanitary city portrayed fresh water as "the universal cleaning agent," under ORSANCO clean water became the "universal growth agent," an elixir for economic development and health with the capacity to spur growth throughout the river basin.

The new Ohio Valley waterways community, containing many different river users, embraced the idea that pollution control administered by an assemblage of local sanitation engineers, public officials, and industrial representatives represented an efficient and advantageous arrangement for the region's continued economic growth. The resilience of this assemblage is evident in the fact that despite their differences, ORSANCO and the Izaak Walton League actually increasingly worked in harmony in the Ohio Valley. G. E. Condo, chair of the Izaak Walton League's Ohio Valley Anti-Pollution Sub-committee, "stated that at one time the league had been doubtful of the effectiveness" of ORSANCO, but that the group's activities had dispelled "such doubts and [given] further evidence of good faith" (ORSANCO 1957, 12–13). Both groups pushed this economic interpretation of clean water in the 1950s, reinforcing one another's messaging. ORSANCO's "Clean Waters Protect Your Health . . . Protect Your Job . . . Protect Your Happiness" motto even gained support from the Izaak Walton League (ORSANCO 1951, 17). By the 1950s in the Ohio Valley, there were few alternatives to ORSANCO's views on "clean water" and its economic potential.

Clean Water and the Cincinnati Riverfront

The Cincinnati Committee on Stream Pollution (CSP) and ORSANCO had little interest in the Cincinnati riverfront. The Ohio River had decreased in importance as a social space over the first half of the twentieth century, with activities like fishing, drawing drinking water directly from the river, and taking pleasure cruises all declining in frequency. According to a recreation and antipollution advocate at the 1935 Ohio Valley Improvement Association convention: "The steamboat age beckoned our fathers and mothers to the river. Another move in another age has called them back ashore" (OVIA 1935, 96).

Many observers pointed to the ways that the Ohio River had changed after the creation of the lock and dam system as the reason for these shifts. The presence of numerous navigational dams along the river contributed to a sluggish flow and growing water pollution, deterring people from enjoying their local waterways. In Cincinnati, health experts advised against bathing or fishing in the Ohio River. After the 1934 drought caused a major typhoid outbreak, Cincinnati officials posted warnings against swimming at popular bathing spots. Across the river, Covington, Kentucky, instituted an outright ban on public bathing (Cleary 1967). The larger Cincinnati riverfront remained a mix of small industry and low-income residential areas, with many structures deteriorating due to lack of investment and sustained exposure to flooding. The Cincinnati CSP and ORSANCO's disinterest reflected larger patterns of riverfront neglect.

The Cincinnati CSP and ORSANCO were therefore at best ambivalent about restoring any intimate social connection to the Ohio River. They did, however, have to account for the general public's interest in recreational opportunities, which had been strongly restricted by increasing levels of pollution. The Izaak Walton League remained a fierce advocate for preserving recreation along public waterways, forcing the CSP to at least address the topic even if the group's overriding focus remained on public health and economic growth.

Once the Ohio Valley states established ORSANCO, staff and commissioners frequently mentioned recreation in the organization's promotional materials, but it was typically treated as a secondary concern in ORSANCO's technical work. At an ORSANCO hearing in 1949 to establish water-quality standards for the Cincinnati Pool—ORSANCO's first set of regulations regarding treatment objectives for a particular section of the river, covering the twenty-two miles in front of the city running between Dam 36 to the east (near the Coney Island amusement park) and Fernbank Dam farther downstream—the committee decided to aim for "a reasonably clean condition" in regard to deoxygenation, where "limited recreation such as boating but not swimming will be inviting," and allowed for conditions that were "lower than recommended for healthy fish life" (ORSANCO 1949a, 13–14).

Despite ORSANCO's general apathy about river recreation, a new generation of river users began to emerge in the decades following the commission's founding. With the economic boom and rapid suburbanization of the postwar years offering increased leisure time, many groups began looking for ways to take advantage of the Cincinnati riverfront as a new space for recreational opportunities. A growing number of urban residents wanted to get out on the river itself for boating excursions and sports such as water skiing. This was aided by new navigation infrastructure that further transformed conditions on the Ohio River. The locks and dams built by the U.S. Army Corps of Engineers in the first decades of the twentieth century to boost navigation were already becoming functionally obsolete as new barge tows grew too large for the original locks. The federal government authorized funds to rebuild most of the navigational system in the 1950s and 1960s, incorporating taller dams and bigger locks in its efforts to modernize the infrastructure (OVIA 1958). These new features further slowed and deepened the river, making the river even more like a series of connected pools. An increasing number of pleasure boaters and fishers demanded access to this lake-like Ohio River; among them was Edward Cleary, ORSANCO's executive director, who was an avid boater.

In tandem, local elites in the city increasingly began calling for riverfront parks as a recreational option for city residents. Urban planning groups had long desired to construct riverfront parks. Although the 1907 Kessler park plan made no mention of a riverfront park, the 1925 and 1948 city plans both called for parks along the Ohio River. These plans called for replacing many lower-income and industrial riverfront areas, including the central riverfront, with beautified promenades and public spaces more welcoming to the leisure activities of upper-class whites. Despite elite interest, these plans produced no real progress in the first half of the twentieth century.

During the postwar period, these efforts picked up new steam. The decision not to build a floodwall along sections of the riverfront had exposed many neighborhoods in the area to long-term flooding. The cumulative effect of this flooding and disinvestment undermined the vitality of these neighborhoods, and city elites were eagerly eyeing these riverfront areas for redevelopment, including as parks. The Cincinnatus Association, which had led investigations into Ohio River flooding and stream pollution in the 1930s, became the lead organization seeking to transform the riverfront into a system of parks. Decades after its founding, the Cincinnatus Association remained a group with one hundred members, overwhelmingly white men representing leading professional and business interests in the city, who investigated municipal issues, presented their recommendations, and then often led reform campaigns. Headed by members Ewart Simpkinson and Robert Acomb, the group held a long-term vision of creating park spaces along the water. For his part, Simpkinson had been advocating for riverfront parks going back all the way to 1929 (Morgan 1993).

Simpkinson, a life insurance agent, and Acomb, an advertising executive, were architects of the Cincinnatus Association's 1962 Symbolon competition. As was noted earlier, the group collected proposals to construct a monument on the central riverfront area, and the process was meant to stimulate visitor interest in the riverfront area as well as provide a showcase attraction to anchor further redevelopment efforts. The Symbolon competition fizzled after a panel of judges declared no submission was of sufficient quality to be declared winner, much to the embarrassment of Simpkinson and Acomb. Despite this failure, the Cincinnatus Association argued the competition had been a success, claiming that the press it generated—and Simpkinson and Acomb's "The park is the spark!" campaign slogan—had led to the passage of a $6.6 million bond issue for urban renewal efforts to demolish buildings on the riverfront and to build a downtown convention center (Tucker 1967).[5]

This work gained traction in the following decade. Cincinnati entering the 1970s had begun to change dramatically. The largely industrial economy that Hudson Biery and early stages of ORSANCO had known no longer dominated the urban landscape. Rather, rapidly accelerating deindustrialization and suburbanization were moving jobs and residents outside the city. Cincinnati's economy moved toward service businesses, including banking and retail, many of which located their offices away from downtown. This era saw the emergence of a local urban growth machine, a coalition of local elites from the real estate, government, industry, culture, and media sectors collectively pursuing strategies intended to boost the city, attract outside capital, and secure governmental redistribution (Logan and Molotch 1987). The deindustrialization then confronting many U.S. cities helped tie an ideology of growth to a belief that cities were in direct competition with one another, putting pressure on urban centers to distinguish themselves or risk the spectacular fall of Detroit or New York (Harvey 1989).

Views of urban centers as dangerous and dirty continued to grow. In response to these challenging conditions, local elites believed that they needed to create healthy and attractive landscapes to draw capital, residents, and tourists back to the city. These shifts had major implications for how residents and city leaders related to industrial activities. Much as historian David Stradling and journalist Richard Stradling (2008) describe for a deindustrializing Cleveland at the same time, these economic transitions brought increased intolerance for the pollution attributed to factories and to waste disposal sites such as junkyards.

In Cincinnati, the status of the central riverfront particularly concerned city officials. Previously known as the Central Bottoms, this area adjacent to downtown had experienced years of flooding and disinvestment that slowly destroyed the original neighborhood. The construction of a new sports stadium on the site in 1970 had helped clean up a portion of the central riverfront and make it attractive to suburban sports fans but scrap heaps, cement plants, abandoned plots, and warehouses made the surrounding area unsightly.

Drawing on Acomb's advertising background and Simpkinson's long booster experience, the Cincinnatus Association made cleaning up the riverfront a key component of its parks messaging strategy, arguing that "Until a few years ago, this Central Riverfront was our run-down 'back yard' flooded area with no one much walking down there. The City has, since then, spent millions making this Central Riverfront our 'front yard' so that private capital would spend millions *more*, which would re-coop this potentially very valuable land so near the heart of downtown" (Simpkinson 1976, 1, emphasis in original).

In addition to the Cincinnatus Association, several other public and private groups had been active in promoting new plans for the riverfront. Seeing limitations to this dispersed approach, Acomb and Simpkinson began to push in 1974 to form one consolidated body to guide the development of this important asset. In February 1975, Cincinnati's city council recognized this new group, the Riverfront Advisory Council (RAC), as an official planning body, with Acomb and Simpkinson on the Executive Committee.

Redeveloping a Healthy Riverfront

The formation of the RAC in many ways exemplified significant shifts in Cincinnati politics at the time. Republicans had dominated municipal politics in the postwar years, holding uninterrupted control over the city council and mayor's office since 1954. Their pro-business policies had reshaped the city's economy, pushing further deference to industry and redeveloping the city center as a haven for white suburban office workers and shoppers increasingly skittish about Cincinnati's safety. In 1971 the Democrats regained power in an alliance with the Charterites, the municipal-level "good government" party that had previously aligned with Republicans. A "new emphasis on revitalizing neighborhoods" and empowering local decision-making contributed to their success (Thomas 1986, 76), a popular position that clashed with the Republican emphasis on technocratic and business control over the city. According to one member of the governing coalition, it was important to provide "something visible which people could rally around," such as recreational facilities or health clinics (76).

The RAC was both the first redevelopment group to cover the entire Cincinnati riverfront and the first community-led effort with this focus. Appointed by the city manager, the council included a mix of industry, conservationists, recreationalists, real estate interests, and neighborhood groups. While the Central Riverfront area had no remaining residential base, especially after the massive Riverfront Stadium opened in June 1970, the string of riverfront neighborhoods to the east and west of the city center continued to be home to a number of low-income Black and white communities.

Unlike past riverfront development plans created without community input, such as the 1967 *Riverfront Plan* created by the Stanley Consultants, the RAC foregrounded pollution as a key issue, highlighting the environment and water quality as important considerations (RAC 1975a; 1975b). RAC members expressed concern that "despite its historic, continuing and projected importance, the city on the whole has tended to treat [the river] as an alley, a place for refuse, rather than as an asset" (RAC 1976, 4). Simpkinson prodded the RAC to focus on the removal of the American Compressed Steel junkyard, located in the central riverfront, as a particularly important target that would show the growing commitment to clean up the riverfront and make it accessible to the city. According to the city's grant application for federal funding to purchase the junkyard, "The project seeks to reclaim and preserve the city's unique and invaluable natural resource—the Ohio riverfront. The area is presently an unsightly scrapyard and a serious environmental blight. The project would remove this eyesore and replace it with open space to be used for park and recreation purposes" (Ahlering 1983, 45). The discovery of the city's Front Street waterworks pumping station under the scrapyard only served to reinforce this message. After being abandoned in 1907 due to pollution concerns, its reclamation offered a powerful symbol for riverfront transformation.

By repackaging the riverfront as a source of "environmental blight," Simpkinson and Acomb, alongside the RAC, secured new supporters and funding to transform the area. Rather than past fears about the blighting effects of low-income Black and white Central Bottoms residents, the concern here revolved around the potential impacts of unattractive and unhealthy sites along the river. The well-being of the region's waterways was thus tied not only to the discharge of pollutants from industries and residences, but also to more general issues like litter and pesticides, called "nonpoint source" pollution.

The RAC's process of positioning the riverfront as a polluted space drew considerable inspiration from ORSANCO's clean-water messaging. The call to stop treating the river and riverfront as the "community dump" (RAC 1976, 13) overtly harkened back to Biery and the Cincinnati CSP's campaign strategies to cultivate shared responsibility to provide healthy conditions that would stimulate economic growth. Simpkinson and Acomb, in their Cincinnatus Association leadership capacity, had been in touch with Biery during the 1960s, learning about the strategies the CSP had used to achieve its objectives, with advice on the importance of publicity and public education (Biery 1963). The RAC also pointed to ORSANCO in order to buttress its own activities, describing how the "Ohio River Sanitation Commission [*sic*] has spent the last two decades enforcing pollution standards," so that "the river is no longer an open sewer" and it was even "clean enough for swimming" in some places (RAC 1976, 8).

In this vein, the RAC incorporated pollution control as part of its planning efforts. The council strategically engaged sanitation experts, including the city's Metropolitan Sewer District (MSD), to provide input on how the riverfront could be redeveloped as a clean and healthy recreational space. The RAC Executive Committee invited the MSD to attend all RAC meetings as a guest, arguing that the district's antipollution efforts directly impacted the RAC's work (RAC 1975c). The RAC collaborated with the MSD in promoting plans to build storm runoff retention ponds along the riverfront; these twenty retention ponds would collect combined sewer overflows—the mix of stormwater and raw sewage discharged without treatment from overwhelmed sewer systems in times of heavy rain—in order to keep the system from being overwhelmed and backing up. Federal budget cutbacks in the late 1970s ruled out the construction of the retention ponds, but the proposal still burnished the water-

FIGURE 3.2. Cover page of the exhibition catalog *Environmental Sculpture: Proposals for Sawyer Point Park*, 1977. The image frames the need for an explicitly "environmental" sculpture as a response to the perceived threat of environmental blight. Photo by Alice Weston. Image courtesy of the Contemporary Arts Center, Cincinnati, Ohio.

front's credentials as an important environmental site, the last line of defense to keep nonpoint source pollution out of the Ohio River (RAC 1976).

While the Cincinnati CSP and ORSANCO had little direct impact on the Cincinnati riverfront, the RAC echoed ORSANCO's notion that "clean water" represented a fundamental precursor to economic growth. Council members believed the construction of parks and green spaces in the area would unlock significant investments and positive health outcomes for the city. Acomb and Simpkinson, through their involvement in the RAC and the Cincinnatus Association, repositioned the riverfront as a fundamentally dirty and polluted space, and riverfront residents and industries as both endangered by pollution and suspect because of their association with these areas. When the RAC identified riverfront neighborhoods and industries as polluted and dirty, it also rendered them a threat to the entire city, requiring extensive demolition and reimagining to restore these areas to a desirable state.[6]

The RAC used ORSANCO's arguments about the economic benefits of "clean water" to argue that environmentally blighted riverfront areas needed to be cleaned up in order to protect the Ohio River and also to make the area desirable for investment. In Cincinnati's East End neighborhood, the eight-mile stretch of riverfront just east of the central riverfront area, city officials used arguments about environmental blight and health to justify disinvestment and displacement in the neighborhood (Halperin 1998), such as with an Environmental Protection Agency investigation that shut down a gas station that doubled as the community's main meeting space, or when "developers attempted to use the [environmental quality control] guidelines to eliminate affordable housing by increasing its cost, again under the guise of 'concern' for the community" (121). In this way cleaning up pollution and improving environmental standards also provided a framework to displace riverfront residents and industries outside of the central riverfront area. Redevelopment became one of the means of sanitizing polluted urban environments, returning them to an appealing and healthy state while legitimizing the need to move out polluting residents and industries (Checker 2011).

In the second half of the 1970s, Simpkinson and Acomb, as part of RAC, finally oversaw parks beginning to open along the central riverfront, featuring promenades and direct access to the water. These new parks—Yeatman's Cove, the Serpentine Wall, and Sawyer Point—became central public spaces in the city, intended to provide wholesome and refreshing natural surroundings. Their design and location catered to high-income white communities who would feel more comfortable entering the city to visit isolated parks with few linkages to the surrounding urban neighborhoods deemed dangerous.

Conclusion

In Cincinnati, these connections between pollution control and economic development presaged a new role for the Ohio River. Industrial elites in Cincinnati and across the region came to appreciate how they could work with the river to achieve their growth goals, rather than trying to control it or ignore it. This goes beyond the perspective described in the previous chapter, where the alignment of the Ohio River's flooding with redevelopment goals for the central riverfront often seemed serendipitous to the public. In terms of ORSANCO and the riverfront park development, local elites felt comfortable arguing that tackling water pollution was not just about public health but also about creating the conditions for continued capitalist expansion. The Ohio River acted as an indispensable partner in this approach. This fed into an ongoing shift in understanding the usefulness of collaboration with particular nonhuman actors such as the Ohio River as a valuable spur to economic activity. Moreover, the vital role played by industry and public relations professionals in determining sanitation conditions for the Ohio Valley received little critique. Rather than being seen as limiting, most technical experts gladly welcomed the participation of nonexperts as a means to strengthen their strategies.

The Riverfront Advisory Council tailored its efforts, based on input from technicians and business interests, to fit with the environmental approach that called for cultivating a proactive care for the natural world (Luke 1995). Environmentalists saw recreation as a way to help cultivate a new mentality, tying together everyday life to care of the environment in numerous new ways. Visual or physical engagement with nature through recreation cultivated this new environmentalist attitude. RAC members argued that the riverfront was unique because visiting "this active natural force . . . refreshes the spirit as well as the mind," making it a "'re-creational' asset of the first importance" (RAC 1976, 10). In this view, contact with the river taught visitors to appreciate the revitalizing effects of the environment and encouraged them to care for the Ohio River, since it in turn took care of them. It also taught visitors to recognize the dangers posed by river pollution and the need to combat it. For industrial elites, this cultivation of care for the Ohio River went beyond a sense of public duty to also encompass an understanding that a collaborative approach could reinforce their own industrial goals and, in important ways, position them as stewards of the Ohio River.

Ultimately, RAC members sought to spur upscale private residential and commercial construction by pushing for riverfront parks as a means of "cleaning up" the area for investment. Despite their efforts, they fell short of making the area desirable to developers in the ways they had expected. City officials and their allies were "successful to the point of cleaning up [this] downward transitional area," but remained frustrated by the slow pace of investment as they "awaited external market forces to generate the required momentum to facilitate the remaining development objectives" (Mitchell 1998, 391). Simpkinson got his parks via massive government funding and private donations, but he never got "millions more" in private investment. When he died in 1993, the central riverfront felt like a disconnected maze of concrete structures and isolated parks, cut off from downtown by Fort Washington Way, a short bypass highway running parallel to the riverfront. On the central riverfront, the RAC only had one riverfront luxury apartment tower, the massive and isolated One Lytle Place, to show for the city's park investments. Farther east on the riverfront, developers did begin to take more initiative to build luxury townhouses and condominiums (Halperin 1998). Extending these successes to the central riverfront would be a major focus of the 1990s.

Meanwhile, even as it met most elite development needs for the region, the

Ohio River remained one of the most polluted rivers in the United States, receiving large quantities of chemical waste annually. The working river once favored by ORSANCO increasingly butted up against a vision of "cleaning up" the riverfront for residential development. Perceiving themselves under threat, Cincinnati's maritime industries felt the need to fight for their place in the city and began to organize to secure more recognition for their contributions. As Cincinnati invested further resources in a bid to finally redevelop the riverfront, these visions of the "working river" and "luxury river" increasingly were at odds with one another.

CHAPTER 4

Reassembling Infrastructure on the Cincinnati Riverfront, 1988–2020

Jack Moreland drove me down to the Taylor Creek Overlook Park. Moreland, president of Southbank Partners, a community development organization serving the six Northern Kentucky cities across the river from Cincinnati, wanted to show me the area's newest park, located on the Ohio River. He turned the car onto the nostalgically named Riverboat Row before pulling up to the one-third-acre pocket park, squeezed between two seafood restaurant chains and a hotel. As we walked around the edge of the park on a clear September afternoon, Moreland offered, "This park's got about as good a view of the city as you can find," letting me take in the prospect for a moment.

Walking down toward the riverbank, Moreland explained that the Kentucky Transportation Cabinet had built the park on top of the discharge point for the Taylor Creek culvert, a tunnel carrying the creek's water underneath the communities of Bellevue and Newport before emptying into the Ohio River. For years, the culvert's discharge had steadily eroded the nearby riverbank, threatening to undermine the restaurants and adjacent street. To prevent further deterioration, the Southbank Partners, along with local officials from Newport and Bellevue, county officials, and state representatives, lobbied together to include a project in the state budget to reengineer the culvert's discharge point and cap the small recess in the riverbank that the erosion had formed. They succeeded in getting a project included in the Kentucky Transportation Cabinet's budget to rebuild and extend the culvert. Afterwards, Southbank Partners secured a grant from the utility provider Duke Energy for basic landscaping on the new land. The city and Southbank Partners hoped to identify further support to include additional park features, including walking paths and seating. Moreland felt proud of the project, citing it as an ideal example of "using infrastructure to turn a liability into an asset." Southbank Partners had seen that the need to fix an infrastructural problem could also double as an opportunity to develop and beautify the riverfront.

Across the river and several months later, I met with Jack Rennekamp at the main offices of the Metropolitan Sewer District of Greater Cincinnati (MSD), located alongside Mill Creek just west of downtown Cincinnati. Rennekamp, an assistant superintendent at the MSD, was explaining to me the goals behind Project Groundwork, a long-term multi-billion-dollar effort to revamp many of Cincinnati's sewers. In 2002 and 2004 a federal judge mandated MSD's upgrades, under what is known as a "consent decree," in order to reduce pollution caused by direct rainwater runoff and combined sewer overflows (CSOS). CSOS discharge raw sewage into local waterways during storms so that the sewer system will not be overwhelmed by excess water, often leading to pollution spikes in affected waterways. The MSD introduced Project Groundwork to combat these issues, including initiatives to replace old sewer lines, treatment facility upgrades, and public education around green alternatives such as water gardens and rain barrels.

Rennekamp was particularly pleased with one component of Project Groundwork: the Lick Run Greenway in South Fairmount, a low-income neighborhood with mostly Black residents. The MSD's plan called for moving Lick Run out of its culvert tunnel and restoring it to its more natural state—a process called daylighting. The restored creek would be the center of landscaped park features intended to help spur redevelopment in the surrounding South Fairmount neighborhood. He described it as a unique proposal, "designed as a consent decree solution, but... it's also hoped to have other consequences, to provide economic development, jobs, growth, community redevelopment to a severely depressed area." While careful to clarify that rate payer funds were only being used to support sewage improvements, Rennekamp expressed pride that this "more comprehensive approach to an engineering problem" went beyond the minimum requirements to embrace a collaborative process. "We could have simply, as an alternative, created a 'detunnel' that would have collected sewage and pumped that out at a later point in time and we're done, we're out of there." Instead the MSD chose to seize the opportunity presented by an infrastructural problem to benefit the community.

These two infrastructural projects bring together technical and economic rationales in surprising ways. In many regards, the MSD plan is eerily similar to the Taylor Creek Overlook Park area that Moreland had taken me to see. With the Lick Creek Greenway in Cincinnati, it is the MSD, a utility agency, driving forward the project, whereas the Southbank Partners, a redevelopment corporation, put the plans in motion for the Taylor Creek Overlook Park. These very analogous projects originated in starkly different contexts.

Previously, it was not uncommon to see practical business approaches and technocratic logics deployed together on the Cincinnati riverfront. When scientists talked about the need to tackle pollution or flooding, it also typically related to efforts to control and benefit from the redevelopment of urban spaces; and vice versa, when developers talked about infrastructure "priming the pump" for economic development, they were also concerned with shaping the conditions of everyday life. An interdependence between technopolitics and redevelopment has intensified in recent years, to the point that it is not uncommon for a redevelopment organization like Southbank Partners to identify and drive forward a sewer repair project, or for utilities like the MSD to propose a community redevelopment project integrated with its environmental remediation program. Practical and technocratic epistemologies have long shaped infrastructural work, but now these rationales have intermingled in ways that make it difficult to separate them out in conversations around new infrastructure proposals.

Whereas previous chapters focused primarily on the histories of specific infrastructural projects, this ethnographic chapter concentrates on two prominent redevelopment efforts in the city in recent decades. The first is The Banks, a by now quite recognizable mixed-use project on the central riverfront with prime residential units, destination shopping, cultural attractions, commercial real estate, and green space. The second is the recently rebranded Ports of Cincinnati & Northern Kentucky, a collection of commercial sites scattered along the riverfront in fifteen Ohio and Kentucky counties, but concentrated in the area stretching westward from Cincinnati's central riverfront. These private businesses have been leading "port development strategies" (Jermier et al. 2016) in an effort to attract additional interest and investment to the region's river industries.

During fieldwork at these two sites, I spoke with developers, engineers, barge and river terminal operators, public officials, environmentalists, and other stakeholders about their involvement in each, as well as about their perception of Cincinnati's riverfront in general. Many of the people I spoke to represent groups discussed in previous chapters, such as with the Ohio River Valley Water Sanitation Commission (ORSANCO), the U.S. Army Corps of Engineers, and the River Advisory Council (RAC, previously known as the Riverfront Advisory Council), while others came from newer groups including the Ohio River Foundation and the Central Ohio River Business Association.

Advocates for The Banks and for the Ports of Cincinnati & Northern Kentucky coexist uneasily, with their visions for the riverfront standing in marked contrast. Developers of The Banks want to portray the Ohio River as a space of leisure and relaxation, while river industries involved in the Ports of Cincinnati & Northern Kentucky stress the economic role of the river, a rugged and utilitarian space of blue-collar work. Most of these river users publicly promote cooperation and sharing the river, yet in practice there are tensions. Condominium owners complain that terminal facilities are dusty, noisy, and ugly. River businesses view with skepticism plans to extend bike paths or parks along their sections of the "working river."

In spite of these tensions, each of these projects is deeply rooted in the same riparian infrastructural systems created over the past century. Both The Banks and the Ports of Cincinnati & Northern Kentucky legitimize their place in the city based on the legacies of the systems created to improve navigation, flood control, and pollution control. Riparian infrastructures have anchored these actors in a common framework, shaping how they relate to the riverfront and each other.

The Banks

When I first returned to Cincinnati in 2015, after having left more than a decade prior, everyone wanted to tell me how much the city had changed. They marveled at Over-the-Rhine, a historic neighborhood located just north of downtown, and how it had rapidly gentrified in recent years, with trendy new restaurants and specialty boutique stores. Despite Over-the-Rhine's hipster cachet, many preferred The Banks, with its newly built apartments, cultural attractions, and popular nightlife destinations. In addition, after years of political drama, the city was building a streetcar line to connect The Banks with Over-the-Rhine.

Of all these developments, The Banks, a totally new neighborhood, perhaps surprised people the most. The central riverfront area had remained obstinately underdeveloped for decades in spite of seemingly never-ending redevelopment proposals. Developers and the city government had repeatedly failed to advance long-cherished plans for amenities on the site such as luxury apartments and destination retail. The city opened a multiuse stadium on the site in 1970, later joined by an indoor arena in 1975 and a system of riverfront parks, but these investments had failed to spur private development in the area. Instead, Cincinnati's central riverfront landscape in the early 1990s was a labyrinthine collection of concrete tunnels, parking garages, staircases, and pedestrian bridges connecting isolated and far-flung sites. Cincinnatians found it hard to imagine any walkable, integrated, urban neighborhood existing on the site.

City officials and business leaders at the beginning of the 1990s saw that the central riverfront needed a change. Even with the 1988 completion of Sawyer Point Park, a flagship riverfront park, it looked unlikely that the current riverfront arrangement would generate transformative private redevelopment. The first step toward resolving these concerns came from a seemingly innocuous community consultation. In the early 1990s traffic engineers from the Cincinnati Department of Public Works began planning for a massive renovation of Fort Washington Way, the 0.9-mile-long connector highway that also separated the city's downtown from its waterfront. Engineers estimated it would cost $20 million to $30 million to resurface the entire section of highway.

As part of the process, City Hall wanted public input. An assistant traffic engineer sent an outline of proposed traffic adjustments over to Downtown Cincinnati, Inc. (DCI), a redevelopment nonprofit launched in 1994 focused on reviving the city center. While the traffic engineer expected DCI to rubber-stamp the plan, the group's Transportation Committee pushed back, rejecting the proposal and urging the city to take the opportunity to rethink Fort Washington Way's whole layout. John Schneider, a local real estate developer and head of the DCI Transportation Committee, assembled a group of what he termed "merry rebels" to formulate alternatives. This group included Jim Duane, the head of the powerful Ohio-Kentucky-Indiana Regional Council of Governments (OKI), which held final approval over all federal transportation funding for highway projects in the region. The group presented its own proposal for Fort Washington Way at a press conference on March 2, 1995 (Curnutte 1995).

When I spoke with developer John Schneider, it had been more than two decades since his involvement in the process, yet the experience was still fresh in his mind. According to Schneider, who headed the DCI Transportation Committee that developed the proposal, a confluence of events in the mid-1990s had finally begun to shift the landscape of possibilities. First, Fort Washington Way, originally opened in 1962, was crumbling and, at a minimum, needed to be completely repaved. The local professional football and baseball teams, which shared the riverfront stadium, both wanted their own new facilities. At the same time, in 1994, the National Conference for Community and Justice proposed the construction of a major museum dedicated to the underground railroad, of which Cincinnati had been a crucial node. A desire to locate the museum on the riverfront proved popular, attracting public and corporate backing for the project. Finally, the Metropolitan Sewer District began developing plans to tackle combined sewer overflows in the central riverfront area, reducing the number of sewer outfalls and annual overflow incidents downtown, estimated at close to 150 per year (Ben 2010).

Schneider's group at DCI, working with the OKI, recommended a complete overhaul of Fort Washington Way, narrowing the highway and sinking it below ground level. This proposed change would not only diminish the break between downtown and the riverfront but would also create fourteen new acres of property to be developed on the riverfront—an attractive prospect. Their proposal ran into opposition from city agencies, which had favored simply repaving the Fort Washington Way as it was. Following the proposals laid out in the *Cincinnati Plan 2000* (published in 1982), the city's urban planning department had already begun drafting its own plans to build a massive concrete platform extending over Fort Washington Way in order to facilitate development of air rights over the riverfront. The joint DCI-OKI plan outraged the city's Department of Public Works and urban planning specialists, as well as the Ohio Department of Transportation (ODOT), which were far advanced in their own planning processes for repaving Fort Washington Way. According to Schneider, the same assistant traffic engineer who had originally requested DCI's approval on Fort Washington Way traffic adjustments—which DCI had rejected in favor of developing its own proposal—later sent an eleven-page letter to the city manager explaining in detail why the DCI-OKI proposal was impractical and undesirable. The city manager refused to sign off on the letter.

In his downtown apartment two decades later, Schneider still conveyed the excitement of the struggle to see which plan would win out, as both groups sought to gain backing from public opinion and from city elites. According to Schneider, "At first there was, you know, outrage. I proposed Fort Washington Way, and the county engineer, Bill Brayshaw, who had actually built [Fort Washington Way] as a young man working for ODOT . . . tried to get me thrown off the board of Downtown Cincinnati, Inc." Schneider shared a scrapbook he had put together with newspaper clippings charting the back and forth, the increasing tensions evident in the stitched-together history. Ultimately, in Schneider's view, the DCI-OKI plan emerged victorious because it represented the possibility to create additional riverfront acreage, whereas previously the "conversation had been so limited because there was so little land down there [on the riverfront]." The influential Cincinnati Business Committee threw its support behind the DCI-OKI plan to reconfigure Fort Washington Way, and eventually City Hall formally endorsed this approach.

City Hall appointed John Deatrick as the supervising engineer to move the project forward. On the back of the Fort Washington Way proposal, in 1996 Hamilton County residents voted to provide public funding for two new sports stadia. The city appointed the Riverfront Steering Commission—yet another group convened to kick-start river redevelopment—and contracted with Urban Design Associates to recommend potential stadium sites, as well as create a master plan for the riverfront redevelopment. A very public debate unfolded around the possible locations for the stadia (in which Schneider again played a prominent role), with the riverfront option facing off against a proposal to build the baseball stadium in the predominantly Black neighborhood of Over-the-Rhine. The perceived safety and accessibility of the riverfront site, contrasted with portrayals of urban crime for Over-the-Rhine, tipped public favor in that direction, formalized by a referendum on the issue in 1998. Eventually both stadia were located on the central riverfront, with the first, a football stadium, intended to be opened in 2000.

Meanwhile, the Fort Washington Way reconstruction advanced rapidly, breaking ground in 1998 and achieving completion in 2000. I spoke with Deatrick, who described how the project managers felt that "to make sure the highway did get done and to add a sense of urgency—that we tie [Fort Washington Way construction] to the opening of the [football] stadium" in 2000, meaning the project had to be fast-tracked, both in terms of securing funding and letting contracts for constructions. I met with Deatrick in his City Hall office, in the midst of supervising the construction of a new streetcar system, Cincinnati's newest major infrastructure project. To show me how the Fort Washington Way project had developed, he pulled out the original funding matrix from among the project files he still kept on hand, outlining the complex operations required to rebuild the Fort Washington Way bypass, which had grown from its estimated original budget of $20–30 million for a simple highway repaving, to a massive $313.4 million effort encompassing the bypass, a public transit station, a floodwall, and other related efforts. During the Fort Washington Way reconstruction, the project engineers were even able to tackle the combined sewer overflow problem, installing a large interceptor sewer on the northern edge of Fort Washington Way, which acted as ad hoc storage for storm runoff and reduced the number of overflow incidents to only a handful each year.

With Fort Washington Way completed, the focus moved to completing the baseball stadium (2003) and opening the National Underground Railroad Freedom Center (2004). In a decade, the city and county officials had been able to realize many of their goals to reconfigure the riverfront. And yet, private development still lagged behind. The city council rejected a development plan put forward by the city manager and economic development director in 1997 for a "mega-entertainment" district, with the mayor decrying it as a "malling" of the riverfront (Donovan and May 1998, A1). As an alternative, the Urban Design Associates consultants developed a plan calling for redevelopment to be built on massive parking garages, raising the site out of the floodplain. In 1999 the City of Cincinnati and Hamilton County appointed another new group, the Riverfront Advisors Commission, with representatives from government and the private sector, which embraced the plan and suggested calling the area The Banks.[1] The commission outlined a timeline to move the project forward and got buy-in from the local city and county governments, the two main entities required to advance the work. Still, bickering between the county and city slowed the construction of the garage infrastructure to a crawl, which in turn delayed the private development that would be built on top of the garages (*Cincinnati Enquirer* 2007). In the absence of progress, across the river in Kentucky a mixed-use development, Newport on the Levee, had opened in 2001, with an aquarium, movie theater, bars, and retail outlets. Much to the chagrin of Cincinnati officials, Newport on the Levee proved extremely popular and drew large crowds down to the Northern Kentucky waterfront.

In 2006 continued delays with building out the garaging infrastructure moved the city and county to form a Banks Working Group, chaired by the CEO of the Cincinnati baseball team, Bob Castellini, who also owned a produce wholesale firm that had previously been located on the riverfront. In November 2007, at the urging of the Banks Working Group, the city and county finally signed a development agreement with Carter and Dawson, two Atlanta-based firms. In addition, the city and county formed a Banks Public Partnership to facilitate work on their joint public infrastructure projects, primarily the parking garages (*Cincinnati Enquirer* 2007). After breaking ground in 2008, The Banks' first commercial and residential tenants moved in during 2011, while the first sections of a new green space along the river, Smale Riverfront Park, opened in 2012. Construction has continued on the parking garages and further phases of development, without any clear timeline for when The Banks will be completed.

The Ports

While The Banks attracted significant public attention, another riverfront redevelopment project involving the city's river industries had been gaining traction outside of the limelight. For a number of years there had been no central organization to represent river industries in Cincinnati. After the modernization of the Ohio River lock and dam system in the 1950s and 1960s, leadership of the Ohio Valley Improvement Association (OVIA), which had long been drawn from Cincinnati's navigation concerns, shifted to Ashland Oil, Inc. (in Ashland, Kentucky) and coal operators in Huntington, West Virginia. In 1983 a much-reduced OVIA merged with DINAMO, a group in Pittsburgh launching a new effort to once again modernize the locks and dams (Murray 2018). Cincinnatians were largely left on the sidelines in this new process.

The city's river industries began to organize again in 2000 or shortly thereafter to gain additional support and investment for their activities. These efforts were connected to the Riverfront Advisory Council —formed by the city government in 1975 to review land use planning and zoning for the entire riverfront, playing a key role in promoting increased recreation and green space along the river. After producing *A Study of the Cincinnati Riverfront* in 1981, the RAC continued to review waterfront zoning decisions and provide advice for the City Planning Commission on waterfront issues. These activities included leading planning for new residential developments in Cincinnati's East End neighborhood (Halperin 1998) and providing input on The Banks plan, though the council increasingly felt excluded from the process (*Cincinnati Enquirer* 1998). After more than two decades of work, the RAC limped toward the millennium with limited funding and an unclear mission. Viewing an opportunity, however, local river industries began to coalesce around the RAC as a vehicle that could represent them.

In 2002 Eric Doepke, a local landscape architect who had been involved in the creation of Sawyer Point Park, among many other area projects, led efforts to reconstitute the faltering Riverfront Advisory Council as the River Advisory Council. In relaunching the RAC, Doepke wanted to improve river trade efficiency as well as watershed management, issues that he felt were slipping off the radar with all the attention on developing The Banks. While primarily drawing participants from the Cincinnati side of the river, Doepke pushed for the new RAC to have a regional focus, encompassing Ohio, Kentucky, and Indiana. Through reports on river industries, site mapping, and prototypes for new river terminals, the RAC brought attention to the "working river," raising awareness among local officials and business leaders about the city's river transportation economy.

The reconstituted RAC's efforts increasingly focused on one primary goal: expanding the boundaries of the federal government's definition of the Cincinnati port area. The existing port designation included just twenty-six miles in the immediate vicinity of the city. New RAC participants agreed that an expanded port area would help official statistics better capture local economic activity on the river. Doepke and others also believed this redesignation would improve local cooperation and help promote the area, since an expanded port zone would bump the entire region up the national trade rankings. In 2000 Huntington, West Virginia, had expanded its port to almost two hundred miles of riverfront located in West Virginia, Kentucky, and Ohio, including stretches on the Ohio River, Big Sandy River, and Kanawha River. The redesignated Port of Huntington Tri-State became the country's largest inland river port and the envy of its neighbors. The process required significant resources and coordination, working with officials from all the implicated counties as well as the U.S. Army Corps of Engineers in order to submit an application for redesignation.

Despite continued discussions, the RAC made little progress toward redesignating the port. I met Doepke at his office in the posh suburb of Hyde Park, cluttered with mementos from past projects. In his view, the main issue was a lack of trust among riverfront industries:

> At the meetings of the RAC, you would have industrial people who owned their machines, terminals, all of it, but they were all looking like frogs, their eyeballs were just this far over the table . . . never saying anything, just trying to suck up everything they could, and they couldn't get their eyes off that jackass over there who's that guy who screwed us out of a nickel per ton. In other words, they were in their competitive mode.

Doepke urged these businesses to embrace collaboration. In 2011 a group of river industries formed the Central Ohio River Business Association (CORBA). According to CORBA's executive director, Eric Thomas, the RAC had been a fundamental first step, but he and many of his colleagues from the private sector had actually had to take the initiative to get things done: "We just got frustrated, because we come here to this [RAC] meeting every month, we talk about issues but we're not doing anything, we don't have any money to get anything done. We need an organization that can take these issues and do something with it."

CORBA took the lead on the redesignation process in conjunction with the Port of Greater Cincinnati Development Authority and the Northern Kentucky Port Authority, building on the RAC's previous efforts and always acknowledging Doepke's early contributions. They were finally successful in early 2015, winning recognition of the expanded Ports of Cincinnati & Northern Kentucky. The new port stretches 226.5 miles across fifteen counties (including along the Licking River). In 2016 government statisticians declared the new Ports of Cincinnati & Northern Kentucky as the busiest inland river port and thirteenth-largest nationally. The redesignation has subsequently garnered significant attention, with the Mid-America Freight Coalition declaring others could "learn from these efforts in Ohio and Kentucky" (Jermier et al. 2016). CORBA moved into promoting the new Ports of Cincinnati & Northern Kentucky as a major shipping destination, with flexible intermodal facilities and access to major industrial regions.

With the redesignation completed, CORBA shifted its focus to raising local, national, and international awareness of Cincinnati's shipping facilities, as well as moving to new projects, including a port asset inventory and debating potential investments in new docking capacities. The decline of coal shipping, long the most important commodity moved on the river, had led to decreasing Ohio River freight tonnage. The Ports of Cincinnati & Northern Kentucky moved thirty-eight million tons of cargo in 2018, which was close to a ten-million-ton decrease from a decade prior, largely driven by the drop in coal shipments. CORBA forecast this could drop another seven million tons by 2027 as local coal plants went offline. A decline of this scale would move The Ports down to being only the fourth- or fifth-largest inland port in the country, a sobering prospect for a group that had only recently acceded to the top spot (Byrne 2020). This change, and the unlikely possibility that coal would return to its previous highs, pushed CORBA to explore alternatives.

These included container-on-barge technology, which could carry consumer goods and would enable the region to develop freight alternatives to the bulk and break-bulk commodities that make up the vast majority of river trade presently. In addition, the local CORBA leadership began contacting other ports and trade associations along the river to discuss the formation of an M-70 Coalition. In 2007 the federal Maritime Administration (MARAD), part of the Department of Transportation, established a Marine Highway Program to encourage freight carriers to move from the overburdened highway system to rivers and coastal waters. MARAD renamed the Ohio River the "M-70 Highway," linking it symbolically with Interstate 70 running parallel to the north. The M-70 Coalition would similarly lead a push to bring new cargo to the Ohio River and coordinate shared promotional efforts.

The Working River and the Luxury River

The Hall of Mirrors is located on the third floor of the Netherlands Plaza Hotel, an extravagant Art Deco building in downtown Cincinnati. According to the hotel's website, the Hall of Mirrors is "often referred to as the most beautiful ballroom in the Midwest," a masterpiece of gilded accents and diffuse lighting. Unsurprisingly, the Hall of Mirrors has been the preferred site for gatherings of powerful people in Cincinnati since it opened in 1931, and thus has featured prominently in the history of the Ohio River and the Cincinnati riverfront. For decades, the Ohio Valley Improvement Association regularly held its meetings there, and in 1948 the eight Ohio Valley governors met there to sign the ORSANCO compact.

In November 2016 the Waterways Council, the national advocacy organization for navigation infrastructure, came to Cincinnati to host its national convention in the Hall of Mirrors. Having the convention in Cincinnati was a homecoming of sorts for the group since it traces its roots back to the Ohio Valley Improvement Association (OVIA), which was founded in Cincinnati in 1895.[2] And just like at the OVIA's first meeting in Cincinnati in 1895, the convention audience featured a mix of rivermen, U.S. Army Corps of Engineers officers, and industry groups including grain wholesalers and cement corporations. They had assembled to discuss the future of the country's inland navigation system, both in terms of infrastructural needs and to forecast the future freight possibilities. At the meeting, I ran into Errin Howard, director of the RiverWorks Discovery educational program, who ushered me over to meet Charlie Jones, nonagenarian chairman of Amherst Madison, a towing and river terminal company based in West Virginia. Jones had been a member of the OVIA from a young age and was happy to regale me with some of his earliest memories of the organization, including attending the massive celebrations in 1929 for the opening of the lock and dam system on the Ohio River.

Moreover, the tone of this most recent Waterways Council convention echoed those early OVIA meetings: an undercurrent of tension fed by multiple years of declining tonnage on the river. The era of King Coal, which had largely been responsible for driving Ohio River trade over the past century, appeared to be ending due to a combination of increased regulations, inroads by natural gas production, and fear of looming transitions to renewable energy sources. Throughout the event, participants were once again pondering how to revive river trade, including discussions of container-on-barge technologies, pushing for more steel freight, and increasing shipments of grain and other products through the expanded Panama Canal.

Proceedings at the current Waterways Council convention were dominated by grizzled veterans of the river trades, many from long-time river families, as well as others who started as deckhands and worked their way up to management roles. Drawn from across the country, they greeted each other as old friends, sharing stories and joking with one another. Reverend David Rider, head of the Seamen's Church Institute, mingled with the crowd in the Hall of Mirrors—his organization has been dedicated to the care of these river workers since 1834, providing counseling and spiritual support, as well as more recently offering professional training and safety certifications. The rivermen were joined by engineers and administrators from the U.S. Army Corps of Engineers (USACE) and from the Maritime Administration command, many in full uniform. Governmental representatives provided updates about their latest plans for the rivers and were eager to reconnect with river business owners.

At lunch, a program honored a USACE Ohio River district officer who was being assigned to a new role. The business owners and USACE officials traded compliments throughout the program, the engineers citing how much they relied on river industries to manage the river and make it productive while the Waterways Council leadership profusely thanked the USACE officer for his fine service and dedication. Throughout the event, this partnership reinscribed the "working river" as a space of white masculinity, based on the combination of governmental technical expertise and parochial industrial knowledge from small-scale regional businesses. As the two groups reaffirmed their bonds, they also demonstrated their commitment to preserving the preeminence of freight navigation on the Ohio River, even in the face of competing claims made by residential developers and environmentalists.[3]

Despite the central role played by the rivermen and male USACE officers, close to 20 percent of the audience were women. A handful came from river companies, and others from governmental offices, but many had backgrounds in communications and the nonprofit sector. In their roles, many of these women were leading public education efforts to connect more people with the "working river": what it contributes to the economy, how the lock and dam system functions, and the possibilities for careers in the sector. Errin Howard's organization, RiverWorks Discovery, has a mission to educate children and adults about river commerce in conjunction with the cultural and ecological histories of the river. Howard has built up RiverWorks Discovery, based in Cincinnati, to reach thousands of individuals each year—including a million-dollar exhibit that tours the region, storyteller programs, and river career days for high school students. The organization is part of National Mississippi River Museum & Aquarium but draws most of its support from more than 150 private sponsors, including almost all of the most prominent river businesses in the Mississippi and Ohio Valleys.

According to Howard, the origin of RiverWorks Discovery, launched in 2004, came from the realization that there is "a disconnect between the public and what they knew and understood about river transportation." Many individuals, even from river communities like Cincinnati, had little idea that there was a lock and dam system that made the river navigable year-round, or the multiple other infrastructures needed to make the river economically profitable. "The idea behind [RiverWorks Discovery] is if you can educate the public, then they can make informed decisions when they go to vote, you know, to support infrastructure on the river." Many women have stepped into similar public relations roles on the "working river," acting as intermediaries between river businesses and communities that have largely forgotten about them or see them as antiquated.

The Banks features a similar gendered division of labor. Despite representing a "luxury river" that is defined in many ways as the opposite of the "working river," there is a tendency for women in public relations roles to promote the successes of the behind-the-scenes work of men. City officials have relied on technical and administrative expertise to move The Banks project forward over more than two decades, with the vast majority of these roles occupied by older white men such as John Schneider, John Deatrick, and others with backgrounds in engineering, urban planning, and private-sector development. Unlike with the rivermen, most of these individuals drew on extensive professional backgrounds. These different formations of practical and expert knowledge mapped onto white masculinity in contingent and interconnected ways, which also filtered through the relative class interests represented by the smaller-scale "working river" enterprises and massive capital-intensive projects of the "luxury river."

While I was in the field, the two primary organizations responsible for continuing to advance The Banks were the master developer Carter and The Banks Public Partnership, which coordinated the city and county's infrastructural efforts, primarily the construction of the garages that served as platforms for The Banks' apartments, hotels, and commercial spaces.[4] The Joint Banks Steering Committee, the group of local officials and corporate executives advising on the project, convinced John Deatrick to return to the city in 2008 to manage The Banks Public Partnership (he had moved to Washington, DC, after completing the Fort Washington Way project). By the time I returned to Cincinnati in 2015, Deatrick had already moved into directing the city's new streetcar project. His role on The Banks had been taken over by Phil Beck, who had a background in architectural design and construction management. The Banks Public Partnership and the developer Carter collaborated closely, coordinating on construction schedules, producing public progress reports, and determining design elements, down to the shape of the curbs and the style of street lamps.

I joined Phil Beck and Marie Gemelli-Carol in The Banks Public Partnership offices, a double-wide trailer tucked into a corner of The Banks footprint that was still awaiting the construction of its parking garage platform, meaning it sat two stories below street-level compared to the other parts of The Banks. Gemelli-Carol, president of Starboard Strategy Corp., described how she became involved in the project, responding to a request for proposals in 2008 to design and implement a public relations plan for The Banks Public Partnership. According to Gemelli-Carol, it was a challenging environment in 2008, first because of the economic downturn, and also because of the inherent difficulties of having to make "concrete sexy" as well as a deeply ingrained belief among the public that The Banks would never happen. "So we came in, and we did some baseline research. We decided that, yeah, people still believed that nothing would ever be built." In response they "took every dollar we could in our budget to show people that it was happening. You don't argue with someone in words, to say 'Oh that's not true,' you know. What you do is you continue to show them. So we tried to tell the story [of The Banks progress]."

Whereas the Waterways Council prefers to project a depersonalized space of river transportation, administered by experienced USACE technocrats and rivermen, the strategy for The Banks has been to project a lively space of fun, relaxation, and coming together, a "magnet for anybody who wants to come downtown and reconnect with the riverfront," in Gemelli-Carol's words. From planning to implementation, the focus has been on highlighting diversity, such as the inclusion of minority- or women-owned businesses in construction and in promoting the multicultural crowd regularly found at The Banks. According to Gemelli-Carol, no one would ever have to "stage" a photo at The Banks to highlight diversity, because it is always on display whenever anyone comes downtown. The combination of technical expertise and development knowledge at The Banks, which Gemelli-Carol and Starboard Strategies interpreted for the public, told a very different story of what the "luxury river" represented to Cincinnati in contrast to the Ports of Cincinnati & Northern Kentucky.

The "working river" is represented as a matter-of-fact space of industry, where aesthetic concerns are subordinate to economic interests. Meeting with terminal owners whose businesses were largely located along the stretch of riverfront stretching west from downtown, they were proud of their ugly enterprises, with "tank farms" for chemical shipments and durable but temporary-looking hoop buildings for storing bulk commodities. They constantly reminded me that it was the river industries that had built Cincinnati and stressed their long roots on the riverfront, with one pointing out to me an on-site loading crane that had been in operation since the 1930s. If the "working river" is a gritty pragmatic vision of the river, the "luxury river" is its inverse, where spaces like The Banks and the cluster of high-end riverfront condominiums extending to the east of downtown celebrate the natural beauty and pleasure-driven side of the Ohio River, with parks, exciting shops, and desirable residences. The developers and engineers I spoke with from The Banks were eager to show how the project represented a new era, solving issues that had long made it difficult to live near the Ohio River.

Claiming the Riverfront

The Banks and the Ports of Cincinnati & Northern Kentucky both strongly assert their rights to the riverfront. Advocates for each believe their projects represent the most practical and productive use of riverfront space. Despite their differences, both projects are deeply rooted in the same infrastructural histories of the Ohio River and the riverfront, shaping how they build relationships with the Ohio River and with one another. The systems developed for navigation, for flood control, and for pollution mitigation are an ever-present reference for both projects. At times celebrated and in other instances haunting, these histories are obviously there but only obliquely discussed. The elite class formations that led efforts to create each of these infrastructure systems have subsequently become embedded in these very systems. Local river industries played a critical role in the building of the Ohio River navigation system, while planning professionals were closely tied to designing flood protection infrastructure for the central riverfront. The perpetuation of each elite class formation is tied to the maintenance of these infrastructures, sustaining both the infrastructure and these elite power bases.

At the same time, the interest of elite groups in riparian infrastructures for the Ohio River has been cumulative rather than successive. Elite class formations are not replacing one another as they establish infrastructural relationships with the Ohio River, but rather adding new layers on top of existing arrangements. The result has been that multiple elite groups claim overlapping relationships to the Ohio River and its riparian infrastructure. River industries can point to the Ohio River lock and dam system to legitimize their arguments, while urban planners can claim flood resilience as part of their right to the riverfront. As one of my informants noted, the riverfront area represents the densest concentration of infrastructure in the city, from sewage to roadways to fiber optics. It contains a disconcertingly complex tangle of different infrastructures that many stakeholders have laid claim to over the years.

This has turned the riverfront area into a morass of relationships, both technological and social, exactly because of its critical role in linking the city and the Ohio River. With this increasing density of infrastructural systems, the riverfront has become more costly to occupy and develop. A local development agency representative told me that due to these past infrastructural legacies, the cost of developing property in Queensgate, a riverfront neighborhood just west of downtown, is roughly twenty times more than the local average. These connections shape the ways that advocates for both The Banks and The Ports of Cincinnati & Northern Kentucky understand and justify their projects, at times in complementary ways and in other instances with divergent viewpoints despite this shared framework.

Both the "luxury river" and "working river" projects prominently feature references to the city's navigational history. For the river industries, it is woven into their daily realities. Terminal owners, barge operators, and other river business elites see themselves as maintaining the traditions of river work that were fundamental to the city's early economy, even as they modernize the industry and incorporate new technologies. In conversations they reaffirm the danger and excitement of "working the river" and interacting with volatile Old Man River. This context makes their jobs more unpredictable than other sectors, reliant on common sense and intuition rather than any particular professional formation.

At The Banks, navigational references predominate in the built landscape, continuing themes first established in the adjacent riverfront parks to its east. While the old sports stadium had been an enclosed bowl, providing an isolating experience for fans, the new baseball stadium opened a wide panorama toward the river so attendees can watch boats pass on the Ohio River, and incorporates steamboat smokestacks in the outfield wall, which belch smoke whenever a player hits a home run. A walkway adjacent to the stadium is home to the National Steamboat Monument, opened in 2002, which includes a massive paddlewheel replica, lofted in the air and surrounded by twenty-four motion-activated pylons that play historic river noises, such as boat whistles, songs, and the shouts of boat hands, re-creating the soundscapes of the river. In the new Smale Riverfront Park, an interactive feature shows how water moves through a scale model of The Banks, including a functional miniature lock

FIGURE 4.1. A lock and dam model placed in front of a relief map of The Banks' grid at Smale Riverfront Park. The unpredictable flow of water is also supposed to pay homage to the history of flooding in the area (Beall 2015). Photograph by author.

and dam built in front of the scaled-down riverfront. All of these references allude to the area's steamboating history as well as its ongoing river shipping activities.

A focus for the Cincinnati Parks Department has been constructing a public marina in front of The Banks. Long-time efforts to create a docking facility for pleasure craft on the Central Riverfront had twice led to the use of wharf boats (converted from a tugboat and a barge) that could be moved during the winter, but both proved largely unpopular and ultimately sank (C. Smith 2016). The newest proposed marina would provide year-round service at an accessible location, attracting pleasure boaters from all across the region to The Banks. Any visitor to the proposed marina would be able to dock in the central riverfront area and walk into the city to enjoy The Banks or the Central Business District.

The incorporation of the historic river reflects the sustained interest in a steamboat "golden age" and its links to modern-day navigation. Proposals dating back to the 1960s recommended including reconstructed steamboats on the shore, even placing one such boat in a pool of water, because it "would lend authenticity" (Stanley Consultants 1967, 37) to the site. The Tall Stacks Music, Arts, and Heritage Festival, held from 1988 to 2006, brought steamboats back to the riverfront and enabled millions of visitors to step back in time. The excitement around bringing a marina to the riverfront has similarly been tied to reopening "the south door to the city," according to one present-day advocate: a return to the origins of the city.

On the part of riverfront industries, there is a feeling of a double standard. According to one river business operator I spoke with,

> You look at the Chamber of Commerce's website, you look at REDI's website, you walk down to the offices of City Hall or whatever, and people like to have pictures of the boats and the barges.[5] You know and everybody likes to say, "Gee we're part of this great riverfront, look at our beautiful riverfront and look at these boats that go by," and so on and so forth. But then when you start saying, "Oh but by the way that boat needs land at that terminal down there to unload sand and gravel and it's a 12-, it's a 24-hour operation, and they're banging and things, making noise all night, and having some dust issues or whatever." Now all of a sudden it's "Oh, wait wait wait, we like to see the boats, we just don't need to see them here."

This ambivalence leads to friction between marine industries and residential developments along the riverfront. The city government is often viewed as disinterested or even actively against the interests of navigation. One isolated terminal facility, located to the east of The Banks, has had several years of disputes with residents who have occupied new condominiums and townhouses in the area since the early 2000s. The city has rezoned the area to restrict the terminal's activities and ability to expand in the future, leading to an unsuccessful lawsuit on the part of the port enterprise to overturn the regulations. While this represents an extreme case, it is well known among the marine industry community as a clear instance of the lack of appreciation for the "working river."

Navigation is not the only issue that connects The Banks and the Ports of Cincinnati & Northern Kentucky. Flooding is another major concern. For its part, The Banks is presented as an elegant solution to the flooding issues that have confounded riverfront developers for more than a hundred years. The garage platforms—already one of the largest contiguous parking facilities in the country and still growing—are the primary response to the issues of flooding. These garages allow high water to pass under The Banks without affecting street life. By emphasizing a flood-resilient approach rather than trying to keep out floodwaters, The Banks is able to work in concert with both the natural and regulatory environments to create a sustainable development. This is seen as especially important in the context of climate change that will likely bring more extreme flooding events (Deatrick 2015).

The parking garages let the Ohio River, when in flood stage, flow through them without disrupting the area's floodplain storage capacity or causing backflow, accommodating the river rather than relying on costly alternatives like energy-hungry pumps to push it back. Phil Beck, the Banks Public Partnership project executive, described it as a kind of infrastructural "martial arts, where you just sort of, you don't resist [the river]. . . . We're just sort of moving with it." The parking garages thus create development podiums raised above the five-hundred-year flood zone, which can be sold to the master developer as air lots outside of the flood zone. This means tenants are not required to hold federal flood insurance, reducing rental costs significantly.

This flood-resilient approach used at The Banks is a point of pride for the engineers and developers. Most presentations of the project start with the area's flood history, describing how the innovative use of garage platforms finally enabled development to take place on the riverfront. Reminders of flooding are built in the infrastructure as well, including a staircase from the bottom of the parking garage up to street level that marks the crests of nine historic floods, as well as the heights of ten, twenty-five, fifty, one hundred, and five-hundred-year floods.

Still, flood resilience is not a core message that The Banks development team or The Banks Public Partnership pushes out when marketing the project. In their view, the association with flooding would generate unnecessary doubts, especially since the modern river monitoring system will give at least a two-day warning if the parking garage needs to be evacuated. According to a lead developer for the project, since tenants are not required to sign up for flood insurance, the topic does not organically arise as part of leasing (though commercial renters tend to be savvier), and they are unlikely to bring it up. According to Beck, "I guarantee you, if you got out there, you're up anywhere on [street level of] our project, maybe, I don't know what percent, but probably over half of the people you talk to, if you say, 'Do you realize there's a two-story parking garage below you right now?,' they'll be like 'Huh?' Most people don't make that connection." While The Banks Public Partnership team is interested in increasing awareness of the parking garage to generate more revenue, there is less need to inform the public that it serves a fundamental flood-related function.

For their part, river businesses have long argued that their port facilities were one of the few riverfront uses that could adapt to regular flooding. Many of the businesses are located directly in the floodplain. The bulk commodi-

FIGURE 4.2. Staircase in The Banks parking garage showing past flood levels. Photograph by author.

ties the ports deal in, such as pig iron and coal, can be immersed in floodwaters without significant issues (though newer bulk commodities like fertilizers pose their own challenges). And flood management plans ensure that most companies can continue operating even during high water. The owner of one facility drove me around his site, pointing out why the operation, which specializes in coal, is able to continue with deliveries even during major high-water events, ensuring that customers receive their shipments on time. Similar to The Banks, CORBA and its port members make little overt use of their flood resilience to market the Ports of Cincinnati & Northern Kentucky. It is an important feature of their worksites but does little to attract business. The few river businesses located outside of the five-hundred-year flood zone are much more likely to market this fact than the other way around.

Perhaps surprisingly though, river businesses are eager to market their environmental credentials when talking about the Ports of Cincinnati & Northern Kentucky. While manufacturing and logistics companies are often portrayed as polluters, CORBA promotes the environmental benefits that come with shipping by barge, since the energy costs per ton mile of freight are significantly lower compared to rail and tractor trailers. According to CORBA's executive director Eric Thomas, the use of barge transportation "alleviates congestion off the highway, which also serves to take the highest polluting mode of transport [trucking] . . . out of the picture, and move it over to the least polluting, which is water. The same with rail to water." Part of this strategy to promote the river as a more environmentally friendly option is represented by the MARAD's M-70 designation. Renaming the Ohio River as the M-70 repositions it as a "green highway," an alternative to the "crumbling" interstate highway and rail systems. According to one river business owner, MARAD's M-70 designation is a way to communicate that the river is an efficient and greener space of transport, as well as to support new approaches like container-on-barge technologies. RiverWorks Discovery also spreads this message, comparing the environmental impacts of river barges versus rail or trucking. Errin Howard highlights the energy efficiency of shipping by river as well as other environmentally sensitive work the industry does, such as on-board recycling programs, organizing riverbank cleanups, and using biodegradable chemicals onboard its vessels.

In terms of The Banks, water pollution plays a less clear-cut role in how the project is promoted. Certainly, most individuals on the development and engineering side recognize that improvements in water quality have been a key factor in enabling the reinvention of the riverfront as a residential and recreational space, even though the vast majority of The Banks' visitors have little direct interaction with the water. Still, this is in line with representations of The Banks as a "healthy" destination according to John Schneider, with wide sunny streets and a gentle slope that draws pedestrians to the river view. The Smale Riverfront Park is fundamental to this perception, helping The Banks cultivate an image as an attractive green space where people can go to relax and enjoy the river view. In recognition of this importance to the success of The Banks, all tenants pay into a fund that helps maintain the park and preserve its green space. At the same time, local groups put on events like Paddlefest (a kayaking and canoeing festival) and the Great Ohio River Swim (a short swimming race across the Ohio River, departing from The Banks to a point near the Kentucky shore and then heading back to The Banks). The Banks and the Ohio River are portrayed as a package offering, where one comes down to the riverfront to enjoy amenities such as bars and shopping but also to connect with nature via the river.

New Approaches to Infrastructure on the Riverfront

The individuals behind The Banks and the Ports of Cincinnati & Northern Kentucky have in numerous ways continued the legacies of earlier groups, building their claims to the riverfront through their relationships to flooding, pollution, and navigation. Yet, the past two decades have seen an important transition in terms of the connections between infrastructure, technical expertise, redevelopment, and the Ohio River on the Cincinnati riverfront. Riparian infrastructure has long mediated relationships with the Ohio River as well as between elite class formations—bringing them together, often in collaboration and occasionally in conflict. In the current moment though, riparian infrastructure not only serves as a focal point for relationship building but also sees elite groups blur the distinctions between expert and practical economic development approaches. Increasingly, technical experts are comfortable adopting developer arguments, and developers are eager to tackle technical problems like erosion and community health. As described at the beginning of this chapter, these rationales go beyond just, for instance, a realtor imitating what an engineer might say, to instead using infrastructure as a means to simultaneously present market-oriented and technocratic logics as interdependent.

This is not to argue that redevelopment knowledge and technical expertise are merging in practice to become a new hybrid formation. In fact, many of the individuals I spoke to continued to point to the differences between their fields—particularly between engineers and developers—as well as the difficulties in bringing them together to collaborate. According to John Schneider, "I think there's always a struggle in infrastructure between the economists, which I support, and the engineers. The economists ask the kind of critical question, 'Why are we doing it this way?' while engineers will just say, 'How can we build it the cheapest? How can we make it the safest?' You know, all that stuff." Another individual described the issue as, "Engineers don't see in gray. They see in black or white. Either it's on or it's off. It's the solution, and this is . . . the best solution based upon their experience and their professional development and their knowledge." One development official I spoke to, when I mentioned my conversations with engineers, simply said, "My condolences." For their part, the engineers and other technical experts I spoke with largely viewed developers as impractical but necessary partners. Throughout projects to create new infrastructure, they are often engaged in what one engineer termed a "dance" between the two sides to secure the information and resources necessary to proceed with work, or in the case of regulatory functions, to ensure that legal requirements were being followed.

Throughout my fieldwork, informants were eager to interpret my interests as conforming to one or the other of their respective viewpoints. Many individuals working in development typically seized on my Cincinnati upbringing and admitted passion for the city to assume I was a booster. They believed I was most interested in understanding the economic impact of the projects we were discussing and that I wanted to ultimately contribute in my own way to local growth. Many of the individuals I interviewed who have a more technical background saw me as a fellow expert. They shared research with me and sought to engage me as an interlocutor similarly concerned with the abstract problems they faced. One waterways lobbyist even told me, "We need more eggheads like you."

My experience with the ways individuals sorted my background pointed to the continued importance of these categories in everyday interactions around waterfront infrastructure, as well as the stark divides in the ways people perceive them. Phil Beck, as lead at The Banks Public Partnership, was very grateful for his professional development in both the technical field of architectural design and the more development-oriented field of construction management. "With my background, I can kind of step in the middle of certain discussions and . . . play referee and figure out exactly what the situation is and how we address it." Such acts of translation and mediation are necessary between developers, engineers, and other stakeholders due to their significant professional differences.[6]

Even given these perceived divides, government officials are increasingly presenting arguments to the public that the conjoining of technical and development logics is fundamental to the success of new projects. The Banks is often portrayed as being made possible only because of a special collaboration between technical and development actors. Cincinnati's urban elites had long seen the central riverfront as an intractable problem, since it contained what was obviously prime real estate but, according to the common view, was limited from reaching its full potential by regular flooding.

Deatrick, the previous director at The Banks Public Partnership, wrote an article for the journal *Water Management* about the benefits of flood-resilient redevelopment and The Banks' parking garage infrastructure. In it, he argues, "Since the founding of Cincinnati on the banks of the Ohio River in 1788, the city's flood-prone central riverside area has been exploited in multiple waves of development, none of which were viewed a success—until now" (Deatrick 2015, 85). In this perspective, the move to build flood-resilient parking garage infrastructure finally unlocked the development potential of the area by also dealing with the more technical issue of preserving floodplain capacity and maintaining a harmonious relationship with the river. The parking garages resolved both issues in one simple solution, managing the flood threat while also creating new air property rights above the parking garage that can be efficiently developed. Furthermore, by generating revenue, the garages help ensure the infrastructure itself is financially sustainable.

The combination of technical expertise and development knowledge deployed at The Banks is seen as a major breakthrough. According to Beck, "Why did it take us two hundred years to figure this out? It just did." It is not just one or the other—many previous proposals could have resolved at least some of these issues—but the integrated approach that makes The Banks a success. In his article, Deatrick describes the importance to the project of "integrating [flood-resilience] into a master plan and, in turn, how it made a dramatic difference to the development of the [Central Riverfront] and turned it from a regional liability to a point of regional pride" (87). For Deatrick and The Banks team, without flood resilience there would be no redevelopment, and without redevelopment there could be no flood resilience. Even though Deatrick, Beck, and other experts involved in the project did not approach it primarily from a development viewpoint, they have been able to powerfully articulate why these two approaches go hand-in-hand and how careful infrastructural design was the key to unlocking the problems posed by the central riverfront.

The effect has been to imbue infrastructure with the capacity to serve as a cure-all, ready to fix any ill. In this usage, infrastructure is an extremely potent and open-ended symbol, its "promise" represented as both a public good and a private good, resolving technical as well as development issues (Anand, Gupta, and Appel 2018). Buoyed by both public and private sources of support, as of 2009 "spending on infrastructure [constituted] the biggest investment boom in history, measured as share of world GDP" (Flyvbjerg 2009, 362). The literature on public-private partnerships has already charted in-depth the allure of approaches bringing together governmental and private-sector actors (Boardman, Greve, and Hodge 2015; Brash 2011), but the reconfiguration of Cincinnati's riparian infrastructure in many ways exceeds these parameters. Whereas infrastructure has very frequently been represented as the "public" component of public-private partnerships, this is not necessarily the case in terms of this new, more flexible approach to infrastructure. The Banks represents a classic example of a public-private partnership, but the Ports of Cincinnati & Northern Kentucky shows a very different path to the infrastructural interweaving of development and technical goals.

Unlike The Banks, there is no discrete location that one can visit with regard to the Ports of Cincinnati & Northern Kentucky. Rather, the redesignated area brings together a collection of disparate river businesses stretched out over 226.5 miles of shoreline on the Ohio River and Licking River. Many of these businesses, organized through CORBA, work closely with the U.S. Army Corps of Engineers and the Waterways Council to advocate for and maintain the lock and dam system on the river. At the same time, they are deeply suspicious of government intervention, with river business owners hotly debating efforts to seek federal support to develop port facilities integrating container-on-barge technologies. According to one terminal director, "We'd be more than happy to put the capital in to go ahead and start unloading [containers]; we'll do it, if there's a deal, we'll do it. What frustrates us a little bit, is sometimes that you know there's government money, and . . . private industry does pretty good. Between us and our competitors in town, all of us want more business, so there's not enough to go around now. There's no need to put public money into another dock that's just going to compete with private industry." For this terminal director, instead of focusing on attracting government funds, CORBA should focus on marketing to bring more business to the Ports of Cincinnati & Northern Kentucky. "Get the business to Cincinnati, then we can all compete for it . . . as opposed to sponsoring an outfit to go bring something in."

Eric Thomas, CORBA's executive director, agreed about the importance of marketing the region in a way that brought attention to the river: "From a marketing perspective . . . everybody likes to brag about the fact that Cincinnati is within a day's drive of 60 percent of the population of the United States and 55 percent of the manufacturing. So what? It's a spot on the map and you can draw a circle. My question is, what does that really mean? And what is the impact of the river?" All these advantages meant nothing if no one knows what Cincinnati has to offer.

Thomas believes that an important first step in this process has been the development of CORBA's Port Asset Inventory, an effort to collect and make accessible data on the region's river industries. Thomas and CORBA envisioned the project to provide logistics information that can be used to attract more commerce to the region, promoting the area's unique local capacities. Called the Central Ohio River Information System (CORIS) and developed in conjunction with the Ohio-Kentucky-Indiana Regional Council of Governments, the database provides granular information about all the river businesses found throughout the Ports of Cincinnati & Northern Kentucky (whether they are CORBA members or not).

In the past decade, Cincinnati has emerged as an important delivery and logistics hub. CORBA is eager to integrate itself as a vibrant part of this booming field. A pivotal part of this strategy has been the message that river businesses are a key component of the region's infrastructure. According to the

CORBA website, CORIS invites users to "explore infrastructure along the Central Ohio River," with an extensive list of the privately owned and operated ports along the Ohio River, sortable by dock type, storage facilities, and their links to other transportation systems like trucking and rail. The port inventory asset has helped reposition river businesses as vital infrastructure in and of themselves, with CORBA using CORIS to make visible and legitimize the presence of private infrastructure on the river.

Thomas has pushed the CORIS project and this infrastructure message through media outreach and public forums, arguing that for the region to effectively market its riparian infrastructure, local officials and the public at large need to understand what already exists. CORBA's infrastructuralization of the river businesses making up the Ports of Cincinnati & Northern Kentucky has driven home repeatedly the public function these port facilities serve, to the point that a reporter for the industry outlet *Marine Link*, in a feature article on CORBA, felt it was necessary to clarify that the group could not actually "officially sponsor projects needing public funds, e.g., serving as the 'public' half of a public-private partnership" (Ewing 2017), since even though it appeared to be acting like a public body, CORBA remains a private entity.

In this sense, this infrastructuralization of river industries can be thought of as a countercurrent (and complement) to the privatization of infrastructure, which seeks to transfer publicly owned infrastructure to private ownership. Instead, here CORBA asks for recognition of the public importance of private businesses, though stopping far short of pushing to transfer these businesses to public control. One of the ways the association has reinforced this argument is through enlisting supply chain and logistics experts from the University of Cincinnati and Northern Kentucky University to help people understand river traffic and legitimize efforts to improve and market the region's assets.

In my conversations with Thomas he insisted on the need to "get somebody analytically answering the question" of the river's impact. Even the much-celebrated redesignation of the Ports of Cincinnati & Northern Kentucky is fundamentally about expert analysis and legibility, involving U.S. Army Corps of Engineers statisticians compiling data about the activities of private river businesses. Like with The Banks, the Ports of Cincinnati & Northern Kentucky is built on the relationship between local river developers and technocratic experts from government and academia. Without one or the other, the Ports of Cincinnati & Northern Kentucky would not exist, literally in this case. Sustaining the ports' interdependence through the symbolic work of "infrastructure" is at the core of CORBA's efforts.

For locals, given this emerging emphasis on infrastructure that fuses together the public and private, it was thus not completely surprising when President Donald Trump visited the Cincinnati riverfront on June 7, 2017, to formally launch his infrastructure push. Infrastructure was a core part of Trump's economic message in both his presidential campaign and during his first administration, but he lauded it in a way that appeared baffling to many observers. On the one hand, he consistently framed infrastructure as a public good, necessary to ensure the country's national strength. His calls for increased federal investment and leadership to rebuild U.S. infrastructure often explicitly criticized past strategies to devolve infrastructural oversight responsibilities to the state or local level. These arguments are based on a form of managerial (though not necessarily scientific) expertise intended to preclude political debate, pointing out how Trump's experience as a builder makes him uniquely suited to these tasks. On the other hand, Trump sought to expand private investment in and control over U.S. infrastructure, as is common in many other countries, while also cutting or streamlining regulations involved in the process. In infrastructure, President Trump had thus found an ideal platform to promote his mixture of a nationalist managerial state and supply-side economics, referred to as Trumponomics.

Appearing at Rivertowne Marina on Cincinnati's East Side in 2017, Trump delivered his infrastructure speech with the Ohio River as a backdrop, the podium positioned so audience members could see a tugboat behind him, draped in a massive U.S. flag, and towing barges loaded with West Virginia coal. His speech led with populist themes about "rivers, like the beautiful Ohio River, [that] carry the lifeblood of our heartland," (Trump 2017, 4), and he made a pointed effort to celebrate the workers and businesses crucial "to help us build the roads, the bridges, the tunnels and the waterways of tomorrow," (1) while also criticizing neoliberal policies that had left infrastructures "crumbling" across the country.

President Trump went to great lengths to highlight the role of developers, inviting "a couple of the greatest builders in America, Steve Roth of Vornado [and] Richard Lefrak of Lefrak" (1) to join him on the stage. This was a marked departure from President Barack Obama's infrastructural message, which stressed new technologies, innovative engineering, and the importance of education (Obama 2010; Obama 2014). Given the location and the focus on waterways infrastructure, notably absent from Trump's speech were mentions of scientists or engineers, as well as any recognition of the U.S. Army Corps of Engineers. But, as Trump delved into praising river transportation, he repeated many of the expert supply chain and logistics arguments that CORBA and others deploy to justify the role of their businesses, stating: "The contents of just one nine-barge towboat, like the one behind me, carries the equivalent of 1,000 semi-tractor trailers," and "More than half of all the American steel is produced within 250 miles of where we're standing right now and its production depends on the inland waterway system" (Trump 2017, 4).

President Trump, much like CORBA and The Banks, pushed forward a new vision of infrastructure built on the interdependence of development knowledge and expertise. Even though each has their distinct arrangements, this emergent view of infrastructure has proven to be widely popular. Despite its blue-collar populist narrative, Trump's approach has also appealed to many members of the "petty bourgeoisie . . . small-business owners, accountants, and pharmacists" (Gusterson 2017, 212), who are invigorated by the patriotic overtones and appeals to free markets, while also feeling reassured by the reliance on business acumen and "analytical" arguments.

On the Cincinnati riverfront, President Trump's visit and a subsequent study of the region by the U.S. Department of Transportation invigorated CORBA, with Thomas stating, "It was a big deal for us to get that kind of prominent mention" (Paeth 2018). The Banks is also reaping the benefits of this fervent belief in infrastructure. Despite delays that saw Carter exit as master developer in 2017, the project has continued to receive massive support for its infrastructural work, resulting in more than $1.3 billion of public investment for the project through 2013 (Deatrick 2015).

This popularity of infrastructure on the Ohio River stands out when contrasted with other contemporary contexts across the globe. Many urban waterfronts are seen as locally and nationally important, but because of crippling state debt, the maintenance needed to make docks, buoys, and waterways economically productive has been lacking, leading to their decay (Bear 2015). Rather than a solution, investment in infrastructure has been seen as a threat to maximizing local revenues. Whereas in Cincinnati infrastructure is seen as a potent force capable of creating new value, infrastructure in these contexts is seen as an undesirable expense, a budget line to be reduced or eliminated to meet the needs of austerity.

Infrastructural Remedies

Through these efforts, infrastructure has gained a new kind of visibility. While sociologist Susan Leigh Star (1999) argues that infrastructure is meant to be invisible or taken for granted, more recent studies have pointed to the need to examine closely how infrastructure is made either invisible or visible in specific contexts (Carse 2012; Larkin 2013). Star's blanket claim has obvious limitations, but at the time it was written it had clear relevance in a neoliberal moment when the private sector far outshone the public sector, and when developers and technocrats relegated discussions about infrastructure and government redistribution to the background (Logan and Molotch 1987).

Clearly, in the current context, infrastructure has returned to the forefront once again, attracting significant new support and attention. It is not the sort of modernist awe-inspiring visibility that geographer Maria Kaika (2005) describes in her study of early twentieth century Greek water infrastructure, where massive dams adorned with classical architectural elements became the site of popular day trips for urban residents to marvel over, representing the victory of the technocratic state over nature. Rather, as infrastructure has become an increasingly flexible tool to bind together developmental and technocratic approaches, it is not the physical site of infrastructure that is so visible, but the act of creating and performing infrastructural functions that attracts attention and value.

For President Trump, the importance of the symbolic role of infrastructure was clear given that he continued to promote his infrastructure plan despite the fact that the "blue-collar" appeal of massive construction projects is often its role as a response to unemployment. During the first Trump administration the United States actually experienced historically high employment levels that would seem to make infrastructure investments less pressing. Infrastructure in this sense appears as the solution that actually goes in search of problems to resolve: "green infrastructure" enables "soft development," and "smart" infrastructure unlocks tech-driven urbanism, and "dynamic infrastructure" turns human waste into renewable energy. Infrastructure serves as a "promise of prosperity to come in spite of the ruins around us" (Venkatesan et al. 2017, 5), apparently brimming with different possibilities. This new symbolic role of infrastructure, rather than being associated exclusively with government investment, makes it accessible to a wide range of private and public actors, and moves beyond any one rationale for why infrastructure is necessary. While still understanding the agency and materiality of specific infrastructures as historically situated (Anand, Gupta, and Appel 2018), the multivalence of infrastructure requires attention as well in the current moment.

In this respect, the current configuration of infrastructure resembles midcentury discussions around housing in the United States.[7] After intense debate about the role of government in guaranteeing a right to housing during the Great Depression (Baxandall and Ewen 2000), the idea of housing that ultimately emerged relied on the private sector leading massive suburban expansion through heavy federal subsidy. This approach combined arguments about private and public benefits that made houses appear as the solution to a range of issues affecting the country, including uncertain economic growth, urban crowding, and the need to cultivate consumer demand. Much as the "house" became increasingly visible as a flexible way to resolve numerous problems in the post–World War II period, the new image of "infrastructure" has seen it portrayed as uniquely situated to resolve a variety of current predicaments of climate change, weak economic growth, and the racial wealth gap. This in turn has led to the embrace of infrastructure by a diverse and apparently conflicting range of actors, from the Obama administration to the Trump administration, and from The Banks to the Ports of Cincinnati & Northern Kentucky.

But, as historian George Lipsitz (2006) points out, despite claims that the new integrated governmental and private sector approach to housing would benefit everyone, the structural conditions of racism means it overwhelmingly accrued benefits to white communities. Ownership of construction companies on the production side, and, on the consumption side, preferential access to mortgages for white homebuyers, redlining, and urban renewal programs that failed to provide relocation services for displaced communities of color, among many other factors, shaped the uneven distribution of housing's benefits.

In terms of how "infrastructure" is presented today, even as it is argued that everyone will benefit from these projects, the reality is that the vast majority of decision-making power remains with the same groups that have always made determinations about the purpose, placement, and scale of infrastructure. The present-day arrangement for creating infrastructure in many ways closely resembles the conditions that produced the infrastructure projects led by the Ohio Valley Improvement Association (OVIA) and the Ohio River Valley Water Sanitation Commission (ORSANCO). Many of the older white men in leadership positions today, from both the technical and development fields, have family connections to the river that stretch back multiple generations.

My own background as a white male from Cincinnati, and in particular my interest in the history of the river, helped me connect with my elite informants in ways that would not have been possible otherwise, providing an entry point to conversations around governmental redistribution, private financing, and local power that are frequently hard to access for social scientists. Rather than as an external observer, many of my informants perceived me as someone equally interested in preserving the city's infrastructural heritage.[8] There have certainly been changes, as with the increased (if circumscribed) participation of women in these discussions, and the increasingly common use during this period of inclusion clauses for publicly funded projects, which stipulate the employment of a certain percentage of minority- or women-owned businesses on projects receiving tax dollars.

These new arrangements have done little to adjust how infrastructural transformations are conceived, negotiated, and maintained; elite class formations continue to use these projects to shape the urban environment to their ends and to meet their goals. When I spoke with John Schneider about the Fort Washington Way project, he emphasized how, after his proposal gained support from the powerful Cincinnati Business Committee, made up of the CEOs of the largest local corporations, the governor's office conveniently "found" $75 million that it had overlooked in the capital budget to advance the project. New support for infrastructure has not meant new power arrangements in deciding what does and does not represent a relevant public and private benefit. Currently, when local organizations and governments in metropolitan Cincinnati want to apply for support for infrastructure projects from the State of Ohio capital budget every two years, the requests must be routed through the same Cincinnati Business Committee, which determines whose requests will be forwarded to the state legislature for consideration.

These infrastructural improvements predominantly benefit wealthier and whiter communities, so that infrastructure becomes a key means of continuing to buttress privilege in Cincinnati. This is clearly the case for The Banks, where the level of investment has created a pressure for financial returns that are only available via luxury housing and hotels, high-end commercial tenants, and larger office tenants. The area has been transformed into an upscale space of consumption. The presence of the new riverfront park is meant to mitigate this exclusivity, yet it can only have limited impacts in terms of making the area accessible to the full community. It is clear that more intense infrastructural investment has been a critical prerequisite to shaping The Banks, as one developer I spoke to called it, as a "luxury brand." Similar developments enabled by new flood-resilient infrastructure now extend along Cincinnati's eastern riverfront, slowly pushing out the remaining pockets of low-income Black and white communities in the area (Halperin 1998). Similar developments are occurring in Northern Kentucky as well.

Meanwhile, the river businesses that make up the Ports of Cincinnati & Northern Kentucky portray themselves as the opposite face of this infrastructural gentrification. While The Banks is the "luxury river," the Ports of Cincinnati & Northern Kentucky represent the "working river." The ports' version of the riverfront, built around private infrastructure, is meant to be more accessible, providing career opportunities for low-income individuals and the possibility to grow the local economy through the logistics sector. However, ultimately, the terminal facility owners are primarily concerned with increasing the value of their business and property. Through its research on riparian infrastructure and its promotional activities, CORBA's port development strategy is enabling these local businesses to grow, and as they are more successful this will make riverfront property more costly and inaccessible, mirroring in many ways the processes taking place at The Banks and other riverfront residential redevelopments that make up the "luxury river."

The parallels between these groups were driven home for me when talking to a terminal operator, well known in the city because of his dispute with condominium owners and the city, who he argued was trying to zone him out of existence. This case is often taken up as an example of the lack of recognition and respect for what the "working river" contributes to the city. In our conversations, this terminal owner also mentioned that his own family had considered redeveloping their property with condominiums but building height restrictions had led them to abandon the plan as unprofitable compared to their current terminal facility. To this river operator, it obviously made good business sense to explore all the options. At the same time, this flexible approach undermines a claim that the infrastructures operated by river industries serve a public good beyond just the profit imperatives of individual business owners.

Under this emerging reconceptualization of infrastructure, these projects bring developers and experts ever closer together, so that it is unlikely what could be considered either a "development" or "expert" justification for an infrastructural project would be put forward by itself. Instead, it is more and more common to see an extended and heterogeneous list of outcomes that an infrastructural project will enable its backers to accomplish. This claim to integrate multiple objectives through a single infrastructural project, which several of my informants referred to as the "comprehensive approach," has proven very alluring, and more difficult for critics to dispute. The relationship between technocratic and developmental logics is often far from straightforward yet also incredibly persuasive in moving forward infrastructure proposals. Even as these engineers and developers compete for control in determining how infrastructure is built, they often reinforce each other and, increasingly, contribute to the perceived potency of infrastructure projects to resolve a broad spectrum of issues (Elyachar 2012). In understanding how assemblages form on the Cincinnati riverfront—that is, tracking the emergence of discordant groups that nonetheless share aligned trajectories around how to relate to the Ohio River—it is clear that infrastructure has increasingly played a central role in knitting together these broad, unstable networks of human and nonhuman actors.

As sustainability researcher Gwen Ottinger (2013) has shown through her study of a Louisiana oil refinery that saw significant local resistance due to health concerns, the company deployed a combination of both economic and expert rationales to stress that it would be taking a responsible and comprehensive approach, a tactic that was extremely successful in muting community pushback. Similarly, in Cincinnati the combination of technical and development expertise has increased public buy-in for these projects. Despite their presentation as a public good that will benefit everyone, these infrastructural projects have largely served to further reinforce white elite control over Cincinnati's built environment. The intermixing of development and expertise knowledge has reinforced white elite control over urban development as well as the conditions of daily life, thus creating and sustaining further forms of social exclusion in Cincinnati. Paradoxically, more infrastructure in places like the riverfront has corresponded with less tangible public control over this area, particularly in terms of the spaces of the river itself, as physical, economic, and bureaucratic entanglements surrounding each new infrastructure turn the landscape into a briar patch of cross-cutting regulations and vested interests. Within such densely layered infrastructural contexts, the capacity to move across and coordinate the operations of these different systems become increasingly important, a skill reserved largely to the elite class formations at the center of these riparian networks (Vertesi 2014).

Since the 1990s infrastructure in Cincinnati has moved from being an afterthought to now being presented as the perfect solution to a host of problems. The interlacing of development goals and technical capacities has been critical to this shift, as each new infrastructural project is accompanied by a magical laundry list of problems it will resolve. Fort Washington Way and The Banks purport to fix sewage problems, simplify traffic, promote public transportation, make flood problems a thing of the past, and on and on. The Ports of Cincinnati & Northern Kentucky claim to reduce pollution, increase transportation efficiency and employment, promote the city, and bring new trade opportunities. Through a planning process, developers and engineers make it seem as if they have considered every angle.

This tactic is beyond being apolitical. Rather, it welcomes public input and debate that can generate additional concerns to be resolved by infrastructure. The construction of Fort Washington Way provided a perfect example of this rationale. When some critics suggested that the project should consider whether light rail could use these routes in the future, or when others argued that ideally Fort Washington Way would be capped one day and enable further development of the potential air lots, the project engineers simply spent tens of millions of extra dollars on reinforcing foundations and expanding throughways. They justified these expenses as "foresight" so that these goals could potentially be realized one day and would save millions in the future (Ben 2010). Today, infrastructure is the solution that goes looking for problems, confident that every issue it can be claimed to resolve will only expand its coalition of supporters.

Conclusion

While this new vision of infrastructure has presented itself as a cure-all, it has done little to change relationships between the Cincinnati riverfront and Ohio River. This chapter has largely avoided a discussion of the Ohio River as an engaged actor in the processes described here. This strategy is to draw attention to the ways that these local projects that are integrating development and technical logics, such as The Banks and the Ports of Cincinnati & Northern Kentucky, have increasingly mediated direct relationships with the Ohio River. As numerous studies have shown, infrastructure has brought water into almost all aspects of urban life, intricately connecting the spaces of the city through pipes, reservoirs, water towers, and numerous other water production technologies (Kaika 2005; Swyngedouw 2004; Gandy 2014). The result has been to interpret the city as a "space of flows" where the impact of water's materiality (alongside the effects of many other nonhuman urban actors) makes it impossible to separate the urban from the natural (Kaika 2005).

In Cincinnati, while the materiality of water and associated infrastructure has increasingly shaped the city, the Ohio River itself has become more marginal. A 2018 article in the *Cincinnati Enquirer* about Paddlefest, the annual Ohio River kayaking and canoeing event, describes the river's role in these terms:

> Two scientists conducted a study where people watched a video of a group of people passing three basketballs in a circle. Half are dressed in white; half in black. Viewers are instructed to count the number of times a player in white passes the ball. While this is going on, a person in a gorilla suit walks into the middle of the game, beats its chest and walks off screen. Only about half of the people who watch the video notice the gorilla. And for 364 days a year, the Ohio River is sort of like that invisible gorilla of Cincinnati, [Paddlefest vol-

> unteer Jerry] Schulte said. It's there, a background of our daily lives. But do we actually notice it? Do we actually see it? (Smith 2018)

Elite groups have moved the physical spaces of the Ohio River farther and farther away from everyday life, even as it has become increasingly important as a setting for urban redevelopment projects in Cincinnati. The Banks and the Ports of Cincinnati & Northern Kentucky represent in many ways a culmination of this process. In vastly different ways, they have positioned the Ohio River as an external object removed from everyday life, while simultaneously increasing its visibility in the city.

The Banks represents the "luxury river" as an object of visual consumption, to be enjoyed from a distance but not up close. One developer termed this view the city's "southern draw," the fact that in recent decades the urban gaze had been pulled back to the river as a beautiful natural space (after decades of pollution abatement). Urban developers cultivated this perspective, building thousands of condominiums and townhouses designed around stunning views of the river. The Banks is a particularly strong example, bringing the river as near as possible without encouraging direct contact. Smale Riverfront Park almost disappears as it descends to the river, with patchy clumps of grass and litter predominating along a muddy shore that no one wants to explore. Meanwhile, the Ports of Cincinnati & Northern Kentucky and CORBA continue to push the message introduced by the Ohio Valley Improvement Association more than a century ago: that the practical experience of rivermen, fused with the technical expertise of U.S. Army Corps of Engineers staff, represents the unique formula that can work with the Ohio River. The practical and technical skills of the rivermen and the corps engineers can best make the river productive by understanding and working with Old Man River's moods. Simultaneously, the Ohio River lock and dam system alters the hydrology of the river and makes the river less useful for waterfront residents, bending the river to the needs of barges and tugs above all else.

In distinct ways, both projects reinforce elite control over relationship building with the Ohio River while making it less hospitable to everyday use. As a result, the people most directly interacting with the river on a regular basis are a limited few: boat hands, waterworks and sanitation engineers, pleasure craft owners, USACE engineers, and dock workers (Coomer 2014). If we think of the riverfront as an assemblage constituted through its relationships, all of Cincinnati's residents are intimately connected to the river through the pipes, sewers, and purification plants that circulate the river's water, but only a limited amount of persons actually deal with the Ohio River itself as a material force, a nonhuman actor shaping the world around it. While the Ohio River once exerted influence on everyday life in Cincinnati—forcing urban residents to respond to its changes in course, the diseases it brought, and the destruction of its floods—the efforts of white male developers and experts have continued to buffer most people from river life.

This is not to claim that the Ohio River has been "tamed" in any sense. The key insight at the center of this book is the difference between dominating the river and dominating relationship building with the river. Elite groups in Cincinnati have often tried to collaborate with the Ohio River and occasionally sought to subordinate it, but they have always worked to cut off more and more of the public from interacting with the Ohio River in consistent ways. The Ohio River has largely gone along with these elite proposals, acting in favor of elite interests on the river, whether through floods that eat away at low-income neighborhoods or increased levels of pollution that make the river unpleasant for recreation or cohabitation. Over the past century, local elites have learned how to work collaboratively with the Ohio River to support the goals of white supremacy, public health, and capitalist development in Cincinnati. It has been a productive partnership that has enabled them to remake the local riverfront and regional economy over the course of decades.

This has not always been a simple or straightforward process for local elite class formations and the individuals that do interact with the river. As local development and technical expert elites have cut off most Cincinnati residents from the Ohio River, they have been the ones who have benefited and learned the most from closely engaging with the river. They have also had to bend themselves to the demands of the Ohio River. Despite its friendlier demeanor, Old Man River is still a demanding and unpredictable force. Ships sink regularly, and barges escape their tows and cause havoc. Floods rage and test the infrastructure built to channel the river's energy. Ice flows strike boats and endanger river workers. In 2011 a popular upscale restaurant on the water in Northern Kentucky, the Waterfront, slipped its moorings and started to float down the river in the middle of the dinner rush, carrying two hundred preoccupied diners and staff. And many river workers, especially boat hands, describe the drab isolation that comes with working on the river, cut off from the liveliness of nearby riverfront communities by relentless logistics schedules. As local elites have dominated relationship building with the Ohio River, the actual relational work has never been easy, requiring significant investment of energy and resources to cultivate this collaborative spirit with the river.

CONCLUSION

Cincinnati's bicentennial took place in 1988. Numerous events, books, and souvenirs marked the anniversary. Unsurprisingly, given the emphasis on the city's origins, the river featured prominently. The inaugural Tall Stacks Music, Arts, and Heritage Festival brought fourteen historic riverboats and more than seven hundred thousand people to the waterfront that year, an event that reminded Cincinnatians of the "river water in our veins" (Goetz 1999). Also, in the newly opened Sawyer Point Park, the local Greater Cincinnati Foundation and Contemporary Art Center unveiled *Cincinnati Gateway*, a massive landscape sculpture, 400 feet long by 145 feet wide, designed to celebrate the waterfront. The sculpture, or "storyscape" as the artist Andrew Leicester called it, is a long narrow earthwork, running parallel to the river and topped by a walkway. A tunnel, capped by an ornate bridge, bisects the earthwork, providing an entrance to the park. Various elements from the Cincinnati area are incorporated into the sculpture, including local Native American iconography and references to the city's geology, although the work is perhaps best known for introducing a new mascot for the city, the flying pig.[1]

However, the project's central imagery is drawn from riverfront infrastructure. The main entryway imitates one of the Miami-Erie Canal locks, the Ohio River terminus of which had been nearby before its closure. The central span represents the city's many bridges, making the Cincinnati area one of the most difficult stretches of the Ohio River for boats to navigate, and the walkway on top of the earthwork includes a scaled replica of the entire Ohio River, on which Leicester chose to mark all twenty-eight of the modern locks and dams operating on the river, from Pittsburgh to Cairo. The earthwork itself is also meant to pay tribute to the series of levees that protect Cincinnati and Northern Kentucky from flooding. Once a visitor passes through the entry tunnel, they reach a small plaza dominated by a towering flood column: the pillar

FIGURE 5.1. On top of *Cincinnati Gateway*, with a scale representation of the Ohio River and the lock-and-dam system. Photograph by author.

marks the height of the city's three highest floods, in 1884, 1937, and 1964. At the top of the column, there is—half-ominously, half-mischievously—a notch at one hundred feet (twenty feet above the flood crest of 1937) next to a question mark, leaving open the possibility of greater disasters in the future. Finally, the sculpture's greenery, particularly the inclusion of riparian plant species, draws attention to the river's ongoing improvements in water quality.

Leicester stated that he intended *Cincinnati Gateway* as an apolitical sculpture, and to do so he leaned extensively on the riverfront's infrastructure to provide the raw material for his storyscape (Doss 1992). The enormous investments in technologies to manage the city's relationship with the river have positioned infrastructure as the omnipresent, neutral, and familiar background to the riverfront. Originally called internal improvements, and then public works, and most recently infrastructure, these Ohio River projects have been promoted by elites in Cincinnati as necessary to facilitate economic growth and also to improve individual well-being in the city.

Cincinnati has become the central node in managing these riparian infrastructures along much of the Ohio River, and consequently, the shape of regional elites' relationship to the Ohio River. The city houses crucial administrative sites like the U.S. Army Corps of Engineers' headquarters for the entire Great Lakes and Ohio River Division, the Ohio River Valley Water Sanitation

Commission (ORSANCO), and the federal Environmental Protection Agency's Andrew W. Breidenbach Environmental Research Center, the agency's largest water and pollution research facility. Cincinnati is now in many ways the quintessential river city, one where a deep relationship with the Ohio River continues to sustain the dominance of white elite class formations.

This is the direct result of the heterogeneous coalitions and alliances in Cincinnati that have pushed a new urban waterways agenda since the late nineteenth century, one that reimagined the definition of a river city. Interactions between groups of Cincinnati elites and the Ohio River also drove changes across the entire 189,422 square mile watershed of the Ohio River (as well as nationally and internationally). The local groups have varied widely in their composition and activities but are also defined by great continuity in terms of class, race, and gender. From the Ohio Valley Improvement Association to the Riverfront Advisory Council, the groups have brought the same technical and development actors together over and over again. As a result, an ideology of growth has influenced the creation of infrastructural systems just as much as an ideology of science. The relationship between these two ideologies has defined the creation of infrastructure in Cincinnati under a capitalist context. In contrast, socialist (Collier 2011) or monarchical (Rademacher 2011) contexts often have starkly different motivations for building infrastructure, such as glorification of the nation, visions of modernity, and legitimation of the state bureaucratic apparatus.

As elite groups of mostly white men in Cincinnati have built closer and closer relationships to the Ohio River, they have excluded lower-income white and Black communities from accessing the river. It is no coincidence that as this book has advanced, the riverfront individuals portrayed have become progressively whiter and wealthier. Black roustabouts and Irish laborers have given way to white sanitation engineers and urban planners. The involvement of elite families like the Tafts and Castellinis have also helped tie together these extended infrastructural conversations, with family members appearing and reappearing as new proposals emerge.

Throughout Cincinnati's history, infrastructure—particularly in its inception and creation—has been an important terrain to connect divergent elite interests under a system of liberal governance—which must constantly balance the desire to govern directly with the need to promote personal freedom (Joyce 2003). Infrastructure has provided an opportunity for elite groups to come together and negotiate regarding their objectives. While an urban planner and a real estate agent, or an industrialist and a sanitary engineer, may have widely differing views about how the city should be governed, through infrastructure they can create concrete compromises that enable them to bring together their discordant visions. Or alternately, one elite group can determine how infrastructure is developed at the expense of another.

The connections enabled by infrastructure, encompassing collaboration and conflict, have transformed both proponents of scientific expertise and local growth in particularized ways. This is not just about developers "using" scientists to advance their own agendas, or urban planners adapting to market necessities by scaling back their visions. Even though most histories have tended to interpret these interactions in this way, the engagements around the creation of distinct infrastructure projects have altered both in this shared practice. Participation in assemblages around controlling pollution or "being flooded" affected all of the actors involved, no matter if one group benefited more from a project's outcomes than another.

Where does the river itself fit in this? An extensive literature has documented how infrastructural projects like those found on the Cincinnati riverfront are intended to control and benefit from nature, even though nonhuman actors constantly upset and transform the infrastructures designed for them (Kaika 2005). More recently, infrastructure has been frequently designed to cooperate with or aid nature, since, as one local environmentalist framed it, "sometimes [nature] needs help." Across these instances, it is still assumed that nature is seen as an externalized nonsocial force, variable in its particulars but essentially comparable across the globe (Tsing 2005). This view reinforces the assertion by anthropologist Timothy Mitchell (2002) that the separation of nature from society is a key means of legitimizing expertise, where experts claim that their capacity for rational thought is what sets them outside of nature and thus makes them capable of manipulating it. Mitchell believes an inert nonsocial nature is a central link in a series of analytical divisions that undergird expertise: "In each case, the place and the claims of expertise are constituted in the separation that seems to open up, opposing nature to technology, reality to its representation, objects to their value" (2002, 15; see also Latour 1993).

However, observing the Ohio River opens up a more complicated view of nature and nonhuman actors. While arguments about the need to control nature have had significant local relevance, in many instances, the history in Cincinnati's riverfront has shown that white elites deployed a cooperative vision in designing the infrastructural proposals related to navigation, flood control, and pollution abatement on the Ohio River. From the first Ohio Valley Improvement Association convention, where a speaker urged that "man must be a co-worker with nature to accomplish its purposes" (1895, 20), to the continued emphasis on learning from "Old Man River," the case for this tendency to separate and control nature has been balanced by multiple and diverse counterexamples of ways elite groups have sought to respect the river and claim they understand its true needs.

The contributions of development actors working at the speculative edges of the economy have been crucial in this sense, representing a more local and contextualized knowledge in these discussions about the Ohio River. These speculative actors, such as real estate developers and terminal operators, have derived their success from experience rather than scientific training. In this view, understanding the Ohio River is not something that can be taught in a classroom. These forms of knowing and working with the river have been used to make riparian infrastructures even more effective in meeting the goals of the elite parties that conceived and pushed forward infrastructure projects, whether for capitalist gain, control over urban space, subjection of Black communities, improved public health, or other ends.

These riparian infrastructures are also explicitly a proactive view of how to engage the Ohio River. Many defenders of the current arrangements on the Ohio River accuse environmental critics of having no concrete plans for what the river should be like, other than returning it to a pristine state. Reflecting several years after his retirement, Edward Cleary—the first director of ORSANCO, the intergovernmental pollution abatement agency launched in Cincinnati in 1948—succinctly summed up the rejection of this drive for pristine environments in 1983, stating that "Congress mandated a national goal of zero discharge of pollutants from municipalities and industries by 1985. Thus far this extravagantly ambitious expectation is far from realization. A professional disturbing aspect of this legislative mandate lies in the value judgment it asserts—namely, that the greatest beneficial use of water resources can be achieved only if they are safe guarded from any man-made alteration of quality. The validity of this assumption is challenged by engineers and economists" (Cleary 1983, 33).

The legacies of riparian infrastructure in Cincinnati demonstrate this elite way of thinking clearly, with infrastructure projects pursued based on a belief that a working relationship with the Ohio River can productively balance a range of human uses. Old Man River may no longer resemble the wildly unpredictable and frequently beautiful riverine force of the nineteenth century, but in this view that does not make it less than what it was. In a pamphlet produced by the Ohio Valley Improvement Association in the late 1960s, the group celebrated regional achievements in the areas of navigation, industry, recreation, and flood control. The pamphlet also proclaims that the Ohio River is "a demanding river, a giant that at times is moved to anger. But at the same time it nurtures an empire without equal in this world of ours" (OVIA, n.d. (b), 1). The Ohio River's unruliness actually underpins its potency; a docile river would never have been able to contribute in the same way. Cincinnati elites argue that this remade Ohio River may not be pristine but it is not broken. According to this view, Old Man River never wanted to be "safe guarded from any man-made alteration." Instead it delighted in interactions with riparian communities and the role its vitality played in bringing prosperity to the heart of the U.S. empire.

While it is important to account for the things that have been lost in the transitions of the previous century (clean water, wildlife diversity, forms of human sociality, and many others), it is also critical to avoid casting the Ohio River as damaged in some fundamental way. As the landscape architect David Fletcher reminds us, what may appear to be "freak ecologies" like the modern-day Ohio River are still dynamic, vital, and even sustainable forces. The Ohio River does not want our pity. Nor does it care whether Cincinnati elites' riparian infrastructure proposals contribute to resource degradation (or even climate warming) in ways that can harm the perpetuation of human life in the region. Building a new, less elite-centric relationship with the Ohio River must keep these realities in mind.

The river is not inherently the dutiful partner of elite white male-dominated groups in Cincinnati. Indigenous groups and other riparian communities have built deep relationships with the Ohio River that continue to the present, subverting claims that ORSANCO, the U.S. Army Corps of Engineers, and other groups have privileged relationships with the river. Moreover, despite Cincinnati elite overtures over decades, the Ohio River as an actor is still profoundly unknowable. The river can help as much as hurt anyone who seeks to engage it. Yes, currently, the river's behavior largely favors the interests of local elite class formations, but this should not be taken for granted. It can and will change. Charting an alternative way forward needs to start by proactively thinking about how to redefine this relationship with the Ohio River as a nonhuman actor, considering the priorities that should structure our mutual engagement.

As geographer Neil Smith (2008) reminds us, this is not about helping the river or other spaces of the environment return to a "natural state." Instead, the focus is on the intrinsic relationship between producing nature and our efforts to reproduce human society (while also recognizing that this does not imply the capacity to "control" nature). The questions for those who would like to seek alternatives are deceivingly simple. How much water does the city want to consume? How do urban residents want to enjoy the river as a space of pleasure? Is navigation important? If current arrangements are preferable, how can more human and nonhuman actors benefit from this relationship? The Ohio River is one of the few commons left in Cincinnati, and residents could much more strongly stake a claim in its future.

While the questions are straightforward, the work is hard. Relatively few individuals engage directly with the river today, and many of them are elite actors (or work the river in service of specific elite class formations). Although they benefit from this engagement, these elites equally must be attendant to the Ohio River's needs and desires. They spend countless hours studying pollution levels, observing flood stages, and navigating its waters. In the celebratory OVIA pamphlet from the late 1960s, the writers point out that the "work, never-ending work it seems, goes on and on. With each step the rolling, tumbling [Ohio River] giant returns more of her wealth and power to land which once she sought to conquer in her more belligerent moods" (OVIA, n.d. (b), 3). Bending the Ohio River to other forms of being is not a simple or painless task. Hundreds of thousands of people in Cincinnati drink the river's water and flush their sewage onto its banks (after treatment) while giving little thought to what they are asking the Ohio River to do. To understand and benefit from the river will require time and work, both to establish new relationships and to unravel the existing behaviors concretized in the thick networks of infrastructure along the riverfront.

Taking up Cleary's challenge, community groups that want to redefine Cincinnati's relationship to the Ohio River need to emerge with new proposals. The lack of existing alternatives was readily apparent in 2019 when ORSANCO, the source of much frustration among environmentalists for decades, announced its plans to reduce its operations and oversight role. Arguing that existing policing functions at the federal level were capable of carrying forward ORSANCO's work, the organization presented itself as redundant. Fierce blowback from environmental groups came immediately, moving ORSANCO's commissioners to reconsider. Activists dismissed the alternatives to ORSANCO's pollution monitoring approach. As a result, they were forced to defend the usefulness of an organization that they had long criticized or, at best, tolerated.

As Cincinnatians look to reinvent the river city once again, it will be critical to both repurpose existing riparian infrastructures and find new ways to build relationships with the Ohio River. There are a range of existing models that foreground the public's role in deciding how to engage local waterways, including democratically elected water boards in the Netherlands and community-driven climate resilience planning (National Association of Climate Resilience Planners 2015). Any of these options could begin to chart new riparian dynamics for the city. Whichever route Cincinnati takes, it is clear the Ohio River will have a major part to play in determining whether the next version of this river city is more equitable and sustainable.

NOTES

INTRODUCTION

1. See, for instance, White 1995; Cioc 2002; Pritchard 2011; Biggs 2012; and Ball 2017. Complementary research in anthropology, geography, and other fields has extended these insights through other methodologies. See, for instance, Alley 2002; Rademacher 2011; Barnes 2014; and Bear 2015.

2. Another important view of infrastructure focuses on it as a supporting feature that enables other activities to take place. In this view, infrastructures such as the means of production, also known as the base, create the conditions for superstructures like political systems or culture. While this is not the operating definition used in this book, it represents an important view on what constitutes infrastructure and is increasingly prevalent as more and more things are classified as infrastructure.

PROLOGUE

1. Others argue that the Ohio River is actually much younger due to the timing of more recent glacial events that had altered the course of sections of the waterway, only finally forming ten thousand to fifteen thousand years ago (Sanders 1991).

2. The decades directly after the Civil War did witness a spike in interest in luxury travel on the Ohio River for passengers who could afford it, reasoning it was more comfortable than travel by rail (Stradling 2013).

CHAPTER 1. Ohio Valley Navigation and the City

1. The last lock and dam in the system was labeled number fifty-three, but two dams had been eliminated when revising the overall plan, leaving the total at fifty-one lock and dam facilities.

2. Though Merrill introduced the idea of the movable dam from France, the proposal to build a series of locks and regular dams along the entire Ohio River to improve navigation had been developed by William Milnor Roberts in 1870 (Johnson 1991), based on well-known precedents, including on Ohio River tributaries.

3. Numerous subsequent studies have further developed the history of the USACE and local water development lobbies during this period without disrupting this narrative (Dodds 1969; Worster 1985; O'Neill 2006; Pisani 2006). Pisani (2006) goes furthest in suggesting that the USACE was right in making its protests because many of the Inland Waterways Commission's conservationist proposals were impractical.

4. Based on listening to the audio from this interview, I have transcribed Evan Bone's quote slightly differently than the original interviewer, John Knoepfle, in the belief that Bone is referring to Old Man River as the source of recurring silt problems. Knoepfle's transcription of the full sentence is as follows: "But then they found out the old man, the trouble with silt came along again, because in the gates when they rolled out away they had to have a gate recess and that's where the gate would, to get the gate out to, not obstruct the entrance into the lock, that recess would fill up with silt, the same thing, problem again" (Bone 1957, 3).

5. This is not to say that all OVIA speakers were consistent in their view of the Ohio River as a nonhuman ally. Rather, in keeping with the OVIA's scattershot approach, many members' perspectives were widely incompatible, with statements ranging from calls to tame nature by "standard-gauging the river" (OVIA 1925, 23) to admonishments to be a "co-worker with nature" (OVIA 1895, 20). The quote here is from a 1904 speech by Captain John Dravo in which he drew on multiple arguments for working with the river, including the responsibility to care for the Ohio River as an element in humanity's duty to steward and improve on God's creation. These opinions varied so widely that another ship captain even asserted in 1898 that "the best plan would be to build boats to suit the river and not ask the Government to build the river to suit boats" (Fleming 2019, 48).

6. Two of the cranes bought by the Cincinnati Rail-Water Transfer Company had come from a failed Muscle Shoals development in Alabama, a site that conservationists had long been pushing for as the ideal location to show the benefits of technocratic natural resource management. Muscle Shoals later became the headquarters of the powerful Tennessee Valley Authority.

7. Shantyboats returned during the Great Depression as a base for a flexible subsistence strategy. In the 1940s shantyboat residents were again legislated against or policed until the boats disappeared, to be replaced later by more respectably named houseboats (Hubbard 1977).

8. There are certainly counterexamples, including The New Cincinnati: Are You Acquainted with It?, a publication of the Cincinnati Convention Committee in 1932, which includes a photograph of the riverfront as part of the book's frontispiece. On the whole though, these waterfront images became much scarcer.

9. In contrast, nonnavigable waters are open to private ownership and are regulated by state laws, which can vary. East Coast states typically employ a riparian rights model where all riverbank property owners have mutual rights, based on English common law, while western states use prior appropriation water rights law, establishing a system of precedent for determining water usage (Johnson 2008).

CHAPTER 2. The Cincinnati Central Bottoms and Flood Control

1. In a rare exception, Mississippi River levees received federal funding in the latter half of the nineteenth century. Officially, the federal government funded these levees

only because they provided navigational improvements by quickening and deepening the river channel. In reality it was an open secret that their primary role was flood prevention (Shallat 1994). The U.S. Congress also provided indirect aid in the form of land grants under the Swamp Land Acts, which financed flood works in many states (O'Neill 2006).

2. After completion of the lock and dam system, the Ohio Valley Improvement Association took a more open stance toward multipurpose water management principles championed by its old conservationist foes including William John McGee. Still, supporting navigation infrastructure remained the primary objective of the OVIA throughout its organizational history.

3. Reportedly, the crest was declared 79.99 feet instead of 80 feet so that insurance companies would not be required to pay out a double indemnity.

4. The City Planning Commission's chairman, Alfred Bettman, expressed disappointment in the preliminary and inconclusive nature of this report. The report was not widely circulated.

5. See also Scott 1998; Smith 2008; Swyngedouw 2004; Gandy 2014; as well as Welky 2011 for the similar arguments used to justify Ohio Valley flood control infrastructure.

6. This response among Cincinnati's professional class aligns with geographer Sarah Whatmore's view of disasters as an "environmental knowledge controversy" (2013). In this view, the defining feature of a disaster is how it causes urban residents to reexamine their spatial assumptions and change their thinking.

7. While Welky identifies some proponents of this approach as "pessimistic observers," representing a "spirit of resignation" in the face of flooding (2011, 229), in Cincinnati this was clearly a case of professional groups seeking to proactively reconfigure riverfront space for their purposes.

8. Following these votes, members of the California Improvement Association challenged the CPC's jurisdiction along the riverfront. The city solicitor upheld the CPC's jurisdiction, eventually confirmed in a case before the Ohio Supreme Court.

9. According to anthropologist Chris Hann (1998), property is frequently understood as "the rights that people hold over things which guarantee them a future 'income stream'" (4). Thus, one of the most serious risks to property is its potential devaluation (Verdery 2004).

10. Craig's plan was later considered alone by the CPC and city council. With numerous absences, the seven-member CPC rejected the Craig plan 2–1. The city council could not meet the required two-thirds majority to overturn this decision. Craig continued to fight for a study of his proposal, but it was also rejected by the USACE as impractical.

11. Similar to anthropologist Catherine Alexander's findings in postsocialist Kazakhstan, "the properties of the property object . . . were redefined and reconstituted while the external form remained constant" (Alexander 2004, 265).

12. Generally, the federal government gave local governments wide leeway in determining what constituted blight (Gordon 2004).

13. Other cities in the region, such as Pittsburgh and St. Louis, passed through very similar situations with their riverfronts during this period, constructing large multisport stadia after clearing out older mixed-race residential and industrial neighborhoods (Cowan 2005).

CHAPTER 3. Stream Pollution and Riverfront Recreation

1. The Cincinnati Chamber of Commerce had a long-standing interest in waterways policy, having played a critical role in the founding of the Ohio Valley Improvement Association in 1895.

2. Ohioans established a state office for the organization in 1924, though the Cincinnati chapter did not form until 1944.

3. Market-oriented economists have claimed that industrialists have long taken the initiative to recycle factory by-products because of the financial incentives involved, but the historical evidence is far from clear that this has been the case (Rosen 2012).

4. The strength of this resistance to adapting a river-basin approach to pollution control in the United States is clearly seen from the example of the Tennessee Valley Authority. It represented the most-advanced and comprehensive vision of technocratic river-basin administration in the nation at the beginning of 1930s, but did not include pollution control among its objectives when the federal government constituted its mandate (Molle 2009).

5. Shortly after the passage of this bond issue, the Cincinnati Park Board created a temporary park in the central riverfront area while city officials developed final urban renewal plans for the area. This was the first riverfront park completed, though the city razed the site when construction began on Riverfront Stadium in 1967 (Payne 1983).

6. The work of anthropologist Mary Douglas (1966) on purity and dirt has also been used productively to understand how portraying certain residents or areas as "unclean" enables key processes of urban disinvestment and redevelopment (Jackson 2010).

CHAPTER 4. Reassembling Infrastructure on the Cincinnati Riverfront

1. Confusingly, the Riverfront Advisors Commission was different from previously established groups called the Riverfront Advisory Council (later renamed as the River Advisory Council) and the Riverfront Steering Commission.

2. After the OVIA merged with DINAMO in 1983, Barry Palmer, the first executive director of DINAMO, helped launch Waterways Council, Inc. in 2003, becoming its president and CEO.

3. According to one local environmentalist I spoke with, the USACE, because of its interests in navigation, has long focused primarily on the Ohio River main stem rather than any of the tributaries or the overall watershed.

4. Carter was in the role of master developer, while Dawson oversaw financing for the project. In 2017 the City of Cincinnati, Hamilton County, and Carter announced they were mutually concluding their relationship for The Banks. Progress on the project had begun to slow down, with difficulty maintaining tenants and finding investors for later stages of the build-out.

5. The Regional Economic Development Initiative (REDI) is responsible for promoting Cincinnati's industrial potential.

6. However, Reuss (2008) has described an increasing expectation for engineers to be involved in public debates directly, so that negotiating ability now sometimes seems more important than technical proficiency.

7. Much appreciation to Dana-Ain Davis for suggesting this line of thought.

8. Although there were also limits in this regard. Despite several efforts, I failed to talk with Bob Castellini, owner of the baseball team located on the riverfront and a major force in pushing forward The Banks project. The Castellini family has deep roots on the riverfront through operating a wholesale grocery business as well as through leadership roles in the Ohio Valley Improvement Association.

CONCLUSION

1. Leicester placed four winged pigs atop steamboat smokestacks, playfully harkening back to the city's early pork processing industry, which had earned it the name "Porkopolis." Despite an initial outcry from some quarters, including a protest at City Hall, the city soon adopted the flying pig as its own, with the symbol appearing everywhere from T-shirts to the name of the city's marathon (Doss 1992).

BIBLIOGRAPHY

Ahlering, Marian L. 1983. "The Story of Sawyer Point." *Queen City Heritage* 41(2): 43–48.

Alexander, Catherine. 2004. "Value, Relations, and Changing Bodies: Privatization and Property Rights in Kazakhstan." In *Property in Question: Value Transformation in the Global Economy*, edited by Katherine Verdery and Caroline Humphrey, 251–74. Bloomsbury Academic.

Allen, Barbara L. 2003. *Uneasy Alchemy: Citizens and Experts in Louisiana's Chemical Corridor Disputes.* MIT Press.

Allen, Michael. 1991. "The Ohio River: Artery of Movement." In *Always a River: The Ohio River and the American Experience*, edited by Robert L. Reid, 105–29. Indiana University Press.

Alley, Kelly D. 2002. *On the Banks of the Gaṅgā: When Wastewater Meets a Sacred River.* University of Michigan Press.

Ambler, Charles H. 1932. *A History of Transportation in the Ohio Valley: With Special Reference to Its Waterways, Trade, and Commerce from the Earliest Period to the Present Time.* Arthur H. Clark Company.

Anand, Nikhil, Akhil Gupta, and Hannah Appel. 2018. *The Promise of Infrastructure.* Duke University Press.

Anderson, Yeatman. 1957. Yeatman Anderson Memoir. Interview by John Knoepfle, August 10. Public Library of Cincinnati and Sangamon State University Inland Rivers Memoir Project. Archives/Special Collections LIB 144. University of Illinois at Springfield, Springfield, Ill.

Andreen, William L. 2003. "The Evolution of Water Pollution Control in the United States—State, Local, and Federal Efforts, 1789–1972: Part I." *Stanford Environmental Law Journal* 22: 145.

Anonymous. 1937. Selection reproduced for Alfred Bettman. Alfred Bettman Papers, Box 7, Folder 20. University of Cincinnati Archives & Rare Books, Cincinnati, Ohio.

Antweiler, Christoph. 1998. "Local Knowledge and Local Knowing: An Anthropological Analysis of Contested 'Cultural Products' in the Context of Development." *Anthropos* 93 (4/6): 469–94.

Arnesen, Eric. 1994. *Waterfront Workers of New Orleans: Race, Class, and Politics, 1863–1923.* University of Illinois Press.

Ball, Philip. 2017. *The Water Kingdom: A Secret History of China.* University of Chicago Press.

Barles, Sabine. 2012. "The Seine and Parisian Metabolism: Growth of Capital Dependencies in the Nineteenth and Twentieth Centuries." In *Urban Rivers: Remaking Rivers, Cities and Space in Europe and North America*, edited by Stéphane Castonguay and Matthew Evenden, 95–112. University of Pittsburgh Press.

Barnes, Jessica. 2014. *Cultivating the Nile: The Everyday Politics of Water in Egypt.* Duke University Press.

Barrios, Robert. 2017. What Does Catastrophe Reveal for Whom? The Anthropology of Crises and Disasters at the Onset of the Anthropocene. *Annual Review of Anthropology* 46: 151–66.

Bauer, Donald. 1988. "Floods to Floodwalls in Newport, Kentucky: 1884–1951." Master's thesis, Xavier University.

Baxandall, Rosalyn, and Elizabeth Ewen. 2000. *Picture Windows: How the Suburbs Happened.* Basic Books.

Beall, Joel M. 2015. "Smale Park's Beginnings, from the Bottoms Up." *Cincinnati Enquirer*, May 2, 12, 14. https://www.cincinnati.com/story/news/local/smale/2015/05/02/smale-parks-beginnings-bottoms/26467481/

Bear, Laura. 2015. *Navigating Austerity: Currents of Debt Along a South Asian River.* Stanford University Press.

Ben, David C. 2010. "Hidden Assets of Fort Washington Way Saving Taxpayers Millions of Dollars." *Urban Cincy*, July 14. http://www.urbancincy.com/2010/07/hidden-assets-of-fort-washington-way-saving-taxpayers-millions-of-dollars/

Bennett, Jane. 2005. The Agency of Assemblages and the North American Blackout. *Public Culture* 17(3): 445–66.

Bettman, Alfred. 1937a. Memorandum from Alfred Bettman to Myron Downs, March 27. Alfred Bettman Papers, Box 2, Folder 19. University of Cincinnati Archives & Rare Books, Cincinnati, Ohio.

Bettman, Alfred. 1937b. Alfred Bettman Draft Memorandum, May 8. Alfred Bettman Papers, Box 2, Folder 20. University of Cincinnati Archives & Rare Books, Cincinnati, Ohio.

Bettman, Alfred. 1938a. Memorandum from Alfred Bettman to City Planning Commission, March 23. Alfred Bettman Papers, Box 2, Folder 28. University of Cincinnati Archives & Rare Books, Cincinnati, Ohio.

Bettman, Alfred. 1938b. Letter from Alfred Bettman to *Cincinnati Enquirer* Editors, April 9. Alfred Bettman Papers, Box 3, Folder 1. University of Cincinnati Archives & Rare Books, Cincinnati, Ohio.

Bettman, Alfred. 1938c. Letter from Alfred Bettman to City Council, April 18. Alfred Bettman Papers, Box 3, Folder 1. University of Cincinnati Archives & Rare Books, Cincinnati, Ohio.

Bettman, Alfred. 1939a. Letter from Alfred Bettman to City Solicitor, April 28. Alfred Bettman Papers, Box 3, Folder 12. University of Cincinnati Archives & Rare Books, Cincinnati, Ohio.

Bettman, Alfred. 1939b. Letter from Alfred Bettman to Myron Downs, June 20. Bettman Papers, Box 3, Folder 15. University of Cincinnati Archives & Rare Books, Cincinnati, Ohio.

Biery, Hudson. n.d. *Federal-State Pattern Stream Pollution Activity Is Getting Results—It Needs Expansion.* Alfred Bettman Papers, Box 14, Folder 26. University of Cincinnati Archives & Rare Books, Cincinnati, Ohio.

Biery, Hudson. 1930. "Street Car 'Dash' Posters." In *The Art of Advertising*, edited by Manuel Rosenberg, 69–71. Harper & Brothers.

Biery, Hudson. 1932. "Can We Sell Public Transit?" *American Electric Railway Association Journal* 23: 1108–10.

Biery, Hudson. 1939. "Success Looms in Chamber's Fight Against Pollution." *Cincinnati Enquirer, Chamber of Commerce Section*, March 23, 1939, 6.

Biery, Hudson. 1940. WLW Radio Interview on Stream Pollution, February 3. Alfred Bettman Papers, Box 14, Folder 29. University of Cincinnati Archives & Rare Books, Cincinnati, Ohio.

Biery, Hudson. 1963. Letter from Hudson Biery to Ewart Simpkinson, December 19. Cincinnatus Association Papers, MSS 617, Box 10, Folder 33. Cincinnati History Library and Archives, Cincinnati, Ohio.

Bigham, Darrel E. 1991. "River of Opportunity: Economic Consequences of the Ohio." In *Always a River: The Ohio River and the American Experience*, edited by Robert L. Reid, 130–79. Indiana University Press.

Biggs, David A. 2012. *Quagmire: Nation-Building and Nature in the Mekong Delta*. University of Washington Press.

Blackbourn, David. 2006. *The Conquest of Nature: Water, Landscape, and the Making of Modern Germany*. W. W. Norton.

Blim, Michael. 2016. "History, Power and the Rise of the United States Ruling Class." In *After the Crisis: Anthropological Thought, Neoliberalism and the Aftermath*, edited by James G. Carrier 77–95. Routledge.

Boardman, Anthony E., Carston Greve, and Graeme A. Hodge. 2015. Comparative Analyses of Infrastructure Public-Private Partnerships. *Journal of Comparative Policy Analysis: Research and Practice* 17(5): 441–47.

Bocking, Stephen. 2006. Constructing Urban Expertise: Professional and Political Authority in Toronto, 1940–1970. *Journal of Urban History* 33(1): 51–76.

Bolin, Robert, and Lois Stanford. 1999. "Constructing Vulnerability in the First World: The Northridge Earthquake in Southern California, 1994." In *The Angry Earth: Disaster in Anthropological Perspective*, edited by Anthony Oliver-Smith and Susannah M. Hoffman, 89–112. Routledge.

Bone, Evan. 1957. Evan Bone Memoir. Interview by John Knoepfle, August 27. Public Library of Cincinnati and Sangamon State University Inland Rivers Memoir Project. Archives/Special Collections LIB 144, University of Illinois at Springfield, Springfield, Ill.

Bourdieu, Pierre. 1984. *Distinction: A Social Critique of the Judgement of Taste*. Harvard University Press.

Boyd, Douglas A. 2011. *Crawfish Bottom: Recovering a Lost Kentucky Community*. University Press of Kentucky.

Brash, Julian. 2011. *Bloomberg's New York: Class and Governance in the Luxury City*. University of Georgia Press.

Braun, Bruce. 2006. Environmental Issues: Global Natures in the Space of Assemblage. *Progress in Human Geography* 30(5): 644–54.

Brooks, Karl B. 2009. *Before Earth Day: The Origins of American Environmental Law, 1945–1970*. University Press of Kansas.

Burnham, Robert A. 1992a. "The Cincinnati Charter Revolt of 1924: Creating City Government for a Pluralistic Society." In *Ethnic Diversity and Civic Identity: Patterns of*

Conflict and Cohesion in Cincinnati Since 1820, edited by Henry D. Shapiro and Jonathan D. Sarna, 202–24. University of Illinois Press.

Burnham, Robert A. 1992b. Planning Versus Administration: The Independent City Planning Commission in Cincinnati, 1918–1940." *Urban History* 19(2): 229–50.

Byrne, Shelley. 2020. "CORBA Discusses Future Of Container Service." *Waterways Journal*, February 21. https://www.waterwaysjournal.net/2020/02/21/corba-discusses-future-of-container-service/

Carse, Ashley. 2012. "Nature as Infrastructure: Making and Managing the Panama Canal Watershed." *Social Studies of Science* 42(4): 539–63.

Carter, Ruth C. 1992. "Cincinnatians and Cholera: Attitudes Toward the Epidemics of 1832 and 1849." *Queen City Heritage* 50: 32–48.

Casner, Nicholas. 1999a. "Angler Activist: Kenneth Reid, the Izaak Walton League, and the Crusade for Federal Water Pollution Control." *Pennsylvania History: A Journal of Mid-Atlantic Studies* 66(4): 535–53.

Casner, Nicholas. 1999b. "Polluter Versus Polluter: The Pennsylvania Railroad and the Manufacturing of Pollution Policies in the 1920s." *Journal of Policy History* 11(2): 179–200.

Central Riverfront Advisory Committee. 1951. *Central Riverfront Advisory Committee Report.* City of Cincinnati.

Checker, Melissa. 2011. "Wiped Out by the 'Greenwave': Environmental Gentrification and the Paradoxical Politics of Urban Sustainability." *City & Society* 23(2): 210–29.

Cincinnati Chamber of Commerce. 1891. *41st and 42d Annual Report of the Cincinnati Chamber of Commerce and Merchants' Exchange for Two Commercial Years, Ending August 31, 1890.* Ohio Valley Company.

Cincinnati Chamber of Commerce. 1896. *Forty-Seventh Annual Report of the Cincinnati Chamber of Commerce and Merchants' Exchange for the Year Ending December 31, 1895.* Ohio Valley Company.

Cincinnati CSP (Committee on Stream Pollution). 1935. *Proceedings—Meeting of Stream Pollution Committee Chamber of Commerce.* July 30.

Cincinnati CSP (Committee on Stream Pollution). 1938. *Communication No. 37: "Let's Take the Dead Horses out of the River"—A Statement by the Committee on Stream Pollution of the Cincinnati Chamber of Commerce*, October 26. Alfred Bettman Papers, Box 14, Folder 25. University of Cincinnati Archives & Rare Books, Cincinnati, Ohio.

Cincinnati Daily Enquirer. 1842. "Beginning and Ending." March 8, 4.

Cincinnati Department of Urban Development. 1965. *Project Area Report.* City of Cincinnati.

Cincinnati Enquirer. 1882. "Terminal Facilities." February 12, 10.

Cincinnati Enquirer. 1884. "The Ohio Booming Again." March 13, 4.

Cincinnati Enquirer. 1887. "The River Traffic." March 6, 9.

Cincinnati Enquirer. 1889. "Tales of the Ohio, as Related by Old Rivermen." July 21, 4.

Cincinnati Enquirer. 1890. "On the Eastern Front." March 24, 1.

Cincinnati Enquirer. 1894. "Freight Bureau Feast: Third Annual Meeting of the Big Traffic Men." December 23, 2.

Cincinnati Enquirer. 1895. "A Call for a Mass Convention of Delegates from all the Towns Along the Ohio." August 14, 8.

Cincinnati Enquirer. 1897a. "Rising Five Inches an Hour." February 23, 10.

Cincinnati Enquirer. 1897b. "Families on the Lower River Road May Be Rendered Homeless." February 24, 10.

Cincinnati Enquirer. 1904a. "Rat Row Will Shortly Be Razed to Make Way for the Erection of a Big Mercantile Plant on Front Street." May 19, 5.

Cincinnati Enquirer. 1904b. "Purchase of Large West End Property by the Moore Oil Company Sets at Rest Rat Row Rumors." June 30, 5.

Cincinnati Enquirer. 1910. "Apprehension as to the Dam's Effect on the Future Water Supply of This City." March 13, 20.

Cincinnati Enquirer. 1911. "Sponsors: At Dedication of Dam Will Be Four of the Fairest Daughters of Ohio Valley." September 2, 18.

Cincinnati Enquirer. 1913. "The Bathing Beach." August 24, 47.

Cincinnati Enquirer. 1916. "May Explain Rumor." November 25, 16.

Cincinnati Enquirer. 1923. "Vast Terminals in Tentative Plan." July 10, 3.

Cincinnati Enquirer. 1935. "Chamber Starts Fight on River Pollution." July 10, 1, 7.

Cincinnati Enquirer. 1936. "Engineers Discuss Proposed Flood Dyke to Protect 'Bottoms' Business Property." February 28, 10.

Cincinnati Enquirer. 1937a. "Valley Is Inferno as Gasoline Burns, Blaze Lights Sky." January 25, 1.

Cincinnati Enquirer. 1937b. "East End Faces Lack of Food as Supplies Run Low in Remaining Stores." January 25, 18.

Cincinnati Enquirer. 1937c. "Army Engineer Explains Flood Protection as Planned for Lower Cincinnati Area." February 25, 16.

Cincinnati Enquirer. 1937d. "River Plan of President Hit." June 17, 3.

Cincinnati Enquirer. 1937e. "Dams Are Suggested for Flood Protection to Cincinnati Area." October 16, 1, 4.

Cincinnati Enquirer. 1937f. "Vote for Judges, Bonds, and Levies." November 4, 3.

Cincinnati Enquirer. 1938. "Flood Plans Are Voted Down." April 28, 3.

Cincinnati Enquirer. 1939a. "Ohio Miners 'Short Sighted' on Pollution, Biery Asserts." March 3, 6.

Cincinnati Enquirer. 1939b. "Council Receives Two Flood Protection Plans." June 28, 3.

Cincinnati Enquirer. 1939c. "Contract for Flood Proofing of California Waterworks Pumping Station Signed by Sherrill." June 28, 13.

Cincinnati Enquirer. 1939d. "Taft Flood Plan Is Approved by Commission's 4–3 vote; Provides for Modified Wall." September 12, 3.

Cincinnati Enquirer. 1939e. "Now Where Are We?" September 13, 6.

Cincinnati Enquirer. 1939f. "Flood Walls Topic of Council for Hour, Then Matter Goes to Committee." September 14, 8.

Cincinnati Enquirer. 1939g. "Opinion Asked by Council of Army Engineers on Flood Wall." December 28, 12.

Cincinnati Enquirer. 1940. "Council Ballots 6 to 3." January 27, 1, 9.

Cincinnati Enquirer. 1948a. "Barrier Dam Is to Go to Work with Crest Due at Noon Tomorrow." April 25, 1.

Cincinnati Enquirer. 1948b. "Eight-State Anti-pollution 'Treaty' Is Hailed by Leaders." July 1, 16.

Cincinnati Enquirer. 1958. "30 Years Bring Big Change in Activities on Ohio Beaches." Kentucky Edition, July 5, 4.

Cincinnati Enquirer. 1998. "City Panel to Discuss Riverfront Development." October 3, B2.

Cincinnati Enquirer. 2007. "A Timeline: Plans for Banks Development Started a Decade Ago." November 2, A10.

Cincinnati Enquirer. 2008. "Ah, the Bottoms: Those Were the Days." April 6, E3.

Cincinnati Post. 1889. "Repulsed with a Revolver." May 31, 3.

Cincinnati Post. 1893. "Filth Heaps Abound Along the River Front." March 17, 4.

Cincinnati Post. 1911a. "Thousands See Fernbank; 'Back-Home' Week Begins." September 4, 1.

Cincinnati Post. 1911b. "Rain Veils the Dam Ceremony from View." September 6, 7.

Cincinnati Post. 1938a. "Hurst Takes Office Amid Council Fight: Republicans and Charterites in Oral Battle over Civil Service Job." January 13, 1, 22.

Cincinnati Post. 1938b. "Hundreds Sign Plea to F.D.R. to End Slump: Cincinnati Business Men Draw Up Petitions Asking Action to Stop Recession." January 13, 21.

Cioc, Mark. 2002. *The Rhine: An Eco-Biography, 1815–2000*. University of Washington Press.

Cist, Charles. 1845. *The Cincinnati Miscellany, Or, Antiquities of the West, and Pioneer History and General and Local Statistics: From October 1st, 1844 to April 1st, 1845*. C. Clark.

Cist, Charles. 1851. *Sketches and Statistics of Cincinnati in 1851*. W. H. Moer.

Citizens' Rehabilitation Committee. 1937. Minutes from Flood Control and Future Planning Committee, March 18. Alfred Bettman Papers, Box 2, Folder 18. University of Cincinnati Archives & Rare Books, Cincinnati, Ohio.

Cleary, Edward J. 1967. *The ORSANCO Story: Water Quality Management in the Ohio Valley Under an Interstate Compact*. Johns Hopkins Press.

Cleary, Edward J. 1983. "An Interview with Edward J. Cleary," by Michael Robinson. Public Works Oral History Interview Number 4, December.

Clemens, Elisabeth S. 1997. *The People's Lobby: Organizational Innovation and the Rise of Interest Group Politics in the United States, 1890–1925*. University Of Chicago Press.

Collier, Stephen J. 2011. *Post-Soviet Social: Neoliberalism, Social Modernity, Biopolitics*. Princeton University Press.

Colten, Craig E., and Peter N. Skinner. 1995. *The Road to Love Canal: Managing Industrial Waste Before EPA*. University of Texas Press.

Conference of Delegates Appointed by Governors of Ohio Valley States. 1936. *Proceedings of Ohio Valley Treaty Conference*, November 20.

Conference of Delegates Appointed by Governors of Ohio Valley States. 1944. *Proceedings of Sixth Conference of Delegates Appointed to Negotiate the Ohio Valley Water Sanitation Compact*, December 7.

Cook, Amy H. 2007. "Troubled Waters: Cincinnati's West End and the Great Flood of 1937." *Ohio Valley History* 7(2): 31–52.

Coomer, James. 2014. *Life on the Ohio*. University Press of Kentucky.

Cowan, Aaron. 2005. "A Whole New Ball Game: Sports Stadiums and Urban Renewal in Cincinnati, Pittsburgh, and St. Louis, 1950–1970." *Ohio Valley History* 5(3): 63–86.

Cowen, Michael, and Robert W. Shenton. 1996. *Doctrines of Development*. Taylor & Francis.

CPC (City Planning Commission). 1925. *The Official City Plan of Cincinnati, Ohio, Adopted by the City Planning Commission, 1925*. Steinhauser Printing Company.

CPC (City Planning Commission). 1937. *The Cincinnati Waterfront: Its Problems and Recommended Future Utilization*. City Planning Commission.

CPC (City Planning Commission). 1938. City Planning Commission letter to City Council, April 18. Alfred Bettman Papers, Box 3, Folder 1. University of Cincinnati Archives & Rare Books, Cincinnati, Ohio.

CPC (City Planning Commission). 1939. *Preliminary Report on a Plan of Redevelopment for the Central River Front*. City Planning Commission.

CPC (City Planning Commission). 1945. Memorandum from the City Planning Commission, January 10. Alfred Bettman Papers, Box 4, Folder 16. University of Cincinnati Archives & Rare Books, Cincinnati, Ohio.

CPC (City Planning Commission). 1946. *Riverfront Redevelopment*. City Planning Commission.

CPC (City Planning Commission). 1948. *The Cincinnati Metropolitan Master Plan—The Official City Plan*. City Planning Commission.

CPC (City Planning Commission). 1961. *Central Riverfront Development: Preliminary Report*. City Planning Commission.

Crissey, Forrest. 1956. *Theodore E. Burton: American Statesman*. World Publishing Company.

Cronon, William. 1992. *Nature's Metropolis: Chicago and the Great West*. W. W. Norton.

Curnutte, Mark. 1995. "Riverfront Renewal Envisioned." *Cincinnati Enquirer*, March 3, 1995, 32.

Dannenbaum, Jed. 1984. *Drink and Disorder: Temperance Reform in Cincinnati from the Washingtonian Revival to the WCTU*. University of Illinois Press.

Davis, John E. 1991. *Contested Ground: Collective Action and the Urban Neighborhood*. Cornell University Press.

Deatrick, John F. 2015. "Flood-Resilient Redevelopment: Cincinnati's Central Riverfront." *Proceedings of the Institution of Civil Engineers—Water Management* 168(2): 85–96.

Deleuze, Gilles, and Félix Guattari. 1987. *A Thousand Plateaus: Capitalism and Schizophrenia*. University of Minnesota Press.

Deligne, Chloé. 2012. "Brussels and Its Rivers, 1770–1880: Reshaping an Urban Landscape." In *Urban Rivers: Remaking Rivers, Cities and Space in Europe and North America*, edited by Stéphane Castonguay and Matthew Evenden, 17–33. University of Pittsburgh Press.

Dixon, Karl S., and Craig Thompson. 1955. "Rebirth of a Great River." *Saturday Evening Post*, December 24, 19, 61–62.

Dodds, Gordon B. 1969. The Stream-Flow Controversy: A Conservation Turning Point. *Journal of American History* 56(1): 59–69.

Donovan, Lisa, and Lucy May. 1998. "Riverfront Plan Sunk, but Shirey Still Afloat." *Cincinnati Enquirer*, April 21, A1, A8.

Doss, Erika. 1992. "Raising Community Consciousness with Public Art: Contrasting Projects by Judy Baca and Andrew Leicester." *American Art* 6(1): 63–81.

Douglas, Mary. 1966. *Purity and Danger: An Analysis of Concepts of Pollution and Taboo*. Psychology Press.

Doukas, Dimitra. 2003. *Worked Over: The Corporate Sabotage of an American Community*. Cornell University Press.

Downs, Myron. 1939. Letter from Myron Downs to Alfred Bettman, March 31. Alfred Bettman Papers, Box 3, Folder 10. University of Cincinnati Archives & Rare Books, Cincinnati, Ohio.

Drake, Daniel. 1834. *Discourse on the History, Character, and Prospects of the West*. Truman and Smith.

Drooker, Penelope. 2002. "The Ohio Valley, 1550–1750: Patterns of Sociopolitical Coalescence and Dispersal." In *The Transformation of the Southeastern Indians, 1540–1760*, edited by Robbie Ethridge and Charles Hudson, 115–33. University Press of Mississippi.

Dunn, J. P. 1912. "Names of the Ohio River." *Indiana Quarterly Magazine of History* 8 (4): 166–70.

Durkheim, Émile. 1995 (1912). *The Elementary Forms of Religious Life*. Free Press.

Edwards, Morris. 1939. "Same Precepts Govern Commerce Activities After Ten Busy Decades—History of Queen City Linked with Organization." *Cincinnati Enquirer*, March 23, 8, 18.

Elyachar, Julia. 2012. "Next Practices: Knowledge, Infrastructure, and Public Goods at the Bottom of the Pyramid." *Public Culture* 24 (1): 109–29.

Ewing, Tom. 2017. "Rolling on the River with CORBA." *Maritime News*, May, 30–35.

Fairbanks, Robert B. 1988. *Making Better Citizens: Housing Reform and the Community Development Strategy in Cincinnati, 1890–1960*. University of Illinois Press.

Fairfield, John D. 1994. "The Scientific Management of Urban Space: Professional City Planning and the Legacy of Progressive Reform." *Journal of Urban History* 20(2): 179–204.

Feck, Luke. 1963. "Reply Soonest." *Cincinnati Enquirer*, September 17, 9.

Ferguson, James. 1990. *The Anti-Politics Machine: "Development," Depoliticization and Bureaucratic Power in Lesotho*. Cambridge University Press.

Findsen, Owen. 1997. "Police Protected District of Brothels." *Cincinnati Enquirer*, September 28, E14.

Fischer, Frank. 2000. *Citizens, Experts, and the Environment: The Politics of Local Knowledge*. Duke University Press.

Fleming, Kristen M. 2019. "Generating a New Ohio River: Ecological Transformation in the Nineteenth and Twentieth Centuries." PhD diss., University of Cincinnati.

Fletcher, David. 2008. "Flood Control Freakology: Los Angeles River Watershed." In *The Infrastructural City: Networked Ecologies in Los Angeles*, edited by Kazys Varnelis, 258–75. Actar.

Flyvbjerg, Bent. 2009. "Survival of the Unfittest: Why the Worst Infrastructure Gets Built—and What We Can Do About It." *Oxford Review of Economic Policy* 25(3): 344–67.

Frey, Bertram. 1974. "The Public Trust in Public Waterways." *Urban Law Annual* 7(1): 219–46.

Gandy, Matthew. 2014. *The Fabric of Space: Water, Modernity, and the Urban Imagination*. MIT Press.

Giglierano, Geoffrey. 1977. "The City and the System: Developing a Municipal Service, 1800–1915." *Cincinnati Historical Society Bulletin* 35: 223–47.

Glass, Pamela. 2017. "Almost 30 Years Later, Olmsted Lock and Dam Projected to Open in 2018," *Work Boat*, June 15. https://www.workboat.com/news/coastal-inland-waterways/olmsted-lock-dam-projected-open-2018/

Goetz, Kristina. 1999. "'River water in our veins.'" *Cincinnati Enquirer*, October 17, A21.

Golden, James T., Jr. 1948. "Here's What and Why of Ohio River Pact." *Cincinnati Enquirer*, March 14, 42.

Goodrich, Ernest. 1937. *Outline of City Planning Commission Investigation Concerning the Cincinnati Flood Problem and the Effect on the Comprehensive City Plan*. Alfred Bettman Papers, Box 7, Folder 19. University of Cincinnati Archives & Rare Books, Cincinnati, Ohio.

Gordon, Colin. 2004. "Blighting the Way: Urban Renewal, Economic Development, and the Elusive Definition of Blight." *Fordham Urban Law Journal* 31(2): 305.

Gordon, Dick. 1948. "Eight States Act Here as Truman OKs Anti-Pollution Bill." *Cincinnati Post*, June 30, 1.

Goss, Charles F. 1912. *Cincinnati, the Queen City, 1788–1912*. S. J. Clarke.

Gottlieb, Robert. 1993. *Forcing the Spring: The Transformation of the American Environmental Movement*. Island Press.

Graham, Stephen. 2010. *Disrupted Cities: When Infrastructure Fails*. Routledge.

Grayson, Frank Y. 1929. *Thrills of the Historic Ohio River*. Cincinnati Times-Star.

Gruenwald, Kim M. 2002. *River of Enterprise: The Commercial Origins of Regional Identity in the Ohio Valley, 1790–1850*. Indiana University Press.

Gusterson, Hugh. 2017. "From Brexit to Trump: Anthropology and the Rise of Nationalist Populism." *American Ethnologist* 44(2): 209–14.

Hahn, Barbara. 2004. "Union Terminal: Business Clubs, Railroads, and City Planning in Cincinnati, 1880–1933." *Journal of Urban History* 30(5): 707–28.

Halperin, Rhoda H. 1998. *Practicing Community: Class Culture and Power in an Urban Neighborhood*. University of Texas Press.

Hann, Chris M. 1998. "Introduction: The Embeddedness of Property." In *Property Relations: Renewing the Anthropological Tradition*, edited by Chris M. Hann, 1–31. Cambridge University Press.

Haraway, Donna J. 1992. "The Promises of Monsters: A Regenerative Politics for Inappropriate/d Others." In *Cultural Studies*, edited by Lawrence Grossberg, Cary Nelson, and Paula Treichler, 295–337. Routledge.

Haraway, Donna J. 2016. *Staying with the Trouble: Making Kin in the Chthulucene*. Duke University Press.

Harper Krista 2005. "'Wild Capitalism' and 'Ecocolonialism': A Tale of Two Rivers." *American Anthropologist* 107(2): 221–33.

Hart, Henry C. 1957. Crisis, Community, and Consent in Water Politics. *Law and Contemporary Problems* 22(3): 510–37.

Harvey, David. 1982. *The Limits to Capital*. Blackwell.

Harvey, David. 1989. "From Managerialism to Entrepreneurialism: The Transformation in Urban Governance in Late Capitalism." *Geografiska Annaler* 71(1): 3–17.

Hatfield, James T., Jr. 1939. Letter from James T. Hatfield Jr. to Alfred Bettman, May 29. Alfred Bettman Papers, Box 3, Folder 14. University of Cincinnati Archives & Rare Books, Cincinnati, Ohio.

Haydu, Jeffrey. 2002. "Business Citizenship at Work: Cultural Transposition and Class Formation in Cincinnati, 1870–1910." *American Journal of Sociology* 107(6): 1424–67.

Hays, Samuel P. 1959. *Conservation and the Gospel of Efficiency: The Progressive Conservation Movement, 1890–1920*. Harvard University Press.

Hearn, Lafcadio. 1953. *Children of the Levee*. University of Kentucky Press.

Hedeen, Stanley. 1994. *The Mill Creek: An Unnatural History of an Urban Stream*. Blue Heron Press.

Hendrickson, Walter B. 1973. "Science and Culture in the American Middle West." *Isis* 64(3): 326–40.

Herzfeld, Michael. 2005. "Political Optics and the Occlusion of Intimate Knowledge." *American Anthropologist* 107(3): 369–76.

Hubbard, Harlan. 1977. *Shantyboat: A River Way of Life*. University Press of Kentucky.

Insurance Journal. 2007. "Kentucky Survivors Recall the Ohio River Valley Flood of 1937." January 16. https://www.insurancejournal.com/news/southeast/2007/01/16/75851.htm

Jackson, John L., Jr. 2010. *Harlemworld: Doing Race and Class in Contemporary Black America*. University of Chicago Press.

Jermier, Aaron, Ernie Perry, Ben Zietlow, and Teresa Adams. 2016. "Port Development Strategies: Learning from the Ports of Cincinnati and Northern Kentucky." *Mid-America Freight Coalition* (blog), March 21. https://midamericafreight.org/index.php/2016/03/21/port-development-strategies-learning-from-the-ports-of-cincinnati-and-northern-kentucky/

Jewell, Katherine Rye. 2017. *Dollars for Dixie: Business and the Transformation of Conservatism in the Twentieth Century*. Cambridge University Press.

Johnson, Herbert A. 2010. *Gibbons v. Ogden: John Marshall, Steamboats, and the Commerce Clause*. University Press of Kansas.

Johnson, John W. 2008. *United States Water Law: An Introduction*. CRC Press.

Johnson, Leland R. 1991. "Engineering the Ohio." In *Always a River: The Ohio River and the American Experience*, edited by Robert L. Reid, 180–219. Indiana University Press.

Johnson, Walter. 2013. *River of Dark Dreams: Slavery and Empire in the Cotton Kingdom*. Harvard University Press.

Joyce, Patrick. 2003. *The Rule of Freedom: Liberalism and the Modern City*. Verso.

Kaika, Maria. 2005. *City of Flows: Modernity, Nature, and the City*. Routledge.

Katz, Wendy J. 2002. *Regionalism and Reform: Art and Class Formation in Antebellum Cincinnati*. Ohio State University Press.

Kehoe, Terence. 1997. *Cleaning Up the Great Lakes: From Cooperation to Confrontation*. Northern Illinois University Press.

Kelman, Ari. 2006. *A River and Its City: The Nature of Landscape in New Orleans*. University of California Press.

Khan, Shamus Rahman. 2012. "The Sociology of Elites." *Annual Review of Sociology* 38: 361–77.

Knoll, Martin, Uwe Lübken, and Dieter Schott. 2017. "Introduction." In *Rivers Lost, Rivers Regained: Rethinking City-River Relations*, edited by Martin Knoll, Uwe Lübken, and Dieter Schott, 3–22. University of Chicago Press.

Kohn, Eduardo. 2013. *How Forests Think: Toward an Anthropology Beyond the Human.* University of California Press.

Kornbluh, Andrea T. 1986. *Lighting the Way: The Woman's Club of Cincinnati, 1915–1965.* Young & Klein.

Koslov, Liz. 2016. "The Case for Retreat." *Public Culture* 28(2): 359–87.

Kreimer, Florence S. 1939. Letter from Florence S. Kreimer to Alfred Bettman, March 31. Alfred Bettman Papers, Box 3, Folder 10. University of Cincinnati Archives & Rare Books, Cincinnati, Ohio.

Kreimer, Ralph A. 1937. Letter from Ralph A. Kreimer to J. V. Maescher, December 16. Louis Coffin Collection, Cincinnatus Association Papers. Cincinnati History Library and Archives, Cincinnati, Ohio.

Laidley, Jennefer. 2007. The Ecosystem Approach and the Global Imperative on Toronto's Central Waterfront. *Cities* 24(4): 259–72.

Landon, Charles E. 1961. Freight Traffic on the Ohio River. *Financial Analysts Journal* 17(3): 51–57.

Larkin, Brian. 2013. "The Politics and Poetics of Infrastructure." *Annual Review of Anthropology* 42(1): 327–43.

Larson, John L. 2001. *Internal Improvement: National Public Works and the Promise of Popular Government in the Early United States.* UNC Press.

Latour, Bruno. 1993. *We Have Never Been Modern.* Harvard University Press.

Latour, Bruno. 2005. *Reassembling the Social: An Introduction to Actor-Network Theory.* Oxford University Press.

Law, John. 1994. *Organizing Modernity.* Blackwell.

Lazzaro, Claudia. 2011. "River Gods: Personifying Nature in Sixteenth-Century Italy." *Renaissance Studies* 25(1): 70–94.

Lewis, Sinclair. 1922. *Babbitt.* Harcourt, Brace.

Lewis, William. 2016. "Building Commerce: Ohio Valley Shipbuilding During the Era of the Early American Republic." *Ohio Valley History* 16(1): 24–44.

Linton, Jamie. 2010. *What Is Water?: The History of a Modern Abstraction.* University of British Columbia Press.

Lippincott, Isaac. 1914. "A History of River Improvement." *Journal of Political Economy* 22(7): 630–60.

Lipsitz, George. 2006. *The Possessive Investment in Whiteness: How White People Profit from Identity Politics.* Temple University Press.

Logan, John R., and Harvey Molotch. 1987. *Urban Fortunes: The Political Economy of Place.* University of California Press.

Low, George S., and Ronald Fullerton. 1994. "Brands, Brand Management, and the Brand Manager System: A Critical-Historical Evaluation." *Journal of Marketing Research* 31(2): 173–90.

Lübken, Uwe. 2012. "Rivers and Risk in the City: The Urban Floodplain as a Contested Space." In *Urban Rivers: Remaking Rivers, Cities and Space in Europe and North*

America, edited by Stéphane Castonguay and Matthew Evenden, 130–44. University of Pittsburgh Press.

Luke, Timothy W. 1995. "On Environmentality: Geo-Power and Eco-Knowledge in the Discourses of Contemporary Environmentalism." *Cultural Critique* (31): 57–81.

Mahoney, Timothy R. 1990. *River Towns in the Great West: The Structure of Provincial Urbanization in the American Midwest, 1820–1870*. Cambridge University Press.

Marchand, Roland. 1985. *Advertising the American Dream: Making Way for Modernity, 1920–1940*. University of California Press.

Marsh, George P. 1864. *Man and Nature: Or, Physical Geography as Modified by Human Action*. C. Scribner.

Marting, W. W. 1939. Letter from W. W. Marting to Alfred Bettman, May 22. Alfred Bettman Papers, Box 3, Folder 14. University of Cincinnati Archives & Rare Books, Cincinnati, Ohio.

Marx, Leo. 1964. *The Machine in the Garden: Technology and the Pastoral Ideal in America*. Oxford University Press.

McGee, William J. 1909. "Water as a Resource." *Annals of the American Academy of Political and Social Science* 33(3): 37–50.

McNeil, Maureen. 1998. "Gender, Expertise and Feminism." In *Exploring Expertise: Issues and Perspectives*, edited by Robin Williams, Wendy Faulkner, and James Fleck. Palgrave Macmillan.

Melosi, Martin V. 2008. *The Sanitary City: Environmental Services in Urban America from Colonial Times to the Present*. University of Pittsburgh Press.

Merchant, Carolyn. 1980. *The Death of Nature: Women, Ecology, and the Scientific Revolution*. Harper & Row.

Merchant, Carolyn. 1984. "Women of the Progressive Conservation Movement: 1900–1916." *Environmental Review* 8(1): 57–85.

Miller, Zane L. 1968. "Boss Cox's Cincinnati: A Study in Urbanization and Politics, 1880–1914." *Journal of American History* 54(4): 823–38.

Miller, Zane L. 1980. *Boss Cox's Cincinnati: Urban Politics in the Progressive Era*. University of Chicago Press.

Mitchell, Lawrence F. 1998. "The Evolution of the Cincinnati Central Business District and Riverfront: An Historical and Architectural Approach, 1900–1989." PhD diss., University of Cincinnati.

Mitchell, Timothy. 2002. *Rule of Experts: Egypt, Techno-Politics, Modernity*. University of California Press.

Molle, François. 2009. "Water, Politics and River Basin Governance: Repoliticizing Approaches to River Basin Management." *Water International* 34(1): 62–70.

Morgan, Sharon. 1993. "'Sink' Simpkinson had a Vision for Cincinnati." *Cincinnati Enquirer*, August 18, B8.

Mukerji, Chandra. 2009. *Impossible Engineering: Technology and Territoriality on the Canal Du Midi*. Princeton University Press.

Muncy, Robyn. 1997. "Trustbusting and White Manhood in America, 1898–1914." *American Studies* 38(3): 21–42.

Murphy, Lindon J. 1932. "Sewage Treatment and the Public." *Sewage Works Journal* 4(2): 296–99.

Murray, David. 2018. "Olmsted Locks and Dam Formally (and Finally) Dedicated." *Waterways Journal Weekly*, August 30. https://www.waterwaysjournal.net/2018/08/30/olmsted-locks-and-dam-formally-and-finally-dedicated/

North American Wildlife Conference. 1947. *Transactions of the Twelfth North American Wildlife Conference*. Wildlife Management Institute.

NRC (National Resources Committee). 1935. "Proceedings of a Meeting," December 7. Alfred Bettman Papers, Box 14, Folder 22. University of Cincinnati Archives & Rare Books, Cincinnati, Ohio.

NRHC (National Rivers and Harbors Congress). 1912. *Proceedings of the Convention, National Rivers and Harbors Congress*. W. F. Roberts Co.

New York Times. 1916. "George B. Cox Dies." May 21, 38.

Obama, Barack. 2010. "Remarks by the President on Rebuilding America's Infrastructure." October 11, transcript, Rose Garden. https://obamawhitehouse.archives.gov/the-press-office/2010/10/11/remarks-president-rebuilding-americas-infrastructure

Obama, Barack. 2014. "Remarks by the President on Building a 21st Century Infrastructure." May 14, transcript, Washington Irving Boat Club. https://obamawhitehouse.archives.gov/the-press-office/2014/05/14/remarks-president-building-21st-century-infrastructure

Oliver-Smith, Anthony. 1999. "'What Is a Disaster?': Anthropological Perspectives on a Persistent Question." In *The Angry Earth: Disaster in Anthropological Perspective*, edited by Anthony Oliver-Smith and Susannah M. Hoffman, 18–34. Routledge.

O'Neill, Karen M. 2006. *Rivers by Design: State Power and the Origins of U.S. Flood Control*. Duke University Press.

ORSANCO (Ohio River Valley Water Sanitation Commission). n.d. *Clean Streams for the Ohio Valley*. Ohio River Valley Water Sanitation Commission.

ORSANCO (Ohio River Valley Water Sanitation Commission). 1949a. *Investigations Leading to Recommended Treatment Standards for Organic Wastes Discharged to the Cincinnati Pool*. Ohio River Valley Water Sanitation Commission.

ORSANCO (Ohio River Valley Water Sanitation Commission). 1949b. *First Annual Report*. ORSANCO.

ORSANCO (Ohio River Valley Water Sanitation Commission). 1950. *Second Annual Report*. ORSANCO.

ORSANCO (Ohio River Valley Water Sanitation Commission). 1951. *Third Annual Report*. ORSANCO.

ORSANCO (Ohio River Valley Water Sanitation Commission). 1952. *Fourth Annual Report*. ORSANCO.

ORSANCO (Ohio River Valley Water Sanitation Commission). 1957. *Ninth Annual Summary*. ORSANCO.

Ostler, Jeffrey. 2015. "'To Extirpate the Indians': An Indigenous Consciousness of Genocide in the Ohio Valley and Lower Great Lakes, 1750s–1810." *William and Mary Quarterly* 72(4): 587–622.

Ottinger, Gwen. 2013. *Refining Expertise: How Responsible Engineers Subvert Environmental Justice Challenges*. NYU Press.

OVIA (Ohio Valley Improvement Association). n.d.(a). "Rail-Water Cooperation." OVIA.

OVIA (Ohio Valley Improvement Association). n.d.(b). "This Is the Empire—the Ohio Valley." OVIA.

OVIA (Ohio Valley Improvement Association). 1895. *Proceedings of the Ohio Valley Improvement Convention.* OVIA.

OVIA (Ohio Valley Improvement Association). 1899. *The Ohio Valley Improvement Association Report of Progress from 1895 to 1899.* W. B. Carpenter Co.

OVIA (Ohio Valley Improvement Association). 1900. *Ohio Valley Improvement Association Proceedings: Sixth Annual Convention.* OVIA.

OVIA (Ohio Valley Improvement Association). 1902. *Proceedings of Ohio Valley Improvement Association Eighth Annual Convention.* OVIA.

OVIA (Ohio Valley Improvement Association). 1903. *Proceedings of the Ninth Annual Convention of the Ohio Valley Improvement Association.* OVIA.

OVIA (Ohio Valley Improvement Association). 1904. *Proceedings of the Tenth Annual Ohio Valley Improvement Association Convention.* OVIA.

OVIA (Ohio Valley Improvement Association). 1905. *Eleventh Annual Ohio Valley Improvement Association Convention—Proceedings.* OVIA.

OVIA (Ohio Valley Improvement Association). 1906. *Proceedings of the Twelfth Annual Ohio Valley Improvement Association Convention.* OVIA.

OVIA (Ohio Valley Improvement Association). 1907. *Proceedings of the Thirteenth Annual Convention of the Ohio Valley Improvement Association.* OVIA.

OVIA (Ohio Valley Improvement Association). 1908. *Proceedings of the Fourteenth Annual Convention of the Ohio Valley Improvement Association.* Ebbert & Richardson Co.

OVIA (Ohio Valley Improvement Association). 1909. *Proceedings of the Fourteenth Annual Convention of the Ohio Valley Improvement Association.* Ebbert & Richardson Co.

OVIA (Ohio Valley Improvement Association). 1910. *Proceedings of the Sixteenth Annual Convention—Ohio Valley Improvement Association.* Ebbert & Richardson Co.

OVIA (Ohio Valley Improvement Association). 1923. *Proceedings of the Twenty-Ninth Annual Convention of the Ohio Valley Improvement Association.* OVIA.

OVIA (Ohio Valley Improvement Association). 1924. *Proceedings of the Thirtieth Annual Convention of the Ohio Valley Improvement Association.* OVIA.

OVIA (Ohio Valley Improvement Association). 1925. *Proceedings of the 31st Annual Convention of the Ohio Valley Improvement Association.* OVIA.

OVIA (Ohio Valley Improvement Association). 1927. *Convention Proceedings 33rd Annual Meeting of the Ohio Valley Improvement Association.* OVIA.

OVIA (Ohio Valley Improvement Association). 1929a. *Official Program and Complete History: Ohio River Pageant and Dedication.* OVIA.

OVIA (Ohio Valley Improvement Association). 1929b. *Ohio River Dedicatory Celebration 1929: Convention Proceedings.* OVIA.

OVIA (Ohio Valley Improvement Association). 1930. *Proceedings of the Thirty-sixth Annual Convention.* OVIA.

OVIA (Ohio Valley Improvement Association). 1934. *Addresses Delivered at the Fortieth Annual Convention of the Ohio Valley Improvement Association.* OVIA.

OVIA (Ohio Valley Improvement Association). 1935. *Addresses Delivered at the Forty-first Annual Convention of the Ohio Valley Improvement Assn.* OVIA.

OVIA (Ohio Valley Improvement Association). 1958. *The Ohio Valley Story.* OVIA.

Paavola, Jouni. 2006. "Interstate Water Pollution Problems and Elusive Federal Water Pollution Policy in the United States, 1900–1948." *Environment and History* 12(4): 435–65.

Paeth, Greg. 2018. "NKyMR18: Billions of Dollars Pouring into an Already Asset-Rich Logistics Scene." *Lane Report—Kentucky Business,* February 2. https://www.lanereport.com/86590/2018/02/nkymr18-billions-of-dollars-pouring-into-an-already-asset-rich-logistics-scene/.

Payne, Frederick L. 1983. "The Evolution of Yeatman's Cove Park." *Queen City Heritage* 41: 35–42.

Pinchot, Gifford. 1947. *Breaking New Ground.* Island Press.

Pisani, Donald J. 1992. *To Reclaim a Divided West: Water, Law, and Public Policy, 1848–1902.* University of New Mexico Press.

Pisani, Donald J. 2006. "Water Planning in the Progressive Era: The Inland Waterways Commission Reconsidered." *Journal of Policy History* 18(4): 389–418.

Pisarski, Genevieve. 1996. "Testing the Limits of the Federal Navigational Servitude." *Ocean and Coastal Law Journal* 2(2): 313–40.

Pohl, H. H. 1937. "Ohio River Flood Control Plan." *Journal (American Water Works Association)* 29(5): 589–96.

Ponder, Stephen. 1990. "'Publicity in the Interest of the People': Theodore Roosevelt's Conservation Crusade." *Presidential Studies Quarterly* 20(3): 547–55.

Postel, Charles. 2007. *The Populist Vision.* Oxford University Press.

Potthoff, Henry A. 1939. Letter from H. A. Potthoff to Alfred Bettman, March 16. Alfred Bettman Papers, Box 3, Folder 9. University of Cincinnati Archives & Rare Books, Cincinnati, Ohio.

Povinelli, Elizabeth A. 2016. *Geontologies: A Requiem to Late Liberalism.* Duke University Press.

Pritchard, Sara B. 2011. *Confluence: The Nature of Technology and the Remaking of the Rhône.* Harvard University Press.

Pritchett, Wendell. 2003. "The 'Public Menace' of Blight: Urban Renewal and the Private Uses of Eminent Domain." *Yale Law and Policy Review* 21(1): 1–52.

Pulido, Laura. 2000. "Rethinking Environmental Racism: White Privilege and Urban Development in Southern California." *Annals of the Association of American Geographers* 90(1): 12–40.

RAC (Riverfront Advisory Council). 1975a. RAC Paper #2, Riverfront Study, February 5. Ewart Simpkinson Papers, MSS 841, Box 5, Folder 4. Cincinnati History Library and Archives, Cincinnati, Ohio.

RAC (Riverfront Advisory Council). 1975b. General Riverfront Council Program—Considerations Involved in Formulation of Riverfront Plan, Policies, and Progress, February 7. Ewart Simpkinson Papers, MSS 841, Box 5, Folder 4. Cincinnati History Library and Archives, Cincinnati, Ohio.

RAC (Riverfront Advisory Council). 1975c. Agenda for Riverfront Advisory Council Executive Committee Meeting, February 27. Ewart Simpkinson Papers, MSS 841, Box 5, Folder 4. Cincinnati History Library and Archives, Cincinnati, Ohio.

RAC (Riverfront Advisory Council). 1976. Draft Report of the Riverfront Advisory Council. Ewart Simpkinson Papers, MSS 841, Box 5, Folder 35. Cincinnati History Library and Archives, Cincinnati, Ohio.

RAC (Riverfront Advisory Council). 1981. *A Study of the Cincinnati Riverfront*. City of Cincinnati.

Radebaugh, Gus H. 1933. "Selling Sewage Treatment." *Sewage Works Journal* 5(6): 988–97.

Rademacher, Anne. 2011. *Reigning the River: Urban Ecologies and Political Transformation in Kathmandu*. Duke University Press.

Rankin, William. 2009. "Infrastructure and the International Governance of Economic Development, 1950–1965." In *Internationalization of Infrastructures: Proceedings of the 12th Annual International Conference on the Economics of Infrastructures*, edited by Jean-François Auger, Jan Jaap Bouma, and Rolf Künneke, 61–75. Delft University of Technology.

Reuss, Martin. 2008. "Seeing Like an Engineer: Water Projects and the Mediation of the Incommensurable." *Technology and Culture* 49(3): 531–46.

Robbins, Christopher. 2016. "Gentrified Aquarium: De Blasio's Streetcar and the Tale of Two Waterfronts." *Village Voice*, September 13. https://www.villagevoice.com/2016/09/13/gentrified-aquarium-de-blasios-streetcar-and-the-tale-of-two-waterfronts/

Robinson, Michael C. 1983. *History of Navigation in the Ohio River Basin*. National Waterways Study.

Rosen, Christine M. 2012. "Fact Versus Conjecture in the History of Industrial Waste Utilization." *Econ Journal Watch* 9(2): 112–21.

Ross, Benjamin, and Steven Amter. 2010. *The Polluters: The Making of Our Chemically Altered Environment*. Oxford University Press.

Ross, Steven J. 1985. *Workers on the Edge: Work, Leisure, and Politics in Industrializing Cincinnati, 1788–1890*. Figueroa Press.

Salafia, Matthew. 2013. *Slavery's Borderland: Freedom and Bondage Along the Ohio River*. University of Pennsylvania Press.

Sanders, Scott R. 1991. "The Force of Moving Water." In *Always a River: The Ohio River and the American Experience*, edited by Robert L. Reid, 1–31. Indiana University Press.

Scarpino, Philip V. 1985. *Great River: An Environmental History of the Upper Mississippi, 1890–1950*. University of Missouri Press.

Schmidt, Jeremy J. 2014. Historicising the Hydrosocial Cycle. *Water Alternatives* 7(1): 220–34.

Schmidt, Jeremy J. 2017. *Water: Abundance, Scarcity, and Security in the Age of Humanity*. NYU Press.

Schroth, Herbert. 1937. *Shall Cincinnati Be Dyked?* Flood Protection Committee Collection, March 9. Cincinnatus Association Papers, MSS 617, Box 1, Folder 1. Cincinnati History Library and Archives, Cincinnati, Ohio.

Scientific American. 1911. "The Largest Movable Wicket Dam." September 2, 204.

Scott, James C. 1985. *Weapons of the Weak: Everyday Forms of Peasant Resistance.* Yale University Press.

Scott, James C. 1998. *Seeing Like a State: How Certain Schemes to Improve the Human Condition Have Failed.* Yale University Press.

Segoe, Ladislas. 1937. *An Inquiry into the Appropriateness of the Ohio Valley Basin as a Region for Planning.* Alfred Bettman Papers, Box 14, Folder 27. University of Cincinnati Archives & Rare Books, Cincinnati, Ohio.

Segoe, Ladislas. 1939. Letter from Ladislas Segoe to City Planning Commission, May 27. Alfred Bettman Papers, Box 3, Folder 14. University of Cincinnati Archives & Rare Books, Cincinnati, Ohio.

Shallat, Todd. 1994. *Structures in the Stream: Water, Science, and the Rise of the U.S. Army Corps of Engineers.* University of Texas Press.

Shanley, Robert A. 1988. "Franklin D. Roosevelt and Water Pollution Control Policy." *Presidential Studies Quarterly* 18(2): 319–30.

Sherrill, Clarence O. 1938a. Letter from Col. Clarence Sherrill to City Council, March 9. Alfred Bettman Papers, Box 2, Folder 26. University of Cincinnati Archives & Rare Books, Cincinnati, Ohio.

Sherrill, Clarence O. 1938b. Letter from Col. Clarence Sherrill to City Council, March 23. Alfred Bettman Papers, Box 2, Folder 27. University of Cincinnati Archives & Rare Books, Cincinnati, Ohio.

Sherrill, Clarence O. 1939. Form IV from City Manager to City Council, March 8. Alfred Bettman Papers, Box 3, Folder 8. University of Cincinnati Archives & Rare Books, Cincinnati, Ohio.

Silver, Christopher. 1997. "The Racial Origins of Zoning in American Cities." In *Urban Planning and the African American Community: In the Shadows*, edited by June M. Thomas and Marsha Ritzdorf, 23–42. SAGE Publications.

Simone, AbdouMaliq. 2004. "People as Infrastructure: Intersecting Fragments in Johannesburg." *Public Culture* 16(3): 407–29.

Simpkinson, Ewart. 1976. Letter from Ewart Simpkinson to DeJager, August 24. Ewart Simpkinson Papers, MSS 841, Box 5, Folder 21. Cincinnati History Library and Archives, Cincinnati, Ohio.

Sleeper-Smith, Susan. 2018. *Indigenous Prosperity and American Conquest: Indian Women of the Ohio River Valley, 1690–1792.* UNC Press.

Sloss, James, and Carl D. Martland. 1984. "Government Intervention in Railroad Freight Car Per Diem: An Historical Perspective." *Transportation Journal* 23(4): 83–95.

Smith, Carrie B. 2016. "Cincinnati Marina Gets Cheers and Jeers." *Cincinnati Enquirer*, June 21. https://www.cincinnati.com/story/news/2016/06/21/cincinnati-marina-gets-cheers-and-jeers/86144026/

Smith, Carrie B. 2018. "How to Ride on Cincinnati's 'Invisible Gorilla.'" *Cincinnati Enquirer*, July 31. https://www.cincinnati.com/story/entertainment/2018/07/31/paddlefest-ohio-river-new-gis-mapping-website/767417002/

Smith, Matthew D. 2016. "The Specter of Cholera in Nineteenth-Century Cincinnati." *Ohio Valley History* 16(2): 21–40.

Smith, Neil. 1996. *The New Urban Frontier: Gentrification and the Revanchist City*. Psychology Press.

Smith, Neil. 2008. *Uneven Development: Nature, Capital, and the Production of Space*. University of Georgia Press.

Souther, Leslie. 1957. Leslie Souther Memoir. Interview by John Knoepfle, August 19. Public Library of Cincinnati and Sangamon State University Inland Rivers Memoir Project. Archives/Special Collections LIB 144, University of Illinois at Springfield, Springfield, Ill.

Stanley Consultants. 1967. *Report on Riverfront Development Plan*. Cincinnati Department of Urban Development.

Star, Susan L. 1999. "The Ethnography of Infrastructure." *American Behavioral Scientist* 43(3): 377–91.

Stimson, George P. 1964. "River on a Rampage: An Account of the Ohio River Flood of 1937." *Cincinnati Historical Society Bulletin* 22(2): 90–109.

Stolz, Robert. 2014. *Bad Water: Nature, Pollution, and Politics in Japan, 1870–1950*. Duke University Press.

Stone, Clarence Nathan. 1989. *Regime Politics: Governing Atlanta, 1946–1988*. University Press of Kansas.

Stradling, David. 2003. *Cincinnati: From River City to Highway Metropolis*. Arcadia.

Stradling, David, and Richard Stradling. 2008. "Perceptions of the Burning River: Deindustrialization and Cleveland's Cuyahoga River." *Environmental History* 13(3): 515–35.

Swyngedouw, Erik. 1999. "Modernity and Hybridity: Nature, Regeneracionismo, and the Production of the Spanish Waterscape, 1890–1930." *Annals of the Association of American Geographers* 89(3): 443–65.

Swyngedouw, Erik. 2004. *Social Power and the Urbanization of Water: Flows of Power*. Oxford University Press.

Tarr, Joel A. 1985. "Industrial Wastes and Public Health: Some Historical Notes, Part I, 1876–1932." *American Journal of Public Health* 75(9): 1059–67.

Taylor, Henry L., Jr. 1993. *Race and the City: Work, Community, and Protest in Cincinnati, 1820–1970*. University of Illinois Press.

Taylor, Nikki M. 2004. *Frontiers of Freedom: Cincinnati's Black Community, 1802–1868*. Ohio University Press.

Thomas, John Clayton. 1986. *Between Citizen and City: Neighborhood Organizations and Urban Politics in Cincinnati*. University Press of Kansas.

Thwaites, Reuben G. 1897. *Afloat on the Ohio: An Historical Pilgrimage of a Thousand Miles in a Skiff, from Redstone to Cairo*. Way & Williams.

Torgersen, Eilin Holtan. 2018. "Waters of Destruction: Mythical Creatures, Boiling Pots and Tourist Encounters at Wailuku River in Hilo, Hawai'i." In *Island Rivers: Fresh Water and Place in Oceania*, edited by John R. Wagner and Jerry K. Jacka, 165–86. ANU Press.

Trollope, Frances Milton. 1832. *Domestic Manners of the Americans*. Whittaker, Treacher, & Co..

Trotter, Joe W., Jr. 1998. *River Jordan: African American Urban Life in the Ohio Valley*. University Press of Kentucky.

Trump, Donald. 2017. "Remarks in Cincinnati, Ohio." June 17, transcript, Rivertowne

Marina. https://www.govinfo.gov/content/pkg/DCPD-201700542/pdf/DCPD-201700542.pdf

Tsing, Anna L. 2005. *Friction: An Ethnography of Global Connection.* Princeton University Press.

Tsing, Anna L. 2015. *The Mushroom at the End of the World: On the Possibility of Life in Capitalist Ruins.* Princeton University Press.

Tucker, Louis L. 1967. *Cincinnati's Citizen Crusaders: A History of the Cincinnatus Association, 1920–1965.* Cincinnati Historical Society.

USACE (U.S. Army Corps of Engineers). 2017. *Waterborne Commerce Statistics for Calendar Year 2016: Waterborne Commerce National Totals and Selected Inland Waterways for Multiple Years.* Waterborne Commerce Statistics Center.

Vaughn, Sarah E. 2012. "Reconstructing the Citizen: Disaster, Citizenship, and Expertise in Racial Guyana." *Critique of Anthropology* 32(4): 359–87.

Venkatesan, Soumhya, Laura Bear, Penny Harvey, Sian Lazar, Laura Rival, and AbdouMaliq Simone. 2017. "Attention to Infrastructure Offers a Welcome Reconfiguration of Anthropological Approaches to the Political." *Critique of Anthropology* 38(1): 3–52.

Verdery, Katherine. 2004. "The Obligations of Ownership: Restoring Rights to Land in Postsocialist Transylvania." In *Property in Question: Value Transformation in the Global Economy*, edited by Katherine Verdery and Caroline Humphrey, 139–60. Bloomsbury Academic.

Vertesi, Janet. 2014. "Seamful Spaces: Heterogeneous Infrastructures in Interaction." *Science, Technology, & Human Values* 39(2): 264–84.

Wade, Richard C. 1959. *The Urban Frontier: The Rise of Western Cities, 1790–1830.* Harvard University Press.

Wadsworth, J. S. 1967. Letter from J. S. Wadsworth to Eugene Ruehlmann, March 27. Eugene Ruehlmann Papers, Box 73, Folder 4. University of Cincinnati Archives & Rare Books, Cincinnati, Ohio.

Walker, Gordon, Rebecca Whittle, Will Medd, and Marion Walker. 2011. "Assembling the Flood: Producing Spaces of Bad Water in the City of Hull." *Environment and Planning A: Economy and Space* 43(10): 2304–20.

Walker, Robert H. 1988. "Gene Ruehlmann and Bob Howsam: Designing a Riverfront Winner." *Queen City Heritage* 46(2): 42–49.

Warner, William L., and Paul S. Lunt. 1941. *The Social Life of a Modern Community.* Yale University Press.

Waugh, Richard, and Judith Hourigan. 1980. *A History of the Board of Engineers for Rivers and Harbors.* U.S. Army Corps of Engineers.

Welky, David. 2011. *The Thousand-Year Flood: The Ohio-Mississippi Disaster of 1937.* University of Chicago Press.

Whatmore, Sarah J. 2013. "Earthly Powers and Affective Environments: An Ontological Politics of Flood Risk." *Theory, Culture & Society* 30(7–8): 33–50.

White, David, Karla Johnston, and Michael Miller. 2011. "Ohio River Basin." In *Rivers of North America*, edited by Arthur Benke and Colbert Cushing, 375–424. Elsevier Science & Technology.

White, John H., Jr. 1999. "The World's Oldest Steamboat Company?: The U.S. Mail Line." *Queen City Heritage* 57(2–3): 50–68.

White, Richard. 1995. *The Organic Machine.* Hill & Wang.

Wiebe, Robert H. 1967. *The Search for Order, 1877–1920.* Hill & Wang.

Wilhelm, Hubert. 1991. "Settlement and Selected Landscape Imprints in the Ohio Valley." In *Always a River: The Ohio River and the American Experience*, edited by Robert L. Reid, 67–104. Indiana University Press.

Wilkinson, Howard. 2008. "Banks' Groundbreaking to Revitalize Riverfront." *Cincinnati Enquirer*, April 2, A1, A5.

Williams, Raymond. 1973. *The Country and the City.* Oxford University Press.

Wolf, Eric R. 1990. "Distinguished Lecture: Facing Power—Old Insights, New Questions." *American Anthropologist* 92(3): 586–96.

Wolff, Raphael G., dir. 1945. *Clean Waters.* General Electric "More Power to America" Series. Raphael G. Wolff Studios.

Worster, Donald. 1985. *Rivers of Empire: Water, Aridity, and the Growth of the American West.* Pantheon Books.

WPA (Work Progress Administration). 1940. *The Ohio Guide.* Oxford University Press.

WPA (Work Progress Administration). 1943. *Cincinnati: A Guide to the Queen City and Its Neighbors.* U.S. History Publishers.

Zimmerman, James. 1972. "Beaches and Bloomers: Bathing and Boating in Cincinnati Waters." *Cincinnati Historical Society Bulletin* 30(2): 130–45.

INDEX

GEOGRAPHIES OF JUSTICE AND SOCIAL TRANSFORMATION

1. *Social Justice and the City, rev.ed.*
BY DAVID HARVEY
2. *Begging as a Path to Progress: Indigenous Women and Children and the Struggle for Ecuador's Urban Spaces*
BY KATE SWANSON
3. *Making the San Fernando Valley: Rural Landscapes, Urban Development, and White Privilege*
BY LAURA R. BARRACLOUGH
4. *Company Towns in the Americas: Landscape, Power, and Working-Class Communities*
EDITED BY OLIVER J. DINIUS AND ANGELA VERGARA
5. *Tremé: Race and Place in a New Orleans Neighborhood*
BY MICHAEL E. CRUTCHER JR.
6. *Bloomberg's New York: Class and Governance in the Luxury City*
BY JULIAN BRASH
7. *Roppongi Crossing: The Demise of a Tokyo Nightclub District and the Reshaping of a Global City*
BY ROMAN ADRIAN CYBRIWSKY
8. *Fitzgerald: Geography of a Revolution*
BY WILLIAM BUNGE
9. *Accumulating Insecurity: Violence and Dispossession in the Making of Everyday Life*
EDITED BY SHELLEY FELDMAN, CHARLES GEISLER, AND GAYATRI A. MENON
10. *They Saved the Crops: Labor, Landscape, and the Struggle over Industrial Farming in Bracero-Era California*
BY DON MITCHELL
11. *Faith Based: Religious Neoliberalism and the Politics of Welfare in the United States*
BY JASON HACKWORTH
12. *Fields and Streams: Stream Restoration, Neoliberalism, and the Future of Environmental Science*
BY REBECCA LAVE
13. *Black, White, and Green: Farmers Markets, Race, and the Green Economy*
BY ALISON HOPE ALKON
14. *Beyond Walls and Cages: Prisons, Borders, and Global Crisis*
EDITED BY JENNA M. LOYD, MATT MITCHELSON, AND ANDREW BURRIDGE
15. *Silent Violence: Food, Famine, and Peasantry in Northern Nigeria*
BY MICHAEL J. WATTS
16. *Development, Security, and Aid: Geopolitics and Geoeconomics at the U.S. Agency for International Development*
BY JAMEY ESSEX
17. *Properties of Violence: Law and Land-Grant Struggle in Northern New Mexico*
BY DAVID CORREIA
18. *Geographical Diversions: Tibetan Trade, Global Transactions*
BY TINA HARRIS

19. *The Politics of the Encounter: Urban Theory and Protest under Planetary Urbanization*
BY ANDY MERRIFIELD

20. *Rethinking the South African Crisis: Nationalism, Populism, Hegemony*
BY GILLIAN HART

21. *The Empires' Edge: Militarization, Resistance, and Transcending Hegemony in the Pacific*
BY SASHA DAVIS

22. *Pain, Pride, and Politics: Social Movement Activism and the Sri Lankan Tamil Diaspora in Canada*
BY AMARNATH AMARASINGAM

23. *Selling the Serengeti: The Cultural Politics of Safari Tourism*
BY BENJAMIN GARDNER

24. *Territories of Poverty: Rethinking North and South*
EDITED BY ANANYA ROY AND EMMA SHAW CRANE

25. *Precarious Worlds: Contested Geographies of Social Reproduction*
EDITED BY KATIE MEEHAN AND KENDRA STRAUSS

26. *Spaces of Danger: Culture and Power in the Everyday*
EDITED BY HEATHER MERRILL AND LISA M. HOFFMAN

27. *Shadows of a Sunbelt City: The Environment, Racism, and the Knowledge Economy in Austin*
BY ELIOT M. TRETTER

28. *Beyond the Kale: Urban Agriculture and Social Justice Activism in New York City*
BY KRISTIN REYNOLDS AND NEVIN COHEN

29. *Calculating Property Relations: Chicago's Wartime Industrial Mobilization, 1940–1950*
BY ROBERT LEWIS

30. *In the Public's Interest: Evictions, Citizenship, and Inequality in Contemporary Delhi*
BY GAUTAM BHAN

31. *The Carpetbaggers of Kabul and Other American-Afghan Entanglements: Intimate Development, Geopolitics, and the Currency of Gender and Grief*
BY JENNIFER L. FLURI AND RACHEL LEHR

32. *Masculinities and Markets: Raced and Gendered Urban Politics in Milwaukee*
BY BRENDA PARKER

33. *We Want Land to Live: Making Political Space for Food Sovereignty*
BY AMY TRAUGER

34. *The Long War: CENTCOM, Grand Strategy, and Global Security*
BY JOHN MORRISSEY

35. *Development Drowned and Reborn: The Blues and Bourbon Restorations in Post-Katrina New Orleans*
BY CLYDE WOODS
EDITED BY JORDAN T. CAMP AND LAURA PULIDO

36. *The Priority of Injustice: Locating Democracy in Critical Theory*
BY CLIVE BARNETT

37. *Spaces of Capital / Spaces of Resistance: Mexico and the Global Political Economy*
BY CHRIS HESKETH

38. *Revolting New York: How 400 Years of Riot, Rebellion, Uprising, and Revolution Shaped a City*
GENERAL EDITORS: NEIL SMITH AND DON MITCHELL
EDITORS: ERIN SIODMAK, JENJOY ROYBAL, MARNIE BRADY, AND BRENDAN O'MALLEY

39. *Relational Poverty Politics: Forms, Struggles, and Possibilities*
EDITED BY VICTORIA LAWSON AND SARAH ELWOOD

40. *Rights in Transit: Public Transportation and the Right to the City in California's East Bay*
BY KAFUI ABLODE ATTOH

41. *Open Borders: In Defense of Free Movement*
EDITED BY REECE JONES

42. *Subaltern Geographies*
EDITED BY TARIQ JAZEEL AND STEPHEN LEGG

43. *Detain and Deport: The Chaotic U.S. Immigration Enforcement Regime*
BY NANCY HIEMSTRA

44. *Global City Futures: Desire and Development in Singapore*
BY NATALIE OSWIN

45. *Public Los Angeles: A Private City's Activist Futures*
BY DON PARSON
EDITED BY ROGER KEIL AND JUDY BRANFMAN

68. *Dispersed Dispossession: Collective Goods, Appropriation and Agency in Rural Russia*
BY ALEXANDER VORBRUGG

70. *Infrastructures of Caring Citizenship: Commoning Social Reproduction in Crisis-Ridden Athens, Greece*
BY ISABEL GUTIÉRREZ SÁNCHEZ

71. *Conservation in Common: Managing Wildlife and Sustaining Community on Tanzania's Maasai Steppe*
BY JUSTIN RAYCRAFT

72. *Reinventing the River City: Riparian Infrastructure, Cincinnati Elites, and the Ohio River*
BY RAYMOND PETTIT

www.ingramcontent.com/pod-product-compliance
Lightning Source LLC
Chambersburg PA
CBHW032347280326
41935CB00008B/474

9780820374918